T0326284

© 1998 by The Haworth Press, Inc. All rights reserved. No part of this work may be reproduced or utilized in any form or by any means, electronic or mechanical, including photocopying, microfilm and recording, or by any information storage and retrieval system, without permission in writing from the publisher.

First published by

The Haworth Press, Inc., 10 Alice Street, Binghamton, NY 13904-1580

This edition published 2012 by Routledge

Routledge
Taylor & Francis Group
711 Third Avenue
New York, NY 10017

Routledge
Taylor & Francis Group
2 Park Square, Milton Park
Abingdon, Oxon OX14 4RN

Cover design by Monica L. Seifert.

Library of Congress Cataloging-in-Publication Data

Kates, Steven M. (Steven Maxwell)
    Twenty million new customers! : understanding gay men's consumer behavior / Steven M. Kates.
      p.   cm.
    Includes bibliographical references and index.
    ISBN 0-7890-0175-6.   (ISBN: 1-56023-903-4)
    1. Gay consumers—United States. I. Title.
HF5415.33.U6K38 1998
306.3'086'6420973—dc21   97-17008
                                                    CIP

To my family: Roberta Addley, Charles Kates, Gordon Addley,
Christine Kates, Shoshanna Addley, and Adam Kates

ABOUT THE AUTHOR

Steven M. Kates, MBA, CA, PhD, is Assistant Professor of Business Administration at the University of Northern British Columbia. Previously a part-time lecturer at York University and an accountant at two different firms, his research interests include the psychological effects of political and product advertising; ethical issues in advertising and consumer behavior; consumption patterns of traditionally marginalized consumers; and services marketing and consumer satisfaction. He has acted as a marketing research consultant for various companies, including the Royal Trust Company, Commemorative Services of Ontario, and Shane Baghai Homes Ltd. Among other projects, Dr. Kates is currently working on a research project on grief, community, and consumer behavior in the context of AIDS, which has been funded by the University of Northern British Columbia.

CONTENTS

Preface

I would like to comment that the data collection, interpretation, and writing of this research was very much a developmental process. In creating this piece of work, I myself experienced two forms of rite of passage—one professional and the other personal. The professional refers to the experience inherent in becoming a competent consumer researcher, worthy of a doctorate. The personal refers to my experience of self-transformation during the last two to three years. During this time, I believe that I have successfully integrated my key identities of an openly gay man and career academic.

The following document relates concepts of community, resistance, and self-concept—concepts consumer researchers are interested in—to various consumer behaviors. It is, upon reflection, both an academic, scholarly work *and* a very political document, considering the views and beliefs I brought to the research process. Quite frankly, at the outset of the project, I believed that gay issues were effectively marginalized in the marketing and consumer research literatures. I still believe that this is so. However, upon the publication of the results of this work, perhaps this sorry state of affairs will be ameliorated somewhat.

I invite the reader to join me on my journey. Gay and lesbian issues have now come out of the closet in the consumer research field. I have promised myself that this particular voice will be silenced no more.

Acknowledgments

I would like to take this opportunity to acknowledge the superb guidance and support I received from the following people: Russ Belk, Pat Bradshaw, Nigel Roome, Tom Beechy, Louise Ripley, and Dan Wardlow. Thanks, folks!

Chapter 1

An Ethnographic Study
of Gay Men's Consumption

The so-called "deviant" consumer behavior of gays and lesbians is a much neglected focus in the mainstream consumer research literature (Sanders 1989; Wardlow 1996) while consumer perspectives are similarly rare in gay and lesbian studies. One dimension that separates these behaviors from other consumer activities is the acceptance of social risk (Sanders 1989): potentially losing important ties to one's friends, families, occupation, and religion (Goode 1990). Risk, in general, is thought to be the probability that an undesirable result will occur; it is a negative phenomenon which is generally avoided if possible (Celsi, Rose, and Leigh 1993). As many gays and lesbians could confirm, assuming the social risk of being "out" may expose a person to insult; public disgrace and censure; loss of status, income, and social ties; and even physical violence by those who discriminate against the social category in question. This work proposes to explore qualitatively the relationships among self-concept dynamics, gay "subculture" or community, resistance, and deviant consumer behavior.

The Specific Focus of This Book

There are many consumer activities which have the potential to brand an individual as a deviant: drug use, cross-dressing, and compulsive buying to name just a few. This book will primarily address the consumption patterns, habits, and styles of gay men (and their accompanying self-concept and community dynamics) as reflected in their feelings, thoughts, values, and experiences. The implications

1

here are that if an individual engages in certain consumer activities such as going to gay bars, wearing certain types of jewelry or clothing that proclaim one's sexual orientation, or marching in Lesbian and Gay Pride Day, he or she may be publicly labeled as a deviant. These consumer behaviors become a meaningful part of the "coming out" experience of gay men and lesbians. More private forms of consumption such as condom use will not necessarily be studied.

GAY CONSUMPTION

Since the end of World War II, gay enclaves have developed in the heavily urban areas of many large, North American cities (D'Emilio 1983) (although it should be noted that there were informal groups of gay men before this time, particularly in the Greenwich Village area of New York City). These areas are characterized by commercial institutions such as gay bars, bathhouses, bookstores, restaurants, travel agencies, clothing stores, and many other kinds of stores. Yet, gay consumption goes further than this. Many gay men take luxury cruises together, wear provocative T-shirts which both gay and heterosexual individuals are free to read, march in very public Gay and Lesbian Pride celebrations, and purchase and use "off-the-wall" products and services such as leather outfits, exotic body piercings, makeup (which is usually considered rather off the wall when a man purchases it for purposes other than performing on the stage!), and drag items. Of course, heterosexual people consume and buy many of these same products (even leather paraphernalia). However, it is expected that there is an important difference which contrasts "gay" from "straight" consumption, and this difference has largely to do with meaning creation, subculture creation, and identity maintenance. When gay men engage in these various consumer behaviors, they are often defining, articulating, expressing (and sometimes hiding) a deviant identity, one considered offensive to many in U.S. society. In other words, certain consumption lifestyles characterize the gay subculture and perform important identity maintenance functions for its members, such as self-concept change, providing affiliation, and symbolizing pride in one's true self, despite the "sticks and stones" (not to mention unkind words) hurled by prejudiced and hostile others.

The coming-out rite of passage (see Troiden 1989; van Gennep 1960) will be discussed later in this book. This is a key process to understand because "coming out of the closet" is the prescribed manner in which many men who possess significant same-sex desires acquire positive, gay social identities. Most important, as in most important rites of passage, goods and services are transformed into ritual artifacts and consumption rituals, invested with significant symbolic power (e.g., Schouten 1991).

Implicit in the mainstream consumer behavior literature is the notion that there is a congruency between the self-concept and products people buy (Sirgy 1982; Sirgy, Johar, and Wood 1986; Wright, Claiborne, and Sirgy 1992). In other words, the brand image of a good or service must "fit" the individual in order for that person to maintain a positive self-conception and communicate that image to others (Holman 1980, 1981; Solomon 1983). Through purchase and use experiences, goods and services assume important symbolic meanings for individuals who incorporate them into their extended selves (Belk 1988). For example, Schouten's (1991) study of aesthetic plastic surgery found that individuals were motivated by their feelings of inadequacy and their desires to create new, positive, "possible selves" (Markus and Nurius 1986, 1987) through engaging in plastic surgery.

There is another small but growing collection of research both in the consumer literature and in the anthropological literature which has made some progress in understanding deviant consumer practices including tattooing (Sanders 1988; 1989), nonmainstream body alteration (Myers 1992), or in exploring semiotically the consumption patterns of social categories such as punks (Hebdige 1979) or other spectacular youth subcultures (Stratton 1985) who focus much of their time and energy upon the singular pursuit of a particular consumer behavior. Important studies in the mainstream consumer literature include a study of addiction (Hirschman 1992), compulsive buying (O'Guinn and Faber 1989), high-risk leisure activity (Celsi, Rose, and Leigh 1993), Harley-Davidson motorcycle use (Schouten and McAlexander 1995), or upon the survival tactics and unique consumption meanings associated with stigmatized groups such as the homeless

(Hill and Stamey 1990; Hill 1991). The literature on deviant consumer behavior might be usefully categorized along the following lines:

Category	Topic, Author
Pathological Consumption	Compulsive buying (O'Guinn and Faber 1989)
Use of Deviant Products	Recreational marijuana use (Becker 1963)
	Tattooing (Sanders 1989)
	Nonmainstream body piercing (Myers 1992)
	Senior citizen discounts (Tepper 1994)
Deviant/Stigmatized Subcultures	Skydiving (Celsi, Rose, and Leigh (1993)
	Harley-Davidson use (Schouten and McAlexander 1995)
	The homeless (Hill and Stamey 1990; Hill 1991)
	Punk style (Hebdige 1979; Fox 1987)
	Bodybuilding (Klein 1985; 1986)
	Youth subcultures (Brake 1985; Rubington 1987; Simmons 1987; Gottdiener 1995)

A review of the literature provokes the following observations. First, there are sets or constellations of consumer behaviors (Solomon 1983; McCracken 1988a) which appear to be lifestyle or subculture defining (or hiding) and which are commonly associated with groups such as punks, openly gay men or lesbians, hippies, or skinheads. What seems to unite these diverse groups is that each possesses a unique set of beliefs and values which are imparted publicly by their consumption styles (Hebdige 1979; McCracken 1986; Schouten and McAlexander 1995). Second, there are significant self-concept dynamics involved in deviant consumer behaviors. Third, these consumers appear to be assuming stigmatized identities (or negative selves) rather than positive, conventional, socially acceptable ones.

This research explores the consumer activities within the Toronto gay men's subculture from a naturalistic research perspective (Lincoln and Guba 1987). This study shares the following with previous efforts: (1) it will study the self-concept dynamics involved with the behaviors; and (2) it will study consumer behaviors that are widely thought of as stigmatized. This study differs from previous efforts in that (1) it will study voluntary consumer behaviors which are very socially risky; (2) it will study phenomenologically a constellation of jointly enacted consumer behaviors which appear to be associated with a particular social identity or subculture (in that they are lifestyle defining or hiding) which are regarded as deviant; and (3) it will study an understudied group of people as consumers—gay men. Hebdige (1979), for example, explored semiotically the political meanings of the punk fashion and style. What he did not do was study this consumer behavior and style at the experiential level of the individual. The other studies in the chart above, moreover, do not really explore voluntary consumer behaviors which, if subject to public disclosure, may have such dire and negative social consequences upon the individual, in that they can associate him or her with a deviant subculture or social category. One could argue that the homeless are involuntarily forced into their circumstances, and that tattoos, skydiving, and piercing are not as intensely stigmatizing as the implication of homosexuality, a widely condemned phenomenon (Goode 1990). This study will make a contribution by gaining a phenomenological understanding of the self-concept dynamics of gay men who engage in socially risky, stigmatized consumer behaviors. In other words, these consumers choose to self-stigmatize. For gay men in particular, coming out is the key rite of passage in constructing a gay identity, and consumer objects and activities are often involved in this process. The Toronto gay subculture is of interest not only for marketers as a consumption venue, but also because it is characterized by visible consumption lifestyles and performs various important identity forming functions for its members.

The research approach is qualitative and naturalistic; data was generated through semistructured personal interviews with gay men and through participant observation at gay consumption venues—bars, events, and the Lesbian and Gay Pride Day festival. A theoretical perspective has been developed, grounded in the data, which describes the findings and the emergent themes and categories.

This study is important for theoretical, pragmatic, and personal reasons. First, as a theoretical contribution, the subcultural defining consumer patterns of gay men, viewed from the perspectives of deviance, have not been studied satisfactorily and related to important issues in consumer behavior such as self-concept dynamics (Solomon 1983; Markus and Nurius 1986, 1987; Belk 1988; Schouten 1991), the affiliative properties of goods and services (Douglas and Isherwood 1979; Csikszentmihalyi and Rochberg Halton 1981; Hill and Stamey 1990; Gainer 1992; Celsi, Rose, and Leigh 1993), and the cultural or subcultural impacts on consumer behavior (Hebdige 1979; McCracken 1986; Wallendorf and Arnould 1991; Peñaloza 1994). Often exploring the extreme examples of behavior inform us about its more normal or usual aspects (O'Guinn and Faber 1989; Schouten 1991). Second, the gay and lesbian population is rapidly emerging as a lucrative market segment for businesses (*Globe and Mail,* August 15, 1992; Fugate 1993; Peñaloza 1996). Third, personally, I am gay and have an enduring interest in the consumer behavior of gays and lesbians.

The following is a brief review of relevant literatures from which I draw various concepts and models for exploring gay urban consumer subculture. Together, these diverse streams of enquiry help provide a meaningful, conceptual, and theoretical background in which to situate and understand the findings of the present study.

DEVIANCE AND DEVIANT SUBCULTURE

The layperson might believe that deviance refers to objective sick, disgusting, or pathological behaviors performed by morally inferior individuals. Rather, deviance refers to any behavior which is widely *considered* or declared by certain groups or societies to be morally objectionable, sick, disgusting, or of an unconventional nature—a serious breach of societal norms (Rubington and Weinberg 1987; Goode 1990). If deviance is discovered, it usually results in punishment, condemnation, or hostility (Goode 1990). This distinction is important to recognize early on because contemporary perspectives on deviance, such as critical theory and the interactionist/labeling perspective, explicitly consider the participation of various societal audiences when exploring deviant phenomenon. In other words, modern views do not reify deviance; they bracket any moral judgments by declaring deviance a socially constructed phenomenon which is relative to certain groups or societies.

Differing Perspectives on Deviance

Over the last two centuries, a number of perspectives have been developed to explain or understand socially unacceptable or rule-breaking activity: demonology and possession, pathology, the positive school, functionalism, and anomie. These branches of thought attempted to explain why deviance arises in a society which was assumed to be ordered. For functionalist theorists, deviance is a kind of "blessing in disguise" in that its very existence protects the majority of society by ensuring order and by setting moral boundaries of behavior (Matza 1969). In this manner, the traditional family is protected, and members of society come to understand that dire consequences may result if they step beyond certain acceptable limits of behavior. The perspective of the anomie theory or strain theory posits that deviance results from contradictory social structures which dictate standards of success. These structures place restrictive conditions upon the individual to accomplish them conventionally (Merton 1957). The positive school is principally interested in explaining why one individual or category of individuals commits deviant activity while another does not. As Becker (1963) describes this branch of the domain, it is primarily interested in isolating (by experimentation, usually) the one or few isolated psychological traits which determines deviant behavior.

There have been many criticisms of the positive school. First, it ignores the critical dimension of the meaning of subjective experiences (Matza 1969; Goode 1975, 1990; Blumer 1969). Second, critics are skeptical of the concept of causality. Becker (1963), in an example of deviants versus nondeviants, raises the issues that the same "causal," motivating psychological trait might be present in both deviant and nondeviant subjects, raising the problematic nature of causality. Finally, positivists have been subjected to questions regarding researcher objectivity (Becker 1967).

From these criticisms has arisen a more subjectivist perspective on deviance—the labeling or interactionist school (Becker 1963)—which is more compatible with the humanistic (Hirschman 1986) orientation of this research. It should be noted that labeling does *not* maintain that psychiatric institutions drive people insane, that prisons cause people to become hardened criminals, or that calling someone a "faggot" causes that individual to engage in same-sex erotic behavior. The premise of the perspective, which developed out of traditional symbolic interactionism (Blumer 1969), is that certain individuals are publicly branded as deviants (Becker 1963) or symbolically label themselves (Pfuhl 1986), and experience and interpret life events through that label. Specific and general audiences of people then behave in a specific manner as to acknowledge the deviant's lower social status and may actually exclude him/her from "normal roles" within a society (Pfuhl 1986). It is interesting to note that an individual need not always undergo a public degradation ceremony (Pfuhl 1986), or ritual such as a trial to assume the role of deviant. Significantly, one can symbolically brand oneself a deviant and internalize a specific label.

The labeling process is critical in understanding the life experiences of individuals who are considered deviant by others and by themselves. Primary deviance is simply the enaction of various proscribed behaviors (Lemert 1951; Pfuhl 1986; Goode 1990). It carries with it no special significance for the individual's general self-concept and is, for the most part, compartmentalized out of the normal life of the man who occasionally experiences a same-sex erotic encounter, for example. Secondary deviance occurs when the individual must cope with either internal self-labeling or societal reaction concerning his/her behavior: "The secondary deviant, as opposed to his actions, is a person whose life and identity are organized around the facts of deviance" (Lemert 1972, p. 63).

The literature in the interactionist perspective suggests that the deviant identity becomes a master status (Pfuhl 1986; Goode 1990) for a "career" deviant, who subsequently adopts the unconventional lifestyle as a matter of course. He/she begins a moral career wherein deviance begets more deviance after public disgrace and condemnation. Pfuhl (1986) calls this phenomenon the "amplification hypothesis" and presents mixed empirical support for such a phenomenon. Overall, he maintains that labeling in itself is sufficient to ensure that those who possess ascribed stigma (i.e., those people whose deviance is highly visible, and in a significant manner defines them to others) launch a deviant career. On the other hand, for those whose stigma is achieved, public labeling is not necessary to set them off on a deviant career (such as homosexuals or drug users).

The implication, therefore, is that gay men can explore gay subculture and/or assume gay identities within that subculture without ever having this fact disclosed to potentially condemning others. Thus one can, as a gay man, choose to be a "closet queen" or secret deviant. In this instance, self-labeling (as opposed to public condemnation) appears to be enough for a deviant career to follow.

An important implication of labeling theory is that audiences— the self, family, important reference groups, and the generalized other (i.e., society)—are critical for the deviant career to progress, consistent with the symbolic interaction notion that self and reality are created interpersonally (Cooley 1902; Mead 1934). Thus, the deviant role is negotiated between the individual and others. Also, consistent with the traditional symbolic interactionist perspective is the idea that moral meanings are created and interpreted from things, people, or behavior. Once a negative moral meaning is placed upon an individual (by self or others—although if one takes a traditional symbolic interactionist perspective it is difficult to meaningfully separate the two), he/she is effectively stigmatized and assumes a lower social status (Goode 1990).

Stigma has been defined as a public mark of shame or dishonor (Goffman 1963), either physical or metaphorical. The difference between stigma and deviance, it should be noted, is rather unclear. Stigma assigns a person to a lower social status. Deviance, generally, has the added negative dimension of inspiring others (i.e., normals or nondeviants) to harm or control the deviant group. Homosexual men, for example, are stigmatized and deviant in that their lives and behavior are largely condemned and illegalized (Goode 1990). It is useful, perhaps, to envision stigma and deviance along a continuum with deviant behavior intensely and pervasively condemned.

For gay men who have been outed or who have chosen to disclose their status, the deviant career entails the everyday management of this stigma in the form of manipulating information relevant to the self (i.e., impression management; see Goffman 1959). Information management takes the forms of various strategies which largely depend upon whether the individual's deviant identity is discreditable (i.e., potentially known, but presently unknown by others) or discredited (i.e., known by others). In the latter example, the identity is termed *spoiled* (Goffman 1963).

Those who possess discreditable identities, such as closeted homosexual men who look and behave straight for the most part, have the option of "passing" (Goffman 1963) as normal. By controlling information about themselves to others, discreditable people may avoid loss of social status. Passing (as straight) requires a high degree of self-control and self-consciousness of gesture, body language, and speech. It also entails the careful avoidance of stigma symbols, which are signs capable of revealing to others one's deviant, homosexual feelings or identity (Goffman 1963). It may also entail the assumption of misleading disidentifers which convince others of one's nondeviant status, such as the case of Mexican homosexual men who date women, wear macho clothing, and engage in heterosexual intercourse with prostitutes (Carrier 1976). It may also entail the leading of a double life for a homosexual man—strictly separating one's interactions with gay friends versus heterosexual friends or workmates. These types of behaviors have significant implications for the purchase, use, and disposition of goods and services, as will be explored further.

The challenge for those who possess discredited or spoiled identities is that of tension management: they must maintain favorable identities when interacting with others. There are a number of strategies available to those whose stigma or deviance is voluntarily disclosed or simply apparent by observation. First, recent research has indicated that people can resist the labels imputed to them by others (Allen 1982) because these labels threaten their self-esteem. Those possessing spoiled identities may also have the option of destigmatizing themselves (Pfuhl 1986) by ridding their lives of the identity in question. Breakwell (1986) suggests that those who cope with "threatened identities" have the options of managing stigma at the intrapsychic, interpersonal, or intergroup level. Intrapsychic coping mechanisms include denial of the identity threat, changing the personally defined value or meaning of the threat, compartmentalizing the threatening condition, or accepting it and fundamentally changing one's identity in a significant manner. Interpersonal coping usually involves engaging in active conflict with those who would judge the condition which threatens identity. Intergroup coping strategies involve people supporting one another in various manners in order to deal with the threat to identity. These coping mechanisms include forming a social movement aimed at changing social norms and revising current ideologies while providing self-esteem and pride to the minority.

Deviant Subcultures

Plummer (1975), in his symbolic interactionist account of the construction of modern homosexuality, maintains that subculture is the consequence of complex, pluralistic societies wherein uniform value systems cannot be taken for granted; thus one might presume that gay urban subcultures, for example, considered along a continuum with the mainstream culture, possesses norms and values which are distinct and which differ from that dominant, heterosexual culture. Hebdige (1979), writing from the British-Marxist (and hence, very political) perspective, argues that subculture may be defined as a form of resistance wherein contradictions and objections to the dominant class or ideology are symbolically represented through style or material objects. Brake (1985) views subcultures as meaning systems (p. 8) which are either extensions of expressions of resistance to larger, dominant class structures. They form constellations of behaviors, actions, and values which have special significances for those involved.

Stratton (1985) differentiates between the spectacular subcultures which have developed in Britain, such as punks, teddyboys, and skinheads, and the more commodity-oriented subcultures of the United States, such as surfies and bikers. From his largely structuralist perspective, Brake (1985) contends that the former group is engaging in "imaginary solutions" to resolve real social problems. By this, presumably, he is asserting that the symbolic resistance of the punks executed through their shocking, offensive style did not in any substantive manner improve their objective economic situation.

Deviant subcultures may be viewed as an accommodation by a group of individuals to their deviant status (Rubington and Weinberg 1987). People who share a common stigma or interest are apt to interact with one another and share various lingos, meanings, institutions, ideologies, dreams, and activities (Pfuhl 1986; Rubington and Weinberg 1987; Simmons 1987). The relevant literature suggests that a subculture is a collective response which aids in the solution to a specific problem of a set of individuals (Rubington 1987). Cohen (1955) asserts that there are five stages in subcultural development: (1) experiencing a problem, (2) communicating it to like others, (3) interacting in the context of the problem, (4) developing a solution, and (5) sustaining and passing on this newly invented tradition.

It should be noted that a subculture can simply be a physical and psychological "place" wherein certain people go periodically (Simmons 1987). One need not become a hard-core punk or "subculture-oriented gay" (Bruce Bawer) to partake of a particular culture. In other words, it is not necessary to raise one's deviant identity to the level of master status to feel *some* identification with a deviant subculture. The literature suggests that there may be differing levels of commitment to subculture among a deviant category (Fox 1987; Rubington and Weinberg 1987; Widdicombe and Wooffitt 1990; Schouten and McAlexander 1995).

Nevertheless, there do appear to be consumption-oriented subcultures, particularly those which involve conspicuous or radical alteration of the body itself, and which are inhabited primarily by hard-core individuals or those who have elevated the activity to that of a master status. The enthusiasts of genital piercing described by Myers (1992) or the bodybuilders studied by Klein (1985, 1986) who display great commitment to their respective activities, are often subject to significant self-concept change in which a particular consumer object or activity takes on great importance and engages the individual in organizing the rest of his/her life and/or identities around it. One interesting notion which arises is that there may be subcultures which one cannot exit (e.g., if one is physically deformed in a radical manner) versus those which people choose not to exit if they wish to be true to themselves. One might presume that the gay men's urban subculture falls into the second category; indeed participants in this study have continually self-selected themselves, constantly defining their gay identities and level of community affiliation, often reflected in consumer patterns.

Gay Urban Subculture

Almost every large urban center in North America possesses a physical area (i.e., a ghetto or the community) in which there may be gay subculture. Historically, in the United States, the demographic upheavals following World War II brought many homosexual individuals together in relatively large numbers for the very first time in port cities such as New York, Los Angeles, and San Francisco. Thus, a sense of shared group identity was formed, particularly through gay bars and through shared oppression (D'Emilio 1983); the latter dimension, homophobia, is key in understanding the formation of gay subculture in response to a problem. Particularly after the Stonewall riots of 1969, a new social invention emerged: the career or ethnic homosexual (D'Emilio 1983; Weeks 1985), someone who is gay for life and spends the majority or a significant portion of his/her time within urban gay enclaves. Gay ghettos emerged in large American and Canadian cities in which many gay men and women congregated. Thus, it has been argued that gays now form communities or minorities as do Blacks, Jews, and Italians (Altman 1982; Paul 1982; D'Emilio 1983; Murray 1992). Murray (1992) argues that the gay enclaves or subcultures possess the distinguishing qualities which qualify them as communities or "peoplehood in a place": spatial boundaries, all basic social services, a concentration of like-minded (in certain limited but significant respects) people, a reproduction of all functions of an entire society (i.e., a microcosm), and a collective memory.

THE GAY IDENTITY ACQUISITION PROCESS: COMING OUT

It is "coming out of the closet" that is the commonly accepted mode of entering and exploring this deviant gay subculture or *gemeinschaft* (or a small social world) and may also be viewed as a rite of passage (Herdt 1992; Herdt and Boxer 1992, 1993; Murray 1992). It is also the critical psychological process or identity crisis (Erikson 1968) by which individuals who possess homosexual desire learn about gay norms and culture and assume a gay identity (Lee 1977; Cass 1979; Troiden 1989). It is also important to note that coming out, as well as being an important rite of passage into gay society, entails a lifelong process of identity management in the face of stigma (Troiden 1989; Herdt and Boxer 1993). Coming out is, quite significantly, the increasingly public disclosure of one's gay identity to others such as friends, family, other gay people, and potentially hostile heterosexuals (Lee 1977; Nungesser 1983).

While homosexuality itself is considered a bodily felt awareness and not a choice (Plummer 1975; Cass 1979; Tripp 1987), in a very profound sense, one does choose to become gay (i.e., take on a new *social*, shared gay identity) by undergoing the coming out rite of passage. This transformation is performed first on an intrapsychic level in that the individual thinks, feels, makes choices, and learns to cope with the management of spoiled (Goffman 1963) or threatened (Breakwell 1986) identity. It is also performed on the interpersonal and intergroup levels in that the individual's behavior is a social phenomenon, open to public scrutiny by specific and generalized others. In spite of considerable social stigma, many gay men do make the critical decision to seek out other gay men, participate in activities (both sexual and social) with gay men, and learn about gay society and what has been labeled the gay community (Herdt 1992; Herdt and Boxer 1993). Within this social context, gay men do travel through a liminal stage in which they unlearn old heterosexual norms and learn new gay ones. This process is the assumption of a societal role or identity which is often heavily stigmatized and is a process quite outside of many people's traditional, expected life development or experience. In this sense, someone chooses to become a social outcast or deviant, in the eyes of some others.

The social meaning of coming out has been transformed during the gay liberation movement, beginning in the 1960s. Previous to this time, coming out meant internally accepting that one was gay (a coming to terms), disclosing it to other gay people, and perhaps quietly disclosing it to some friends and family. However, after the advent of gay liberation, the subcultural meaning of coming out was transformed into one involving an essentially political process by which one challenged the dominant sexual hegemony by one's disclosure, which was to be done with pride and defiance (D'Emilio 1983).

Minton and McDonald (1984) present a particularly interesting model of gay identity formation, based upon Habermas' model of ego development (1979). Habermas identifies four stages of the complete process: symbiotic, egocentric, sociocentric, and universalistic. During the first stage, the individual is an infant and has no sense of independent bodily awareness. During the egocentric stage, the child differentiates between himself/herself and the environment. At this stage (labeled the sensitization stage in the models of Plummer [1975] and Troiden [1989]), a person achieves an understanding that he/she might be homosexual, but does not make a connection between personal feelings of being different and the label of homosexual. During the sociocentric stage of the Minton and McDonald (1984) model, also called signification by Plummer (1975), social norms are internalized, and the person often feels anxiety and confusion about his or her homosexual feelings. Cass (1979) calls this the identity confusion stage. During the universalistic stage, according to Habermas, the individual realizes that societal norms can be evaluated and criticized. Thus, the soon-to-be gay individual comes to accept his or her homosexual feelings, develops a social identity of being gay, and criticizes society's negative evaluation of homosexuality (e.g., pride). Finally, he or she may decide to commit to a gay identity for an indeterminate period of time. Minton and McDonald (1984): also identify a last substage, which entails the individual incorporating the gay identity as just one more dimension of the self, and which they call identity synthesis. Pride in one's identity is another possible developmental occurrence (Cass 1979; Minton and McDonald 1984): often those who consider themselves extremely out (or willing to disclose their gay identity to anyone and everyone) are proud to call themselves queer (Browning 1993).

A number of interesting observations may be made about the coming out process. First it reflects the psychological development of a form of social identity (i.e., in this case, relating to a social category): one increasingly accepts a gay identity as a part of one's self-concept. Second, it is the progressive disclosure of one's (previously) secret deviant status to various audiences: self, gay others, heterosexual others, and a generalized other (Lee 1977); it is a willful, most often voluntary form of self-stigmatization. Third, it usually entails some form of exploration of gay consumption venues and meeting other gay men (Troiden 1987) within the subculture, whether in an urban or even suburban setting (Lynch 1987). Fourth, as reflected explicitly in the Minton and McDonald (1984) model, the coming out process incorporates both the voluntaristic experience of (re)interpreting the external world (or gay subculture) and moving toward a new possible self which was previously thought of as negative and shameful, *and* the more deterministic experience of internalizing alternative subcultural norms and values.

CAPITALISM, CONSUMER BEHAVIOR, GAY IDENTITY, AND SUBCULTURE: CRITICAL AND INTERPRETIVE PERSPECTIVES

During the Victorian Age, the dominant masculine/heterosexual discourse was developed (Foucault 1980). Sexual relations between a man and his wife which resulted in reproduction was deemed the (only) norm and all other conceivable acts, including homosexual ones, were marginalized as perversions. Underlying this discourse is the often unspoken assumption that there existed a natural or true sexual identity in men and women which directed them to their proper biological roles (Weeks 1985, 1987). This medicalization of sexuality reinforced the social order of the era. Before this time, it was acknowledged that particular acts of an erotic substance which differed from the prescribed norm certainly took place between individuals. Following the works of the early scientists and sexologists, however, classes of people were defined primarily by their so-called aberrant behavior; from these works of sexual research, which constituted a dominant sexual and social discourse, the modern homosexual was born (Foucault 1980). According to Foucault (1980), certain discourses—that is, "the structuring of reality . . . which is the complex of historical, social, cultural, and linguistic settings that shape our sense of the world and, therefore, our possibilities in it" (Pronger 1990, p. 85)—become the dominant or privileged ones within society (Cooper 1991). While the discourse of reproductive normality which has dominated Western thought for the past 200 years or so definitely has a specific place for queers, this social space has been relegated as deviant or dirty (Visano 1987). In the view of some authors, heterosexuality has set itself up as the dominant norm within this discourse (Jackson 1987; Kinsman 1991). Moreover, this heterosexual/homosexual, normal/deviant, masculine/feminine, queer/straight discourse of dialectic opposites sets behavioral boundaries for all people—not just homosexuals. The latter have been viewed as those who embody impurity and perversity. Women and the feminine gender are tolerated, but are subordinated to the male sex and are usually granted the status of property (Hirschon 1984; Whitehead 1984). Even heterosexual men—those who seem to be the indisputed beneficiaries of the marginalization, subordination, or demonization of everyone else—are powerful only within their rigid, narrow, and traditionally masculine roles; they too may face negative consequences as prisoners of this master-and-servant discourse: alienation from their own feelings and from others, usually their own children and female companions, and a constant anxiety concerning their own masculinity (Lewis 1978; Seidler 1987). One of the stated goals of the new men's movement is to disalienate men from their emotions.

It has been noted that there can be no heterosexual, male-dominated, superior norm without the condition to which it is constantly compared as superior (Kinsman 1991). Queerness, by challenging and subverting heterosexual, masculine hegemony and by violating the most rigidly held conformist sexual myths in our society (i.e., the separation of women from men along the socio-political construct of gender, and the domination of the latter by the former) has been historically reviled. Significantly, coming out (disclosing one's queer identity to others) is "really to be in—inside the realm of the visible, the speakable, and the culturally intelligible" (Fuss 1991) and is an open challenge to the dominant sexual discourse. Gay men, by defining their sexuality by choosing those of their own sex, identify themselves with women and are construed to be inferior because of this. Thus, an interesting paradox emerges: homosexuality both eroticizes hegemonic masculinity and yet violates it (Pronger 1990).

What is important to note is that coming out and the very existence of open gay subculture challenges and breaks down the homophobic, rigid gender roles, and hegemonic masculinity. Ironically, in response to the stigma of femininity, a hypermasculine style of dress and behavior was adopted by many gays in the 1970s (Kleinberg

1992); this may be interpreted as an acquiescence to hegemonic masculinity by gays themselves, even once they have come out. The threat posed by homosexuality and gay culture to traditional masculinity and patriarchy (Millett 1969) is a theme found throughout the literature in men's studies and homosexual studies, and it is a challenge to sexual orthodoxy which provides one of the primary cornerstones of gay political activism (D'Emilio 1983; Weeks 1985; Kinsman 1991, 1992).

This radical stance is perhaps best embodied in the political action group which called itself Queer Nation, founded in the late 1980s to battle homophobia, heterosexism, and queerbashing in American and Canadian cities such as Los Angeles, San Francisco, New York, and Toronto. Browning (1993), in his qualititative exploration of contemporary gay culture, explores some of their more obviously agitative measures. Interestingly, the groups often used consumption venues and activities to express their hostility and anger toward straight society. In Browning's (1993) research, the members of San Francisco Queer Nation visited a suburban shopping mall, handed out leaflets, shopped, strolled hand in hand with their same sex partners, and culminated their excursion with a massive "kiss-in" where, in full view of many other shoppers, they proceeded to kiss one another on the lips.

Political actions were not restricted to public shopping malls. In 1990, members of Queer Nation Toronto, in response to a public advertisement which was construed as homophobic and heterosexist, invaded the straight space of the Loose Moose restaurant, drank, dined, danced with and kissed their same-sex partners in full view of the other (presumably) heterosexual patrons. The Loose Moose subsequently published a full-page ad in the same weekly, apologizing to the gay and lesbian community. Thus, there appears to be a very extreme or political stage of being accepting of one's identity and being out (for some but not all gay people) which is not fully developed in the gay identity formation literature. This might be referred to as the queer identity stage. Consistent with the emergence of this social phenomenon, it has been argued by some authors including Altman (1982) and Minton and McDonald (1984) that the assertion of a gay, social identity is also a political act due to shared oppression. It has been further argued that many gays share these subversive norms and values and thus, constitute a subculture.

It is unsurprising that such acts of rebellion occurred in consumption venues. Certain authors have recognized the importance of the relationship between capitalism, consumer behavior, and the development of gay subculture and shared social identity. Altman (1982), for example, argues that "the collapse of traditional values, whether in regard to sex, work, or authority, are in a sense the result of the very success of the capitalist societies these value systems had helped engender" (pp. 90-91). This is a paradox because early capitalism demanded conformity to the nuclear family model (Foucault 1980) and to rigid gender roles for social control to be successfully accomplished. Weeks (1985) argues that capitalism colonizes various spheres of private life. However, in doing so, capitalism weakens the traditional family because free laborers (as opposed to lowly serfs) are able to work, live, spend, and engage in sexual encounters however they please, within certain constraints. Thus, capitalism paradoxically provides choices and a degree of freedom to the individual (Thompson, Locander, and Pollio 1989, 1990) while also demanding conformity to certain traditional producer/consumer roles (Gough 1989), an example of the classic contradiction which Marxists have identified (Burrell and Morgan 1979).

There have been critics of the free choice philosophy, of course. As Weeks (1985) states, Herbert Marcuse maintained that a state of repressive desublimation or unfreedom may evolve as individuals believe they have freedom in one area (e.g., as consumers) but are socially controlled in another area (e.g., as free citizens) unbeknownst to them. Seabrook (1976) argues that gays pioneered modern consumer values of luxury and hedonism and comes very close to claiming that the gay community exists only as a market or consumer phenomenon. Lasch (1979), perhaps the harshest of all social critics of consumerism, has argued that consumers are the passive agents of advertisers, swept up by modern capitalism, a part of the phenomenon which he labels the culture of narcissism.

All of these critics, nonetheless, have missed some critical points which underlie the importance of consumer behavior in the modern gay subculture, and which other authors point out. First, human beings are not necessarily passive agents of the forces of capitalism but are free to interpret (as opposed to accept) the information in their environments (Giddens 1991). Second, Seabrook (1976) and Lasch (1979) both ignore the omnipresent dimension of political struggle within modern gay communities (Altman 1982). For example, the Queer Nation members in Browning's (1993) account of modern gay culture were shopping, but they were also proclaiming their gay identities to other people, breaking the silence and shattering the illusion that homosexuals do not exist. Finally, Lasch (1979) particularly ignores the truly liberating aspects of consumer capitalism for the gay minority: materialism, acquisitiveness, choice, and affluence (Altman 1982). As Altman observes, "thus not only does modern capitalism create the socioeconomic conditions for the emergence of a homosexual identity, it creates the psychological ones as well. In short, the new homosexual could only emerge in the conditions created by modern capitalism" (p. 93). Finally, critics such as Lasch and Seabrook (who are quite Marxist in their orientations and thus prone to a more deterministic view of human nature; see Burrell and Morgan 1979) completely overlook the subjective, creative (and often subversive) elements involved in consumers' uses of their products (Hebdige 1979; Peñaloza and Price 1992).

Marxists would concur that capitalism, on the one hand, has generally demanded conformity to rigid gender roles and traditional family structure. On the other hand, it has given individuals the financial means and opportunities to reject, and subsequently subvert, those constraining structures. Thus, from a Marxist perspective, the emergence, existence, and success of urban gay subcultures are indicative of this classic contradiction. On the other hand, Marxists engaging in a more "vulgar" (Goode 1990) point of view, might argue that the gay consumer subculture is an example of false consciousness (see Hirschman 1993) or repressive desublimation in its power to persuade individuals that they are free, while objectively, these individuals are oppressed by dominant social structures. From a more humanistic point of view, moreover, one could argue that capitalism has offered various oppressed individuals such as gays and lesbians the subjectively felt freedom to express themselves in important manners through the creative use of products or services.

CONSUMER PRODUCTS AND SYMBOLIC MEANING

The idea that goods and services have sociocultural meanings which go above and beyond their basic functional utilities is not a new one in marketing (Levy 1959). Furthermore, Goffman (1951) suggested that products possess symbolic properties which are somehow congruent with an individual's self-concept. Consumer objects, activities, ads, places, and situations may be considered signifiers which are arbitrarily and historically associated with underlying ideologies, ideas, emotions, and thoughts, and with other objects (see Mick 1986; McCracken 1988a). While individuals may bestow very unique meanings upon their possessions, there usually exists a collective understanding of a product's underlying meaning. In this way, people within a particular culture are able to communicate symbolically. For example, when traditional Coca-Cola was taken off the market in 1985, a flurry of negative publicity occurred; the company may not have fully appreciated the importance of deep-seated cultural meanings which the American public associated with their original product (Hartley 1992). Thus, brands and products acquire significant sociocultural meanings over time which provide links between people and a marketer's offerings. Further, recent research supports the notion that the symbolic meaning or artifacts, which are indicative of shared cultural meanings and/or experiences, are learned early during childhood (Belk, Bahn, and Mayer 1982).

The Process of Consumer Meaning Movement: A Cultural Perspective

In McCracken's (1986, 1989) theoretical account relating goods, people, and conduits of meaning, culturally constituted meanings are transmitted from the culturally constituted world by means of advertising and the fashion system to consumer goods, and from products to the individual consumer, via possession, exchange, grooming, and divestment rituals, illustrated as such:

CULTURALLY   Ads   CONSUMER   Rituals
CONSTITUTED   GOODS   CONSUMER
WORLD   Fashion
           System

The importance of meaning as reflected by certain kinds of possessions or activities is one of the important themes found in the literature. For example, gender differences and consumption has been one area of inquiry, and the findings seem to reinforce the notion that certain kinds of possessions and/or consumption activities may be strongly associated with one group of people as opposed to another, according to the dictates of the culture involved. It has been suggested that material objects that symbolize achievement or communicate an instrumental message are generally important to men, as opposed to women (Csikszentmihalyi and Rochberg-Halton 1981; Wallendorf and Arnould 1988). In contrast, it has been demonstrated that women usually value those objects which symbolize their connectedness to others within relationships, indicating a more communal orientation (Wallendorf and Arnould 1988; Hirschman 1993).

Yet, it is also critical to note that the notion of culture as a wholly unifying and homogenizing force is often implicitly challenged within the consumer behavior literature; in other words, the culturally constituted meanings for some people and/or groups are not the same as for others. For instance, Wallendorf and Arnould (1991), in their exploration of the Thanksgiving Day feast ritual, maintain that consumption is not a passive result of external factors but is an active force which helps mold culture itself. In this respect, a particular dialectic tension is constructed between self and culture wherein appropriate manners of celebrating Thanksgiving are imposed by culture (as a molding force) but are, in turn, molded by individuals. Preparers of the Thanksgiving meal, for example, may combine traditional store-bought ingredients and their own efforts to create a meal that is homemade.

This dialectic tension between the self and society or between the dominant culture and various subcultures is also demonstrated in Hirschman's (1985) work on primitive consumption. Her work is interesting in that it challenges the widely held notion that the United States is characterized by a monolithic, secular consumption ethos. On the other hand, she presents evidence which suggests that various ethnic cultures—Jews, blacks, Italians, and WASPS—have in significant ways resisted homogenizing cultural forces, and consume in order to enforce community bonds and preserve a spiritual dimension in their lives. Belk, Wallendorf, and Sherry's (1989) research on the sacred and the profane in consumer behavior also reinforces the notion that certain ancient, primitive elements remain hidden in the consumption practices of modern individuals, particularly when they engage in special activities such as collecting or gift-giving. Other researchers such as Mehta and Belk (1991), O'Guinn and Belk (1989), and Hill and Stamey (1990) have provided empirical studies which challenge the notion of the monolithic nature of cultural forces. O'Guinn and Belk (1989), for example, conducted on-site interviews at the PTL's Heritage Village, and attempted to reconcile the seemingly opposing forces of consumption and worship, transforming meanings in a particular consumption context. Another example of how certain groups redefine cultural categories and principles (i.e., transforming meanings) to suit the conditions of their lives is provided by Hill and Stamey (1990) and Hill (1991) wherein the researchers study the consumption patterns of homeless individuals and homeless women living in a shelter, respectively. In these two latter studies, the universalistic meaning of home is challenged and a particularistic one, appropriate to these marginalized groups, is developed. Relevant to this study, the camp sensibility or aesthetic may be considered the particularistic homosexual meaning system (Sontag 1964).

Product Symbolism, the Self-Concept, and Deviant Consumer Behavior

Deviant consumer behavior, by its nature, is very symbolic. For a certain product to symbolize unconventional, socially unacceptable, or immoral behavior, it must convey negative messages to various audiences (including the self audience) who, in turn, pass judgments upon the behavior and the individual. The literature on various forms of deviant consumer behavior confirms this observation.

Recently, some deviant consumer behavior has been explored in the consumer behavior literature. Hirschman (1992) phenomenologically explored addiction and observed that this form of consumption is *in extremis*, well beyond the realm of normal consumer behavior. One of her important findings is that the self-concept of addicted persons becomes narrowly confined and defined by the substance itself; drugs become the focal point of the person's entire existence. Moreover, much time and energy is invested in hiding the addiction from the shame and discovery by family, friends, and workmates. In another study, O'Guinn and Faber (1989) explored compulsive buying, and consistent with the notion that consumer behavior has important implications for self-concept maintenance, it was found that compulsive buyers suffer from low self-esteem and often experience a personal sense of shame and alienation from significant others.

In studies of the homeless (Hill and Stamey 1990; Hill 1991), the authors explored the difficult task of positive self-concept maintenance for a group whose members have not necessarily chosen their impoverished and stigmatized situations. The former study demonstrates that the homeless use self-talk as well as various consumer activities to bolster their threatened sense of self-esteem. The alternative forms of work (such as recycling) are viewed positively by the homeless, particularly in contrast to those homeless who live on welfare. Thus, in order to insulate themselves from the hurtful judgments which they perceive others are thinking (the looking-glass self), the homeless invest personal, positive meanings into their activities.

The anthropological literature offers a number of examples of the self-stigmatizing experience of certain consumer behaviors. Activities such as recreational marijuana use (Becker 1963), tattooing (Sanders 1988, 1989), bodybuilding (Klein 1985, 1986), and non-mainstream body piercing (Myers 1992) (i.e., piercing one's genitals, eyebrows, lips, tongue, nipples, navel, etc.) are all symbolic in that they convey to the self and to others that the consumer in question is apart from those who are perceived as straight or mainstream, indicating the social category in which the individual wishes to be placed (Csikszentmihalyi and Rochberg-Halton 1981). As important parts of consumer's identity kits (Goffman 1961), these sorts of purchases act as symbols of unconventionality and disaffiliation (from normals) and as stigma symbols (Goffman 1963). From the emic view of the participant, such behavior makes them feel different or special. Also, such activities serve as rites of passage (van Gennep 1960) into certain groups, or as badges of association (Douglas and Isherwood 1979).

The literature on culture and consumption raises some very interesting issues, relevant to the present research. It suggests that culture is not only a monolithic, shaping force which inevitably influences consumption norms, but rather, culture and self must be viewed as acting within dialectical tension wherein both shape each other. Moreover, consumption must not necessarily be viewed strictly as a passive response of the self to cultural forces (Wallendorf and Arnould 1991) but rather as a negotiation of meaning between self and culture. McCracken's (1986) theory can be judged quite robust in that it can shed light on the perplexing notion that not all meanings or practices are uniform throughout the consumer world. Not only do meanings flow down from the world to products and then to consumers, but also meanings flow up from consumers to products and then to the culturally constituted world. McCracken (1986) maintains that individuals may play with culture and invent new meanings; for example, "groups responsible for the radical reform of cultural meaning are those existing at the margins of society, e.g., hippies, punks, or *gays*" (p. 76; italics mine). In other words, one way new cultural meanings are created is through the creativity of certain radical or stigmatized groups.

METHODS USED IN THIS RESEARCH

I began the participant observation aspect of the study in June 1993 by observing the Lesbian and Gay Pride Day celebrations. I continued informally observing various gay events for the next nine months until March 1994, when I entered the next phase of the research. I obtained official permission from Lesbian, Gay, and Bisexual Youth of Toronto (LGBYT) to sit in on their sessions, and informed the board of directors of The Fraternity that I would like to interview some of their members. The formal interviews of informants from LGBYT and The Fraternity were conducted from May 1994 to November 1994. During this time, I continued to visit LGBYT and attend functions at The Fraternity, taking notes, interacting with members, and performing the functions as outlined below. The study concluded officially on December 2, 1994 when I attended The Fraternity's "Winter Wonderland" holiday dinner and dance, performing participant observation.

Snowball sampling is usually used in studying stigmatized and hard-to-locate groups of individuals; Troiden (1987), in his study of gay men's coming-out patterns, also used this technique. In Nardi's (1992) quantitative study on gay men's friendships, however, he used a social outcropping technique whereby he contacted gay and lesbian organizations in order to find participants and avoid bias.

The two organizations where I began the journey described in this research are a gay and lesbian youth group and a gay men's social activities organization. I have had extensive past involvements in both organizations. First, the steering committees of both organizations were notified of the existence and nature of the study. Permission was obtained from both groups, and a general announcement was made informing the general memberships of both groups of the nature of the study. It should be noted that due to the stigmatized and private nature of the phenomenon being investigated, considerations for both confidentiality and anonymity were strictly observed. Members of both groups were asked to volunteer only if they had no reservations concerning participating in this study. From that point, the sample snowballed to additional participants by asking present participants to refer gay acquaintances outside of the groups who would feel comfortable about volunteering information. I also networked among my own gay friends and acquaintances in order to find willing informants. The sample itself is comprised of gay men aged from sixteen to fifty-three. A number of men in their sixties and older were asked to participate but refused. One had experienced a heart attack in the last six months and responded that he did not feel "up to the task." Another man in his sixties, an academic, objected to the naturalistic perspective of the study, and upon examination of the interview questionnaire, refused to participate on the grounds that the questionnaire was not scientific enough. A few older men declined to participate because they were not quite comfortable with the process, despite my assurances of strict confidentiality.

Another goal of the study was to have at least 20 percent of the participants to be of black or Asian ethnicity in order to obtain a diversity of views which would challenge and reinforce interpretations. (See Appendix 3.)

Data Generation

Long, semistructured interviews (McCracken 1988) as well as participant observation were used to explore the consumer research of gay men who belong to a gay men's social group known as The Fraternity. I have been a member of this group for almost four years and have served as Treasurer of this group for two years. The primary purpose of this group is for gay men to engage in various forms of consumer behaviors: listening to talks by certain popular public figures; going to movie nights and house parties at members' homes; going on ski trips; having competitive mini-Olympics; and participating in special charitable events such as Winter Wonderland (the Christmas/Chanukah party), and Music, Magic, and Men (an evening of song, dance, and a slave auction to benefit the Lesbian and Gay Community Appeal). (Please see Appendixes 1 and 2 for the interview questionnaires.)

Interviews with members of Lesbian, Gay, and Bisexual Youth of Toronto were also performed. It should be noted that these potential participants were between the ages of fifteen to twenty-five, and extreme discretion and caution had been used in approaching and interacting with them, respecting their privacy and feelings.

Participant observation was performed at the gay and lesbian youth group called Lesbian and Gay Youth of Toronto. It should be emphasized that participant observation of the youth group was necessary here in order to enable the researcher to engage in the primary mode of data collection: long interviews. Otherwise, new-comers and other group members may not have felt comfortable enough to speak to the interviewer in an interview situation. When possible, I interviewed friends of friends, networking among my gay friends and acquaintances for interested participants. This was also a very successful tactic.

In 1994, Lesbian and Gay Pride Day (LGPD), was held on July 3. I observed the parade (and indeed the entire Lesbian and Gay Pride Week which "traditionally" precedes the day itself), participating in various activities such as brunch, marching, buying memorabilia while observing others doing the same activities. The long inter-views described above contained portions devoted specifically to LGPD festivities.

Data Interpretation

The data generated from the above methods was read over several times and sifted (see Hirschman 1992) for emergent themes. Essentially, the data was transcribed and treated as text, illuminating the phenomenon of consumer behavior as critical in the coming out process. As interviews progressed, tentative themes were generated and tested on subsequent informants' interviews.

All themes—that is, patterns which emerged from the data once it was generated—were grounded in the data itself (Glaser and Strauss 1967). During the progress of the interviews and participant observation, and particularly after the completion of the actual fieldwork, it was necessary for me to read the transcribed interviews and field notes over and over, regarding the notes as text to be interpreted (Ricoeur 1976; Bleicher 1980; Hirschman 1992). I endeavoured to understand each individual interview and subsequently began a part-to-whole phase in which I related data items across interviews, searching for common patterns of experience. It should be noted that I did not transcribe interviews until all were completed in the field. However, during the fieldwork, I relied upon my notes taken during the interviews to direct further interviewing and questioning efforts.

At this point during the research, I broke down the data into categories and topics, looking for similarities and differences across the participants' contributions. The data was then put back together in a meaningful manner which described and illuminated the phenomenon. Jorgensen (1989) calls this arrangement of the facts a theory or an interpretation. The analysis of the data involved the method of constant comparison (Glaser and Strauss 1967; Lincoln and Guba 1987; Belk, Sherry, and Wallendorf 1988). New data was compared to my own prior conceptions and interpretations as the research progressed and unfolded. From this continuous process, patterns emerged and were elaborated upon. Also, since it is necessary to provide a thick, rich description (Geertz 1973) of the participants' consumer lives, I used many, many of their actual quotes and my own field notes to convey the meanings within the interpretation.

Trustworthiness of my interpretations of the data was ensured by methods of peer debriefing, prolonged engagement, and member checks with participants (Lincoln and Guba 1987). What follows is an ethnographic account of the lived experiences of the informants' consumer behaviors, supplemented by my own perspectives gained from participant observation.

Chapter 2

Meet the Informants

In this chapter, I offer brief biographies, including the coming-out stories of ten of the informants who contributed to this study. Space limitations would preclude biographies of all forty-four informants interviewed in the project. Thus, I selected ten of them in order to convey a sense of diversity on the bases of age, race, occupation, and the level of "outness" or willingness to disclose sexual orientation. For a brief synopsis of these characteristics for all the informants, please turn to Appendix 3.

I attempted to obtain a very diverse sample of gay men with differing perspectives on and involvement in the gay subculture. A critical issue involving the following portraits involves confidentiality and privacy. During the past twenty-five years, the gay movement has adamantly stressed being out and proud and the extensive disclosure of one's homosexual status. However, not all of the informants have reached the stage of being out to everyone. Thus, as in virtually all interpretive work, in order to preserve everyone's privacy, I have disguised the informants' identities with pseudonyms. Moreover, when necessary, I have disguised other details of their biographies such as locations where significant life events took place. Aside from these necessary fictions, other details concerning the informants' lives are accurate, according to their own self-reports.

Jeff

Coming out? I realize that really was only a couple years ago [laughs]. I never really considered myself to come out of the closet. I never really was in the closet. Really, like . . . um, mind you, as a young person, I was never very flamboyant or anything, like I wasn't a Liberace type, I guess you might say . . . [laughs].

As we used to say in school. I was . . . people would question me about that type of thing. I was young, and I just told them, "Look, I like guys, you know, so what?" I've never had to come out of the closet . . .

When I interviewed Jeff, he was twenty-five years old and working in a warehouse. I met him at Lesbian, Gay, and Bisexual Youth of Toronto (LGBYT) and was struck by the fact that every time I saw him, he appeared very different. On some days, he would be dressed in a leather jacket and punk garb. Sometimes he had dyed hair (blond, green, and other interesting shades). On other days, he would be dressed very neatly and preppy. During the discussions which took place in the youth group, he was always outspoken, candid, and friendly. I decided that the study would be enriched by his contribution since he always seemed so forthcoming and open about his life and opinions.

I interviewed him on two occasions. In his late teens and early twenties, Jeff lived his life as a hard-core punker who was somewhat open about his bisexual status with his punk friends. During this time, he regularly wore punk clothing and accessories including leather jacket, dyed hair, fourteen earrings on his left ear, a full mohawk hairstyle, pierced nose, and antiaesthetic clothing. He found that the punks were too closed-minded, however, and then decided to come out into the gay community in Toronto. He considers himself a "gay bisexual" which he defines as a person who is able to have sexual relations with women but does not choose to since "something is missing."

After an initial period of disorientation and shock, he began to enjoy the gay community very much, fit right in, and spend the majority of his time in the Church and Wellesley area of Toronto. He disclosed his sexual orientation to his family, who have not quite accepted it. Jeff attributes this lack of full acceptance to the fact that his family is strongly Pentecostal Christian. Despite his rebellious leanings, Jeff still respects Christians because he believes "that's the way they were brought up."

It is interesting to note that Jeff's realization of same sex attraction and subsequent coming out did not cause him a great deal of trauma or emotional upheaval. First, according to his self-report, he has always been very laid-back, relaxed, and good-humored. Second, in spite of his Christian roots (or maybe because of them), he has always been a rebel, as he expressed it, and becoming a punk and then an openly gay man were not viewed as overly negative or hostile possible selves. Looked at from Jeff's own perspective, he never attached a negative meaning to his sexual feelings or possible gay sexual self and was not disturbed by its development and realization. Shame, a devastating and pervasive emotion for many gay men, was never really a problem for this particular man.

Jeff states unequivocally that he identifies with gay life and subculture. Despite the fact that he lives and works in a suburb community over an hour away from the gay ghetto of Toronto, he likes to spend most of his free time within the borders of the gay area, socializing with other gay men, and seeing his boyfriend.

At the time of this writing, Jeff made a career change and is now designing fashion chain mail for clothing stores in the gay community. He has moved into the area and is seeing someone new. Jeff's high level of identification with the gay community has led him to focus his livelihood and everyday life within it—work, living, leisure, and shopping.

Lennie

And um, and I remember the thought occurring to me, "Does this mean I'm gay?" Which never really occurred to me before because growing up, calling someone a fag was the worst thing that you could call them. So I had never . . . thought of myself as being gay until that point in time, and when I thought about it, I thought, well, yeah. I mean, uh, it seemed clear to me that I was gay. And I figured that this was just some . . . I figured this was horrible. This was the worst possible thing that could have happened to me. Um, you know, I thought God was playing some cruel joke on me although I'm not sure I believed in God. I guess I tend to believe in God when bad things happen. Um, uh, anyway, I just . . . I knew I think that I would have to deal with it someday, but I decided that I did not want to deal with it. I just would not tell a soul, and um . . . and that was it!

In contrast to Jeff, Lennie felt extreme shame and emotional disturbance connected to his same sex desires, as the above quote vividly illustrates. By contrast, Lennie was raised in a relatively liberal, secularly Jewish family.

Lennie was thirty-two when I interviewed him. At the time, he lived in a spacious, nicely furnished flat on a quiet street in one of Toronto's older, more desirable residential areas. From the one long interview I conducted with him, it became apparent that Lennie's first twenty-five years or so were almost completely preoccupied with avoiding this negative possible identity. He was born into an upper-middle-class Jewish family, and Lennie's parents divorced when he was a teenager. He made many long-term friendships with other Jewish children his own age, and many of them went to the same university with him. By coincidence, they all moved to Toronto as well. His friends formed a very tightly knit, close group, and as Lennie expressed it, they all knew what the rest of the group was doing, "every minute of the day almost." It is not surprising then that his one greatest fear was that his friends would find out about his same sex attraction and then cruelly reject him for it.

Despite his fears and self-loathing, Lennie excelled in school, earning both a BA and an MBA, specializing in real property management. After a short search during the prerecession boom years in Toronto, he found a well-paying job as a real estate manager for a very large company. At the time of the interview, he still held the same job.

Lennie's reports that his psychological journey from being a self-loathing, unhappy individual to a very out and proud gay man was a traumatic one. During his late teens, he often "hung around" with some of his close friends who were heavy hashish and marijuana consumers. After a few years of resisting the temptation to use drugs himself, he eventually did begin to experiment with them, and in his own words, quickly became an addict, smoking up every day after school and work. Lennie found that using drugs was a very effective way to avoid the unhappiness, fear, and pain surrounding his perceived socially objectionable sexual needs. His friends, who were also heavily into drugs, were generally supportive of the addiction.

In 1990, Lennie decided to explore his sexual feelings more actively. He consulted a counselor, went to a coming-out group, and eventually joined Narcotics Anonymous. At the time of the interview, he had been clean for approximately four years, had disclosed his sexual identity to all of his friends, work colleagues, and family, was heavily involved in gay rights activism, and was planning to apply to law school.

While Lennie is currently involved in the Campaign for Equal Families, he does not identify heavily with the gay subculture or spend much time in "gay space" (e.g., bars or bathhouses), as he dislikes bars, as he puts it. Like many gay men I have met, he is one who enjoys participating in gay politics without getting too heavily involved in other aspects of the gay subculture.

Cameron

It [coming out of the closet] was . . . it wasn't like a big event. It was sort of like . . . it was always like an understood thing. That Cam has a boyfriend now or whatever. And it wasn't really like it was a momentous decision. It wasn't like I gathered all my friends together and said, "You might be wondering why I've gathered you all here today." Um, I don't think I particularly made a big deal of saying to anyone, "I'm gay" or "I like boys" or whatever. It was sort of . . . I guess because our crowd was very . . . sexuality was a very . . . I don't want to say unimportant because it was a very big part of our socialization, but it wasn't . . . an issue that people put emphasis on, any more than you have black hair and blue eyes or whatever. It was just something that was there, and it wasn't particularly discussed but sort of . . . background. The same as what race you were or what gender you were or if you had a disability or if you wore glasses, or whatever. It was just sort of a characteristic that you would list along with all your other characteristics. And it would obviously be taken into account if you were in a relationship with that person, you would have to say, you know, "I'm compatible with this person," and you wouldn't just think, "Do we like the same music, do we go to the same movies?," you'd also think, "Well, are our sexualities compatible?" And it was just something that we never thought about. Just like, I guess, straight people don't think about the fact that they're straight before they get into a relationship. It's just kind of there. I didn't have a problem with it [laughs]. I was very lucky. I had a good high school, I had good friends . . .

Steven Kates: Do your parents know?

Cameron: Yup! Um, my parents knew later on. I told my friends first. Most of us did. With one notable exception who told his parents first and they didn't have a problem with it. He was out to them for two years before he told all his friends. But that was unusual. Most of us came out to each other first.

Cameron is a twenty-two-year-old Canadian-born Chinese gay man from "an upper-middle-class to upper-class household" in the suburbs of Toronto, as he chooses to describe himself. At the times of this project, he was working as a graphic designer and production manager for a new, gay fashion and entertainment glossy magazine.

I interviewed Cam twice during my study and his interviews together comprise the longest texts from any of the informants. The interviews revealed some very interesting insights about Cam and his life. It should be noted that he is out to everyone he knows: his parents, family, friends, and work. Another important finding is that Cam is another one of those younger gay men who have had virtually no significant problems in accepting his sexual orientation. He adamantly reported that he felt no real guilt or shame when he came out of the closet. This might be attributed to the support and nature of his peer group. The high school he attended, situated in a middle-class, heavily Chinese and Jewish area of a Toronto suburb, is reknowned for its artistic accomplishments and liberal climate. Being gay was considered just another ordinary facet of life. In spite of the fact that Cam spends much of his working and leisure time in the gay area of downtown Toronto, he has chosen to live with his parents at home because he likes it there and because the rent is cheap (i.e., nonexistent). This may be interpreted as evidence of Cam's high level of comfort with his sexual identity. There are significant places for both gay subculture and his more traditional Chinese family in his life. He stressed to me that while he does enjoy spending time with gay friends and in the gay area of Toronto, he could not do this all of the time. He enjoys going to straight bars and baseball games some of the time.

Viewed holistically, Cam's interviews were remarkably incisive and observant. During the four hours of his two interviews, he was able to communicate a distinctive body of gay cultural knowledge that he has learned and, in a sense, collected, over the last few years. He is a virtual fount of gay folk knowledge which encompasses trends, fashion, ideology, manners, and history. In order to understand more about Cam and his life, I carefully read several issues of the magazine which he works at producing. The magazine itself is a composite of gay pop culture—entertainment listings, fashion spreads, Top Ten Club music lists—which is targeted toward the club kids or young gay males who frequent gay venues such as bars or nightclubs. It appears that Cam is able to use his vast knowledge of the gay community, gathered over a number of years of personal experience, reflecting it back to the relevant market niche. In this manner, the knowledge gained from consumption is converted into a productive enterprise.

Gareth

Oh, I must have been eighteen, maybe [when he told his mother he was gay]. Maybe eighteen-and-a-half, nineteen. Don't really remember, but I was not twenty. I know I was still in my teens, then I remember going into . . . I cried and cried and cried for a long time. I had actually gone to the Church and just sort of cried. I was so angry at God because he hurt my mom's feelings. I got over that fairly . . . it was never discussed really, for many, many, many years, and then I got into a serious relationship, moved in with someone and moved to Toronto, and that's when . . . I must say . . . it's only been . . . now that I've been out for so long and uh . . . but only now in the last couple years have I become really, really confident and secure about my being gay. I don't think about it as much as I used to, and I feel very normal, and I don't care who disapproves or who approves, you know. It's very different now. It's a different feeling. I don't know if that comes with getting older and becoming more . . . established and mature or . . . it's just a reflection of the times that we're going through. So many [people] are um, are choosing to . . . to confront . . . to be more confrontational and much more aggressive about the rights of homosexuals and the whole same sex spousal benefit stuff. I'm certainly much more tied to my community now than I've ever been, and I identify strongly with the community which I never used to.

At the age of thirty-four, after almost fifteen years of living as a gay man, Gareth is "becoming a fag," in his own words. He comes from a large, closely knit, athletic family which regularly goes on sporting holidays such as skiing in the winter. The family is also religious in an unconventional manner. Gareth's parents are Protestant. His brother has converted to fundamental born-again Christianity, and Gareth himself converted to Catholicism just before he decided to explore his sexual orientation at the age of eighteen. Despite the mix of different faiths within the same nuclear family, he reports that they all get along very well and that both his parents and his siblings acknowledge and accept his sexuality.

This acceptance, nevertheless, was not earned without pain. While his father accepted the disclosure quite easily, his mother had a more difficult experience. To complicate matters, Gareth's first tentative sexual explorations and ruminations occurred almost at the same time that he experienced a poignant crisis of religious faith which resulted in his ultimate conversion to the Catholic religion. Fortunately, his family accepted the situation fairly well within a relatively short number of years, and Gareth settled down to live quite happily with his first lover for the next ten years. After that relationship ended, he lived with another man for three years.

Gareth is now single for the first time in his adult life. He is making a career change to social work, and living as a student for the first time in ten years, he must learn to live on less money. Second, he is now beginning to identify heavily with the gay community. He now lives almost at the corner of Church and Wellesley, the heart of Toronto's gay area. He is more involved in gay politics and is making an effort to learn about same sex spousal rights. In his own personal view, this is also making a difference in his consumer spending patterns.

In sum, Gareth believes he is becoming a fag. He views a gay man as someone who is rather conservative, in a committed relationship, and spends both time and money in keeping the romance in that relationship. A fag, on the other hand, is much less conservative and even somewhat daring and risque. As Gareth told me, he is more politically aware now and angrier at the injustices which are inflicted upon gays and lesbians (and fags, presumably).

Gareth's anger, moreover, has also turned inward toward the community itself. As a gay man approaching thirty-five years of age, he is worried about becoming a *persona non grata*—undesirable and unimportant to other gay men and to a subculture which, he believes, unduly values youth and beauty over maturity and wisdom. During his one interview with me, he passionately communicated his fears and criticisms about a community which he thinks is fraught with dangerous and self-destructive habits, pain, and self-doubt.

Lance

I've been out for over four years. I guess I came out when I was in, okay, um, hmm, actually, maybe I sort of acknowledged to myself that I was gay when I was in my last year of high school. And before then, I just didn't want to put a label to it. I kind of knew, but I didn't want to say anything about it or even to myself. And then for first year and university, I was going through the confused stage, I guess, at times, you could almost say suicidal. But I don't think I would have done that.

Um, I guess . . . one thing is that when I came to this gay community, I expected to be . . . I just I guess I had this kinda utopian view that all right, finally accepted, like um, for what I am, right? For my sexuality? But I guess I caught on pretty fast that just because I'm accepted for my sexuality, um, that, just like there are like um, people from my culture [Jamaica] who are homophobic, there are like gays and lesbians who are racist as well.

Lance, who was twenty-four and just graduated from university when I met him, experiences life as a minority person within a minority—for Lance is black and was born in Jamaica. He considers himself "pretty well Canadianized" however. Now that he has graduated, Lance is working in a community theatre which performs productions on political themes such as racism, sexism, and homophobia. While he would eventually like to become a playwright, he finds that acting work is more available, and at this stage in his career, he is taking the work where he can find it.

His very first step in coming out, self-acceptance, was very difficult. He reports on feeling "confused." His previous self-conception of being heterosexual (however incorrect) was being challenged by sexual feelings and doubts that refused to remain buried. The contradiction between Lance's old straight self and the new possible self as substantiated by growing sexual, bodily awareness generated in him serious and frightening self-doubts, enough to make him feel suicidal. Lance chose to deal with his self-doubts and fears by exploring them and meeting others who might "be like him."

Four years ago, in order to explore his sexuality, Lance went to LGBYT and participated in the newcomers group. He decided to stay with the group and when I met him during the study, he was a newcomers facilitator himself. When he first entered university, he felt he had the freedom to come out, as he had moved out of the house and lived in a university dorm. After gaining some confidence, he told a number of his friends and dormmates about his sexuality and eventually told his mother. His father, however, still does not know.

Since moving out of his parents' house, change and self-exploration has been constant for Lance. When he first came out into the community, he reported that he was quite overweight. Over the last few years, he has been dieting and exercising in order to change this. When I met him, he appeared to be in good condition, but he still believes he has quite a ways to go.

Lance found himself in a curious double bind. On the one hand, he disclosed that he was used to experiencing culture from both a heterosexual and white perspective through mainstream education, film, books, and art. Once he came out, he found that his sexuality was accepted in the gay community but his race was not. After expecting to find an accepting utopia in the gay community, he realized that the gay community was really the "gay men's white community" and most of the culture—such as advertisements in the bimonthly gay magazine *Xtra!*—depicted and seemed to be targeted to white, young, blond, smooth torsoed, gay males. Even when he dated, he found that he experienced a subtle form of discrimination in that when he dated someone from another race, other gay men would "give them looks." Lance is now aware of this kind of pressure and has decided to resist it and work for change within his own community—just as he does by battling homophobia in his theatre productions.

Chretien

> I denied it. No, I didn't deny it. I said, "Yes, it's true at this point." Having studied Greek culture in the Roman time and so on, what I knew from Greek is that when they were going to war at fourteen, fifteen, they were doing a lot of homosexual experiences, and then by the age of twenty-five, they would come out of the war, or the army, and then they would get married and have their heterosexual . . . I thought it was the same thing! I really believe . . . like, I was not really lying to my mother. I really believe that it was a phase, and I remember using the word, *une phase,* a phase, a new . . . or I believe it was a period of time in my life where I would be like that, and then at the age of twenty-three, twenty-five, I would come out of the army or so to speak, and become heterosexual. At this time, I thought it was a normal thing. That it would be because the Greeks has done it that way.

Chretien is an extremely good-looking twenty-eight-year-old Quebecois Native, originally from a reservation near Quebec City. English is his second language. When I interviewed him, I was struck by his perceptiveness, intelligence, and increasing candor. When he was eight years old, his mother divorced his father and moved from the reserve to Montreal. When Chretien was eighteen, he moved from Montreal to Toronto where he attended university for mathematics. He is currently working as a human resources professional for the government and lives with his lover downtown.

Chretien honestly believed that his homosexuality was just a phase. When he was attending school in Montreal, he was reunited with his best childhood friend, Bill, and soon the two began a love affair and great friendship. After the relationship ended during the summer before Chretien went to university, Chretien experienced a very difficult period in his life. He was dissatisfied with his school and with Toronto. During this period, his mother, who had also moved to Ontario with her second husband, asked him if he was gay—if he would like to "embrace a man." Chretien was shocked, and he told her that for this stage in his life, he *would* like to embrace a man, but as soon as he got older, he would emerge heterosexual. His mother took this news very well, and suggested that he might like to inform his stepfather when he was ready. He now acknowledges that she knew and accepted all along that he was really gay and was trying to inspire him to accept it too.

After the first hour of our three-hour-long continuous interview, I remember that I began to feel uncomfortable about something that I could not pinpoint. Chretien had confided that during his early time in Toronto, he felt "no longer alive," and my feeling may very well have been one of misapprehension: what could be so awful about his life that he was dead, I wondered. But the uneasy feeling went deeper than that. I felt that something vital and important was missing from his narrative which would help place everything into some sort of perspective. Finally, Chretien disclosed this piece of information:

> Weekdays I would go out . . . and I was very happy. YES!!!!! We were very, very, very, very, very ecstatically happy. Um, Bill was a year older than I was so I guess he was nineteen at that point. Um, July of that year, Bill passed away. He had a motorcycle accident on the . . . the equivalent of the Don Valley . . . not the Don Valley Parkway, yeah, I guess the equivalent of the north south highway, most of it the 427. The . . . in Montreal. It was raining, and he was on a motorcyle, and obviously slipped and passed away. Um [pause], what we were talking about earlier that I was dead for two years.

As could be expected, Chretien went through "hell" the two years after. He described the funeral during which he cried and was acknowledged not as Bill's "friend" but as Bill's friend; the relationship had gone completely undisclosed.

After the death of his lover, Chretien explored gay subculture: bars, parties, and other consumption venues, and did not enjoy them at all. Instead, he made friends outside these venues, attended occasional parties or events, and eventually met the lover with whom he now lives. For the most part, he ignores manifestations of gay subculture and overall, regards it as *unimportant.* His locus of control is inward, as demonstrated by his intense concentration on his thoughts and ideas, that he seems influenced very little by external forces. His favorite possessions reinforce this notion: his dog and his ideas. In terms of coming out, he does not feel obliged in the least to come out to people who are *unimportant* to him. It is sufficient that his friends and his family know, although he will not deny his sexual orientation if asked. He does not condemn gay politics, but he is not interested in the topic either. His belief is that gay activists are too interested in telling other gays and lesbians what to believe and do, without concentrating appropriately on their own self-development. In his view, by overstepping themselves and intruding on others' rights to make decisions, they are concentrating too much on outward things—the things that do not matter much.

Ben

> I was brought up a Catholic, and I didn't want to go to hell, and get excommunicated from the Church, and all this shit. So I tried . . . I lived in fear, I guess, most of my younger life. Say, from the age of twelve when I realized there was something different about me 'til I was about seventeen, really, for at least four years or five years. I actually lived in fear of being gay. And what was going to happen to me, and that there was probably something wrong. Because it was the stories you heard from other people that weren't gay . . . My life was really . . . like, I was running through that period that I really wanted to die, commit suicide. I mean, which I didn't, I didn't try or anything. There was that period I really wanted to do something with my life—like end it. You know, because I felt like I was alone in the world, really. You know, 'cause at that time, I didn't really know . . . a large number of gay people, coming from a small town, you gotta keep it quiet, you couldn't talk . . .

Ben provides a very unique perspective for this study, as he is fifty-three years of age and came out in a small Canadian Maritime city in the late 1950s. He comes from a large Catholic family and has one gay brother and one lesbian sister. Currently, he has lived in Toronto for over thirty years and works as a counselor.

Coming out was a very traumatic experience for Ben, as he was forced to cope with his sexuality in the repressive 1950s. After contemplating suicide and spending a month in a psychiatric ward for depression, he began to meet men in his home city in eastern Canada. Soon, every weekend, he would socialize with other gay men, drinking and having sex. It was at this time that he developed his addiction to alcohol. During this period, he married a woman and entered the Canadian Navy. After learning that his wife was "fooling around" on him, he obtained a divorce and moved to Toronto where he currently lives.

Religion has played a problematic role in Ben's life. Ben was raised a Catholic in a large family, and the religious influence appears to have been pervasive and significant during his first years. He was frightened about "going to hell" if he was exposed as gay and excommunicated. When he left the small town where he was born and moved to a larger Maritime city and then to Toronto, the direct influence of his faith seems to have lessened. Nevertheless, the feelings of guilt and shame remained and like many other gay men, he escaped into alcohol abuse in order to avoid the pain.

During the 1950s and the 1960s, he reports that people "just didn't talk" about homosexuality, and disclosures would have seemed both shocking and inappropriate. Ben describes a time when gay life or subculture was considerably more hidden and closeted than it is now in most urban centers. There were fewer bars and places for men to meet, and exposure to heterosexuals was a very dangerous, frightening possibility. Yet, there was one bar, the Scarborough Bluffs, and the beach at Hanlan's Point where gay men regularly congregated.

Over the last five or six years, Ben has become more open about his sexuality and has come to trust other people more, a difficult issue for him previously. He reports that he has quit drinking completely and currently organizes alcohol-free conferences for the gay and lesbian chapter of Alcoholics Anonymous. His community work includes talks about AIDS and safer sex and shows where he performs in full drag. During our interview, he spoke repeatedly on how much more comfortable and satisfied he was feeling with his life as it is, as opposed to as recently as five years ago. Achieving self-esteem has been a difficult struggle for him, given his upbringing and life experiences. But as he puts it "I guess that's when [coming out fully as a gay man] I started to feel a little bit more acceptance of myself . . . when my life started to take a turnaround, but not a complete turn . . . I wasn't looking for approval from anybody else. That's the way to say it. I approve of myself, and that's what counts!"

François

> For me, gay people are some people who are outside from the community. They are not . . . I mean, they are . . . who are people . . . I wouldn't say sick people, no. Because they are born like that, that's the way they are. I think that they must be accepted. Accepted and that's it. I don't agree with the fact that they should have certain privilege. As soon as you give them privilege, it's going to be abusing people, and it's going to go overboard, automatically. If all the people that I saw yesterday [at the Lesbian and Gay Pride Day festivities] would be in charge of the government and things like that, my goodness! It doesn't look serious. Gay people, to me, they don't look serious. There seems to be only lots of tea party. Life would be a tea party. It would be with dancing and chanting and marching and nothing will be done.

François does not fully approve of himself, and many of his attitudes appear internally homophobic. He feels some contempt for other gay people and their struggle for equality and does not believe that same sex rights are appropriate; to him these kinds of items are "privileges." Moreover, François votes for the openly homophobic, socially and economically right wing Reform Party of Canada and, as he phrases it, will always side with the "establishment" or "law and order," even if these institutions oppress him in certain ways.

François came to Canada from France over twenty-five years ago, and at the time of the interview, he was fifty years old. His parents were solidly middle class, and he was sent to boarding school while living in France. He is a self-employed dental technician who makes molds for false teeth. His great hobby in life is ballroom dancing, and he rehearses for competitions several times per week.

François is almost completely closeted to heterosexuals. Only his close gay friends, a few relatives, and a few "lady friends" from ballroom dancing know about his sexual orientation. "Years ago," he attempted to approach his parents, but they refused to discuss the sexuality issue. He is certain that his parents and siblings know that he is homosexual, but no one discusses it. In other words, while his sexuality is known, it is not acknowledged or considered a topic of proper conversation. Moreover, if his friends who "surround" the French consulate knew that he was openly gay, they would "shut their doors" to him, and he would no longer be invited to cocktail and dinner parties. He chooses to live an entirely "straight life" outside of his social circles within The Fraternity, the gay men's club that I observed. He told me that he needs to live in a straight life, and he could not be gay "all the time." As a result, he takes elaborate precautions to ensure that his different "lives" do not meet and that there is nothing flamboyant about his appearance whatsoever. He also consciously limits and restricts his involvement with the organizations and venues within the gay subculture.

Five years before our interview, François almost married a woman, following pressure from his parents. He reports that she was "a French girl from France" and that he liked the girl. However, he began to feel very uncomfortable with his engagement, and eventually canceled it, deciding to "approach life differently." He joined the gay tennis club, made some friends, and eventually joined The Fraternity where he is able to relax "a little bit." Everything, he emphasized, was done discreetly.

François' choice to remain closeted is not the only important dynamic working within his self-concept. It is important to stress that his loyalties and attitudes side with those who would oppress him, and he openly acknowledges this fact. That part of his self-concept which encompasses being normal and socially accepted is more important to him than the relatively less important—and esteemed—gay identity. He accepts his own marginalization when he acknowledges that he is "not sick" but not entirely part of the community either. For him, gays must somehow remain "apart" from others. When he claims that they are not serious, he is coming as close as he dares to implying that gays are inferior to the more serious and important heterosexuals.

Ron

> That was really tough for me because with um, with telling other people, I think you've really admitted it to yourself, and there's so much inner conflict with that. The whole psychology behind um, growing up and being told that gay is wrong and it's evil and it's perverted and sick, and of course you're not going to make those associations with yourself, and finally when you do come to terms with this is what I am, but your heart of hearts tell you you're not those things, you're not evil, and you're not corrupt, and you're not sick. It was really tough, because um, a really big part of me really believed all that that I've been told. So I must be a really terrible person, and on top of being . . . on top of admitting to myself or thinking to myself that I'm this terrible person, I have to go tell everybody else that I'm this terrible person too. So it was really, really hard. I told my closest sister first.

Ron, a twenty-nine-year-old waiter who also teaches dancefit classes, was born to a large Catholic family. I was very much struck with his excellent sense of humor, sharp wit, and his candor in elaborating how he feels and what he believes. During our interview at his downtown apartment, I think I laughed more than during all of the other interviews.

His father died when Ron was sixteen, and by some fluke of circumstances, had won a trip down the Nile in Egypt at the same time. Since his father was not able to go, Ron took his place and had his first sexual experiences with a man. He then realized that he was gay and had a very difficult time dealing with it. He lived in a suburb of Toronto and felt very bored, isolated, and restless there. When he learned to drive, he regularly started to go to "seedy, low-life" bars, as he calls them. He did not make any "quality friends" until a few years later. Instead, he had to rely on bars where they allowed underaged teenagers to enter.

When he first understood his sexual feelings, he attempted to convince himself that they were part of "just a stage"; he maintains that he denied that he was "really gay." It was important to him to grow up normal and get married. He believed himself to be sick and perverse, but he knew "deep down" that he was not. Yet, he found it very difficult to convince himself of his worth when so many external forces seemed to be relaying the same negative message.

Ron is out to almost everyone in his life. The first person he told was his girlfriend at the time. Then he told his best friend. Following these disclosures, they "had a threesome." He continued to tell his four sisters and his mother. He is also out at work. Moreover, he does not care in the least if strangers believe or know that he is gay.

Ron spoke extensively about something he calls the "lover syndrome." He believes that there is an abundance of tension in the gay men's community due to the typically frantic search for companionship. He vividly describes the panic and insecurity he thinks gay men experience when they do not have a date for a long period of time. He firmly believes that gay men and straight men dress and consume very differently. Gays, he maintains, are more flamboyant and take more risks with their spending. In his own life, he confessed to using "beauty products."

Overall, Ron feels very secure with his life in the present. He enjoys his work (except for the overly demanding customers) as well as his sidelines as a dancefit instructor and a makeup artist. He keeps himself constantly busy with these jobs and his other hobby, music.

Antonio

I think I reacted like a lot of gay men when I first came out, especially if they enter a relationship for the very first time. Um, I still hadn't accepted it completely. Let's say I hadn't accepted the gay lifestyle. Not that there was a lifestyle to accept, it was a little different than today. Today you have a whole infrastructure, community, and everything. Back then, there wasn't. It wasn't as extensive and as obvious, so for me, being gay was still something shameful, it wasn't right, it was something that was a little antisocial, so what I had with my friend was um, our own little, and he had the same thing, trouble accepting the fact that he was gay. We found that we were only gay to each other and not to anybody else. I mean, take us out of that situation, we were perfectly normal. And well, this relationship was our own little secret, our own little world, and it was only limited to each other, we certainly didn't embrace the rest of it, didn't embrace the lifestyle, and I even avoided gay people, not that I knew many, except for my two closest friends, I didn't associate with any gay people, certainly with flamboyant gay people, who were obviously gay, you know, who sort of accepted this lifestyle. I was still out of it. So it was just my two friends, who sort of reacted the same way that I did. And this guy I was seeing, and you know, we weren't really gay, we just liked to sleep with each other and that's what we told each other.

Antonio, who was thirty-eight at the time of the study, was born in a small city in central Ontario to Italian immigrant parents. Antonio reports that it took him a very long time to accept his sexuality, and while he is now out to almost everyone in his life, he still has not told his parents.

When Antonio was in his first year of university, he had an affair with one of his professors. When this professor left for a year in France, Antonio decided to follow him to do a year's study there. This relationship ended after his study term in a small French city, and Antonio remarks that neither of them really accepted that they were gay; they simply lived together and enjoyed sleeping with one another. Once he graduated from university, Antonio returned to live in Paris for four years. During this time, he felt quite isolated and lonely, and even "flirted with the idea of going straight." He decided against this option, however, and when he returned to Toronto, he participated actively in the gay community there. He maintains that he finally "acquired a gay identity," went to bars frequently, and became involved in the AIDS Committee of Toronto as a volunteer.

During his affair with his professor, Antonio did not self-identify as gay even though he was regularly sleeping and living with another man. However, near the end of his four years in Paris, he was becoming "connected" to other gay men and just starting to "break into" gay social circles. As with many other informants, it appears that the novel experience of socialization with one's own kind provides a positive alternative to previous societal conditioning which resulted in Antonio's condemning himself so cruelly.

Nevertheless, the acquisition of a gay identity and a healthy measure of self-acceptance was by no means the end of Antonio's growth and development. By the end of the decade, he began to feel "confined and limited." He was bored with going to the same places. He then started to frequent other kinds of restaurants and bars for variety. He notes that he did not make a conscious decision to do this at the time. When Antonio makes a major decision in his life, he does it "by attrition." By this, he means that he gets bored with one experience after doing it many, many times and moves onto something new.

Antonio works very hard as an interpreter, and he finds that he is very often busy with this work. He speaks English, French, and Italian, and he is currently learning some Spanish as well. Often he must travel out of town to serve his clients. During the study, he was in the process of buying a new house in the Cabbagetown area of Toronto and living with his partner.

The previous text is no more than a series of brief sketches of the lives of some of the informants. It is presented only to convey a notion of who these men are and some of their important life experiences. I now turn to the focus of this book—consumer behavior. The next chapter describes in-depth the consumer subculture, which is an essential and integral aspect of the gay men's community in Toronto. The subsequent chapters describe the consumer rituals which help to create, change, and maintain this complex subcultural meaning system. Both sections will illustrate and examine the gay man as a consumer, emphasizing consumer behavior as a realm of everyday, lived experience.

Chapter 3

The Creation and Maintenance
of Gay Consumer Subculture

Gay subculture is largely a socially constructed phenomenon (see Brake 1985). That is, as a separate world, it exists as a collection of articulated, coherent meanings that are culturally shared among many out gays and lesbians and even among some heterosexuals who are "in the know." If the meanings that constituted the subculture were so radically different and dramatically varied from person to person, there would be a failure to communicate (both verbally and otherwise) and understand the contents of subculture, such that the subculture *could not exist at all* as a separate, meaningful social phenomenon. By contents, I refer to the unique meanings, language (i.e., the vernacular or lingo), norms, values, customs, mores, activities, and traditions which are generally thought to constitute a subculture (Pfuhl 1986; Rubington and Weinberg 1987; Simmons 1987).

Consumer rituals and their accompanying subcultural artifacts are important in the construction and maintenance of this gemeinschaft with respect to its place within the larger cultural world. The great concepts, ideas, and ideologies that describe much of the human condition—love, hatred, oppression, power, affluence, liberation, and struggle—are all intangible and cannot be represented visually per se. Thus, they must be either represented or symbolized by things (i.e., products and possessions) or enacted within the context of certain activities (i.e., rituals), into which people symbolically pour these meanings (McCracken 1986, 1988a). As represented visually and materially, gay subculture becomes manifest in various patterns of good and service consumption which play certain roles within the lives of the informants, in a manner previously described by Solomon (1983) in his discussion of consumer behavior and symbolic interactionism. Not only do goods and services used within the gay subculture constitute the means by which impression and identity management are accomplished, but also material possessions and activities serve as tangible "clues and cues" (particularly to the neophyte or the newly out gay man) as to appropriate social behavior and cultural meanings.

Just how is this subculture represented in the lives of the informants? How is it organized? What are the various meanings attached to the purchase, use, display, and disposition of consumer goods and services? In reply to these questions, the following discussion will elaborate upon the role of subculture as a lens (McCracken 1986) or way of viewing an important portion of the informants' shared worldview.

THE ACCULTURATION
TO GAY CONSUMPTION NORMS

The process of acquiring new meanings, beliefs, and stereotypes concerning the purchase and use of consumer goods within the context of a gay, social world is not analogous to a quantum leap. Rather, over a period of months or even years, gay men come out of the closet and come out into a new social milieu in which they are exposed to new people, objects, meanings, and places (particularly including commercial venues). It is almost as if the physical world takes on a whole new appearance; in fact, it is the individual's perspective that changes. As some of the participants of the study communicated this experience, it is as if one is a child again. One sees part of the world for the very first time in a new, fresh light. Their particular phrasing of this phenomenon is strongly reminiscent of literature reviewed for this study (e.g., Herdt and Boxer 1992, 1993). The old selves associated with gay youth are, in a sense, considered dead to their parents, and a new one is created, or in a sense, *reborn*. The consumer acculturation process constitutes a significant part of this modern, social rite of passage as described by van Gennep (1960) wherein an individual undergoes a transition period and finally incorporates a new social status. Brendan, a twenty-eight-year-old gay male I interviewed who is currently going back to university to major in psychology, revealed the workings of a similar process when he spoke about Levi's loose fitting jeans:

Brendan, 28: I'm sure the people that are marketing that product are going after the gay audience, especially if its something gay people would be inclined to buy, like designer type jeans, or um, even like a silk product or whatever. I guess I firmly believe this. I know I'm biased in saying it, but I firmly believe that um, they're going after a gay audience even though they would justify it saying that they're going after women and women are consumers.

Brendan noted that he has no real, objective basis for believing that this product is being targeted to gay men; he simply believes it. In fact, Brendan stated that he is "biased"; the bias may be interpreted as the results of six years of his being out and having had acquired knowledge and meanings within the gay social world. Thus, a product such as Levi's loose fitting jeans which feature billboard ads with the barechested men or the Calvin Klein advertisements featuring Marky Mark in various states of undress acquire an extra meaning for gay men, as acquired through the consumer socialization process: "Straights think they're for them, but they're *really* for us." In so doing, gay consumers develop a lens or perspective for viewing not only the gay subculture or their own gemeinschaft, but also one for viewing the larger culturally constituted consumer world. The informants learned gay meanings from ads and other people who, in turn, helped them interpret them, and a mindset is developed from these initial experiences; this perspective is often reinforced by subsequent experiences in which the informants' developing mindsets interpret events in a particular, somewhat stereotypic manner. In another study, Freitas, Kaiser, and Hammidi (1996) note that certain marketers code advertisements with ambiguous images to invite both gay and heterosexual readings.

Cody, a thirty-one-year-old teacher whose main passions in life are writing music, playing guitar, and singing, has also experienced a shift in the manner that he views certain products in various contexts. Some time before the study, he became interested in tattoos after a close friend got one:

Cody, 31: Tattoos used to be a prison thing, really, and before that . . . I think when I look through cultures and society when you look at things, people who are in subcultures did things more artistically to their bodies and things. I mean subcultures back centuries ago were pirates, and they wore earrings and tattoos. Tattoo . . . I think the tattoo has always been the symbol of the ultimate controversial thing . . . style thing you can do to your body. I don't think you can do much more than a tattoo. That's visible, anyway. A tattoo is really uh, kind of rebellious. I was in a band called World Tattoo and specifically . . . my friend . . . has books about men who have tattoos on them. And um, we're called World Tattoo because the tattoo is the symbol of people being . . . of people being unique and pushing that sort of envelope of acceptability and the world part being a world consciousness view. So, I, yeah, but then again, you see tattoos, and you go to something like, you know uh, what's it called? The CNE [Canadian National Exhibition], now you'll see adolescents who'll put on temporary tattoos and then they'll fade away. So I think there's always this inner play. And not just gay culture, black culture with rap . . . not just black culture but rap black culture did a lot of things with gold chains, especially, you know. So . . . So there are little trends that happen . . . well, tattoos, no, because heterosexual men who are seen as more you know rugged and rough and you know, prison culture and drug culture will have tattoos. Interestingly enough, *I always think that heterosexual men who do some of these styles are viewed as being more dark and dangerous and that if a gay man does it, at least amongst gay society, it's viewed as a lot more benign and not dangerous at all, and trendy and artsy.* (italics mine)

The meaning of tattoos, for Cody, is largely dependent upon their context. Relevant literature also claims that tattoos and other forms of body transformation such as piercings are strong symbols of disaffiliation and rebellion (Sanders 1988, 1989). Yet, in Cody's view, when gay men use these same products, their meanings are somehow modulated. Fascinatingly, a fashion that gay men have appropriated from other subcultures such as pirates and prisoners has been sanitized such that the original meanings have been changed or even inverted so that this product is fit for gay men to consume. Some of the informants believed that the process occurs the other way around: gay men start trends which the larger culture adapts after a meaning cleansing process. Like the great majority of the informants interviewed, Cody's view on various products—his relevant net of associations and beliefs—has altered during his seven years as an out gay man.

Acculturation to gay consumption norms and meanings takes place in other situations as well during the coming out process. Visiting a gay bar for the first time—that important rite of passage into gay society—was mentioned by many informants including both Brendan and Martin, who experienced similar moments upon their first excursions, as illustrated:

Brendan, 28: I had about three weeks off on holidays, so I decided to go to a gay bar in Toronto, 'cause I didn't have any established circles of friends or anything. And uh, I remember, I phoned up the equivalent . . . the gay line type of thing in the newspaper, and I asked the person . . . I sort of described myself, and I asked where a bar would be, just a normal bar that I could go to that um, there would be sort of people like me, he suggested Chaps at the time. I remember, I walked by it like four times without breaking stride, like just looking straight ahead, terrified to go in, and I guess, well, on the fourth time, I finally just said, this is ridiculous, and I took a deep breath, and turned and went in, and uh . . . I was pretty nervous about going in because I didn't know, really that much about the gay world, and I remember seeing a dreadful movie when I was younger. Al Pacino in *Cruising.* Oh, I hate that movie! I've subsequently seen it, and I realized that there was this disclaimer at the front saying, "this represents a very small portion of the leather scene, represents a very small portion of the gay world, blah, blah, blah, blah, blah," but when I was younger, I don't remember reading that, and I don't remember seeing it. I remember renting the movie. I'd heard it was a gay movie, and I'd rented it sort of secretly and watched it, and I was just like, "holy shit!," you know? I mean, this whole leather, S&M scene. I just thought, oh my God!!! I think that put me back . . . kept me in the closet for many more years than otherwise. *So when I walked in, I didn't know what to expect, but I thought there would probably all sorts of different rules and . . . and you sort of . . . it was kind of like the idea in the movie, that the sort of handkerchief on this, certain pocket meant something, I guess I thought that . . . that different things would have different meanings, and I was really nervous,* because I didn't know if someone would come up and say, would you like . . . could I buy you a drink? If that meant something? I had all these things going through my head, totally out of realistic proportion. And uh, I was in the bar for um, for the night, and I was just petrified, you know, standing sort of in the corner, just absolutely shaking. And um, just before the lights were going on at the end of the night, someone tapped me on the shoulder, and said would you like to go for coffee, and I hesitated for like . . . a minute, 'cause I thought, what does this mean, you know, am I like agreeing to go and have sex with this person?

Martin, 25: I was scared to go to a gay club. I had this . . . I had this perception that a gay club was gonna be a lot of leather and a lot of . . . a lot of, you know, leathermen and um, just that it was gonna be very scary. I didn't know what to expect. I thought that men would be all over each other, and and you know, it would be maybe very seedy and dirty. Because I had no idea. I had never been to a gay club. I didn't know. I had just heard stories, you know, here and there are read bits and pieces, but I didn't really know. So I was scared to go. So the first couple of times [my best friend who was also gay] asked me. I sort of declined, and gave a stupid reason. But finally he said, "It's Friday night, let's go downtown. You've gotta meet some men. You've gotta get into the action, because you know, you're very depressed," so I said, "Okay, sure." So we went downtown, and we went to Komrads. The first time.

SK: How'd you feel, going in?

M: *Nervous, really nervous.* I remember . . . when I was . . . when I was at the door, the bouncer, um, looked at [my friend] and looked at me and asked me for my ID, and uh, I had blond hair then, and I guess I looked like an impressionable young adult male, whatever, I was blond, I guess I was considered good-looking, fresh meat, whatever. So the bouncer said to me, he took my driver's license, and said, "Oh! Cute," whatever. And [my friend] said, "Don't you want to see my ID?" and the guy was like, "No, don't flatter yourself" and as I walked in . . . he pinched my ass or something. And I walked in. I was just like, wait a minute! What's going on? This is very strange. This is like, you know, I've never had this kind of contact with a man before. Really . . . some people looked at me and went, well, you know, you're really attractive, and kind of hitting on me. Teasing, flirting, whatever it was. So I was nervous. But I went in and it wasn't anything like I thought it was gonna be. Like, there was things that I did expect and things I didn't expect. So . . .

SK: Can you tell me what you did expect and what you didn't expect?

M: Sure. I expected . . . I expected there obviously to be a lot of men and there were. I didn't expect there to be any women. And there were women there. I'd never seen a drag queen before in my life, and there was a show going on that night. Um, this drag queen that now . . . since I know is a friend of mine, and uh, her name's Vida, and she has professional runway work and this kind of stuff, and she was doing, *Don't Cry for Me, Argentina*, and she was wearing like this like, boa, and this feathered hat, and she did this number, and it was incredible. And I just sat there, mesmerized by it. I couldn't get over it. I couldn't get over that the person on stage was actually a man. What I didn't expect was it to be as friendly as it was. Like, it was very friendly and very down to earth. Like, it wasn't like I thought . . . you know, just eyes all over the place and staring and you know, just cruisy and pickup. There was that, but it wasn't as intense as I thought it would be and people were just hanging out and having a drink and having a good time, you know. People went after work for a drink or went for a dance, or whatever it might be. But it was like . . . a *normal* club. It was like a straight club, um, except for the fact that you knew when you walked in that you were on the menu.

Brendan and Martin, like several of the informants, first viewed the gay bar as a dark, frightening, and potentially harmful stereotype, due primarily to negative images communicated in media and social interactions. Once they acquired personal knowledge, however, the old stereotypes were shattered; as part of an ongoing process of acculturation new, usually more positive, tolerant meanings took their places. While the instances here were not quite as dramatically self-revelatory as some, it is notable that both Brendan and Martin experienced both a change in their viewpoints regarding gay bars and a corresponding subtle shift in their self-concepts. During those hours spent in the gay bars, they had conquered previous fears and felt more comfortable about *themselves*. This ease or comfort often marks the beginning of a new self-esteem, a crucial aspect of the self-concept which acts as a global evaluator.

For the most part, all of the informants in the study left the gay bar with at least slightly different perspectives on the bar and on themselves. Similar to Schouten's (1991) study of cosmetic surgery and self-concept transformation, the first few visits to the gay bar may constitute an important rite of passage for gay men whereby one acquires a new social status after a period of separation and liminality. During this period, a slow acceptance of one's sexual orientation occurs and a gay identity begins to form. However, the gay bar is not the *only* consumer rite of passage that inspires meaning acquisition and consumer acculturation. A walk down Church Street, it seems, is enough to gain a nascent appreciation of the open display of certain gay fashions and consumer fetishes, as vividly described in the following:

Jeff, 25: Well, I can't remember the first time I met with gay people, but I remember one of the first times that I came into the community and I was somewhat disgusted because the first thing I saw was a bunch of queens on the corner, looking and talking and acting and being sluts, and it was a dirty attitude to me because I grew up in a Christian household, and I was always taught properness. You know, it's not proper to be that way. And if you're to be that way, it's not in a public place, and they were flaunting it in a way where . . . you know, like, well, fuck you attitude [laughs]. If you don't like it . . . well, they were flaunting their sexual orientation. They're being gay or bisexual or lesbian. They were . . . just like, just being rude, all out rude. And to me, uh, rude also has to do with the fact that coming out in public and saying, "I'm gay, everybody, I'm gay!" You know, if you don't like it, fuck you, the rest of it! You know, being crude and crass, so to speak in that way. Although I was crude and crass in many ways, but in that way, I thought that was . . . the peak. That takes the cake. Kinda thing . . . Well, the queens, the transvestites, as well as the leathermen, [they were in] all this in leather, carrying their whips and chains around, dressed in studs and not in a punk rock way but in a . . . in a sadomasochistic way, and I took it as a threat. I didn't know what they were all about. It scared me. It was scary because . . . I . . . you hear all these stories in the heterosexual community about what gay people are all about, and you know, me being gay, I knew what I was like, but I could have been just one in a million, you know what I mean. I didn't know that . . . just anybody was gonna walk up to me, drag me in a back alley and rape me or what . . . you know? [laughs] You hear all these stories about washroom sex and the rest of it? Oh, don't use the public washroom, somebody's gonna rape you or whatnot, this kind of thing, you know? And in the gay community where you expect it most. Go to a public washroom in the gay community? Oh, I côuldn't! Forget that! You know that kind of thing? As an experience, or . . . or uh, you hear all these stories about the Second Cup [a very popular local coffee shop where many gay men and lesbians frequent] whereas back then I didn't hear much about it, but these days, you would . . . walking into the Second Cup for the first time would . . . *to me it seems like nothing now. Right? I'm used to it and I know the people, so I know they're not really . . . they're not bad people. They don't . . . it's a joking thing.* You know, it's a humorous thing to talk and joke about being gay and being a transvestite and being a leatherman and whatnot. You know, but for someone who doesn't know all that much about the gay community, and gay people, even being gay is completely scary. It's a threat to life, you know! And I mean, the styles and the fashions that go through the community, as well. Saying, oh, does that mean I have to be like that? A role model. Role models, you know? *They buy all these dresses and the fancy leathers and the boots, and whatnot, and I thought to myself, I have a Mohawk, does that mean I don't fit in? Am I not..you know. Maybe I'm not gay!* [laughs] *Maybe I'm just a man who likes men.* What are they gonna classify me as? Or what if one of them calls me over and starts talking to me, what do I say? You know, it's almost like going to a new school, except that it's a bigger threat. It's not just being beat up after school. It's being personally abused or verbally . . . not verbally, mentally abused where they're doing it and not knowing it, you know. Like, me even coming from a Christian household. One of the first conversations I heard at the Second Cup, was these guys putting down Christians like you wouldn't believe! And they were like complete anti-Christ. You know what I'm saying? And uh, they were . . . it went on and on and on. And I was disgusted in a way because . . . I have respect for Christians. They believe what they believe because they were taught that and they stuck to it. It's simple lives for simple people and simple homes. You know, picket fences and the rest. You know, but . . . um, being where they are and like, everyone believes in their own politics. Everyone has their own politics. You know, you can't . . . you can change it in some ways, but you can't change a person altogether, and you can put a different type of clothing on them, but the way they think is one way. That's what I thought when I came into the community. I was thinking, these people are just not for me, you know? And I was just scared because I didn't know what to expect. I was more scared in the gay community than I was in the heterosexual community. You know [laughs], when I first came in. *I changed over time.* As I got to know more people and understand that really, you know, gay people as a whole are not like that. It's just that . . . individuals, you know . . . that make up a mass of such.

SK: I was going to ask you . . . how do you feel now? Your feelings were quite negative.

J: Right now, *I'm basically the opposite of the way I was.* I was always open about my sexuality and stuff, you know, but uh, I can look back and say I've come so far. You know? I've come from being scared in the community to wanting to live here! For safety. So, like, a lot has happened, you know?

Brendan and Martin enjoyed their first boosts in self-esteem and reductions in fear, and Jeff's coming out experience and shift in consumer perspective was qualitatively much different. As a young punk rocker starting to come out of the closet, his Christian roots inspired him to feel extreme disgust and contempt for the deviant queens dressed in drag and leather which he saw during a visit to the gay ghetto. In contrast, his first introduction to punk subculture was marked by feelings of curiousity and attraction. His reaction was also one of perplexity: how could he be gay if he did not look at all like these particular people on the street? This appears to be a common issue for many of the informants: since they personally did not fit into certain public consumption stereotypes (drag, leather, chains, tight clothing, etc.), *how could they be gay?* Often, a fuller, more sophisticated understanding and appreciation of the wide diversity of gay men which follows these first experiences is subsequently acquired.

A deeper understanding of Jeff's feelings is gained from a review of some of the literature on spectacular subcultures like punks. According to Fox (1987), hard-core punks often evaluate the authenticity and commitment of other punks according to both stated adherence to punk ideology and manner of dress. A shocking, strange haircut such as a full mohawk is usually considered evidence of true punk commitment by most punks within the subculture. These consumption cues often, but not always, indicate whether the individual is devoted to the nihilistic, anarchistic punk ideology. According to Fox (1987), moreover, use of dangerous drugs like glue is a surefire indication. Jeff, upon viewing the queens, and having been conditioned by punk subculture to believe that ideology is invariably openly displayed and reflected in physical appearances, may have experienced a fundamental misunderstanding typical of neophytes within the gay subculture: not all gays "look gay" in a stereotypical manner (as manifested in leather, an effeminate or campy manner, and drag). He had not yet come to appreciate that the gay men he saw were, most likely, members of smaller subcultures within the gay subculture (drag and leather, respectively). As Jeff expressed to me in his interview, in the punk world, "your ideology is expressed on your jacket." He had entered the gay milieu expecting this dictum to be invariably true there as well. However, when he realized that the walking, animated stereotypes on Church Street had nothing in common with him, he began to doubt that he was a part of this social category or subculture. He was correct; at the time, all he shared was a same sex attraction. What followed in his life was a years'-long learning process which changed his view of the gay consumer world. Ironically, one year after the interview, Jeff started his own business making and selling chain mail vests targeted toward gay leathermen. Moreover, his self-concept has kept pace with his acquired complex of meanings: he is now completely out and committed to the well-being of his community.

It has been argued here that the gay men interviewed have experienced an important acculturation process as pertaining to various consumer goods and experiences. According to the data collected, "things just don't seem the same" after coming out. McCracken (1986) refers to a culture as a lens through which individuals view their worlds. On a microcosmic level, once gay men begin the coming out process—undoubtedly one of the most significant social learning processes in their entire lives—their various thoughts, feelings, opinions, attitudes, dispositions, and associations regarding some products (i.e., the various manifestations of consumer meaning) undergo serious, self-reflective change. This finding is thoroughly consistent with the literature on subculture as reviewed previously. Recall that the relevant literature posits that people with a common problem gather together in response to societal domination and develop their own meaning systems (Brake 1985) as one possible solution. The social interaction that ensues results in shared meanings, vernaculars, and ideologies. This social interaction, evidently, inspires a learning process of new consumer meanings as recounted here.

THE DEEP MEANINGS
OF CONSUMER GOODS AND SERVICES

It has been argued above that a certain process of meaning acculturation occurs upon entrance to the gay community studied herein. As found from the data, this is a course of development which involves social learning via advertisements and media, conversations with gay others, and public display and subsequent observations. It will be argued below that a complex of meanings is the result of such a transformation within the minds and cultural worldviews of the gay consumers interviewed here. The following important meanings (i.e., subcultural categories and principles) were identified by several of the informants and will be discussed in turn: political beliefs and consumer goods, and consumer stereotypes.

Political Beliefs and Consumer Goods

As stated previously, coming out is a process that embraces many events or aspects of development within the lives of gay men, such as disclosure to others and internal self-acceptance. One of the developmental steps (Minton and McDonald 1984) as described by the informants is the eventual questioning and challenging of societal beliefs or norms. Internalized homophobia, one important aspect of hegemonic culture which entails considerable self-loathing due to one's stigma, is progressively exposed and labeled as the problem itself. Coming out is usefully viewed as the unlearning of old, self-destructive thinking patterns and beliefs imposed by others and by society at large. Once these previous beliefs and accompanying attitudes are challenged and partially eradicated, new beliefs may replace them. Many informants such as Ben and Lennie asserted that they feel more comfortable with themselves and happier with their lives than ever before. This is not surprising, as they used to hate themselves for being gay. In a profound sense, almost all of the informants (François, whose biography was briefly outlined in the previous chapter, is the only exception) experienced an ideological shift. This shift is also interesting because it often represents a significant inversion of the conventional order. Gay people and subculture are now considered positive, for example. Further, sometimes this inversion process progresses beyond acceptance of oneself and other gays; frequently during the interviews, informants would "bash back" at heterosexuals for prejudice, closed-mindedness, and poor fashion sense.

Such ideological meanings are often embodied within goods and consumer rituals (e.g., see McCracken 1988a). Moreover, goods themselves usually carry prescribed manners of use or avoidance. Various informants reported on the political ideologies embodied in particular consumer products in their own lives: goods which also served to represent their gay identities. Nigel, twenty-eight, had recently graduated teachers college in Montreal when I interviewed him for the study. Coming out during his early twenties was a very difficult process for him, but in a sense this struggle may have begun even earlier in his life; at the age of fifteen, Nigel developed anorexia while dealing with the loss of his best friend who had moved away. Looking back, he realized that he must have had an adolescent crush on this friend. Before this bout with illness, he recalled his early puberty and the upsetting challenges it presented to him:

Nigel, 28: I remember, um, well I was . . . I mean, when I think back to like, when I became . . . sexually mature. Um, I mean my first fantasies were always about other guys in my classes, and they were consistently about guys, but I still had this thing about, I'm not gay, I'm not gay. Because when I was that age, around twelve, even though I kind of had the feeling before I was different, um, I remember walking downtown in Toronto at the end of the seventies, and all you'd see is these clones everywhere. Wearing leather with the handlebar moustaches, like outside of St. Charles Tavern and The

Quest. I believe, was the other name of the bar at the time. And it's like, oh, if that's what it means to be gay, well, I mean, I didn't really . . . think about it. But I didn't say it and think it in so many words, but if that's what it's like to be gay, I don't want a part of that. Please make me straight.

At the time, Nigel was preoccupied with harmful stereotypes of gay men, and it was through these manifested stereotypes that homophobic ideology was able to influence him. The gay bars and the men's manner of dress and grooming were matched to existing negative stereotypes which were indicative of homophobic ideology. Now that he is in his late twenties and feels secure in his gay identity, the constellation of largely political meanings surrounding various products are very positive, by contrast; he mentioned that he feels "empowered" when using or enjoying products which he associates with gay life. For example, listening to music is Nigel's favorite hobby. Recently, he has begun to listen to "queer-themed music," as he calls it, and particularly to a band called the Pansy Division which openly and energetically celebrates queer sex, love, and identity through their music. One of their songs, "Smells like Queer Spirit," is a blatant takeoff on Nirvana's song, "Smells like Teen Spirit," and this fact is strongly indicative of the strong, proud, and queer political meanings which Nigel now embraces with considerable alacrity. Consistent with the proud poltical meanings described above, Nigel invests considerable political meaning in his T-shirts, preferring ones that openly declare his sexual orientation. Here again, the ideological meaning is clear: no fear of heterosexuals or homophobia.

Russ, a twenty-nine-year-old accountant originally from a small city in Ontario, also considers himself quite attuned to the strong political beliefs invested in the products in his environment. The thoughtfulness of the quote below illustrates the involvement which many of the informants feel with some of their product choices. It is evident from the data that after years of experiencing abuse from others and from oneself, it is important for informants to take a strong stand on beliefs which pertain to being gay, coming out, and oppression:

Russ, 29: I tend to uh, read the T-shirt or the message that they're trying to state or the button they're wearing. See where it's coming from and then . . . why would someone be wearing something of that nature? And then try and fit it to that person. I find that the same button on one person does not mean the same thing on another one. The red ribbons, for instance. They mean various things on different people. When the red ribbon campaign first came out and the pink ribbon campaign, and all the rest of them, it was to raise money and awareness. Those were the two key issues, and I found that it was very, very effective, in that sense. Well, years have gone by, and I found that it doesn't have the same meaning it once did. And I find that, with myself, the only times I will wear a red ribbon is when I'm in mourning from someone who died of AIDS or during their main campaign in December. I find that it's too much of a fashion state-ment for some people. Some people support the cause, not with their dollars, not with knowing someone or doing anything for anyone, but rather, they feel that . . . they want to do something, they want a voice, they want to be a part of something, but they're not. And so by wearing this red ribbon which they purchased for a dollar, they feel that, "Oh! wow! This is just . . . it's given me a purpose in life," and I found that . . . I mean, I go deeper than that. I want to help people if I can. I want to do the silent things in life rather than going around and you know, "Look at me! Look at what I stand for! Look at my beliefs!"

It is important to note that Russ has been extensively involved in many organizations and causes within the gay community. Using his skills as an accountant, he has done the books for Lesbian and Gay Youth of Toronto, the Gay Community Dance Committee, and the Pride Day Committee. Doing constructive activities has always been more important than making fashion statements, although he recognizes the political ideology inherent in both types of actions. For Russ, wearing a red ribbon in honor and support of people living with AIDS and who have died of it is too important an ideological issue to degrade into a simple fashion statement. Thus, he wears his red ribbon only during occasions he believes are appro-priate, such as after the death of a friend from AIDS; this is another example of consumer ideology as defined in Wallendorf and Arnould (1991). Thus, Russ' actions neatly illustrate two concepts:

consumer ideology (i.e., the way products should be used or bought), and the potential political nature of products (i.e., the deeper, often political meanings which products symbolize).

Russ' passage above also reveals a very important process which occurs within the context of the gay subculture. The last section deals with meaning changes of products once an individual has come out of the closet and the way culture-as-lens transforms. Moreover, consumer ideological meanings may change continuously after one is out. First, the red ribbon was an important form of remembrance and protest, as interpreted by Russ. Then after a number of years of personal experience, the meaning changed into a fashion statement. In other words, an originally powerful, inspiring, and important symbol was diluted and lost the power attached to its complex of ideological meanings. During this process of meaning dilution, something very important—the power behind the symbol—was lost. In a profound sense, constant use of the red ribbon by many people transformed the ideological meaning from a statement of enormous loss and unthinkable interruption of humanity to something one puts on in the morning to appear trendy and cool. The degradation of meanings has been recorded in other studies. For example, Schouten and McAlexander (1995) note how the increased diffusion of Harley-Davidson bikes among "inauthentic" bikers has diluted the original, wild ideology and mystique surrounding the product. Belk, Wallendorf, and Sherry (1989) elaborated upon consumers' division between the sacred versus the profane in the discipline, and assert that a previously sacred good can become contaminated and lose its preciousness if used in proscribed manners.

One of the most prevalent and powerful political ideologies underlying various products as identified in the study involves the in-your-face display of politically-oriented T-shirts which feature slogans such as: "Heterosexuality is not normal. Just common," "Fag," "Dyke," "I'm not gay but my boyfriend is," "Friend of Dorothy's," "I don't mind straights as long as they act gay in public," and many others which might be considered very shocking and offensive to some. During the participant observation portion of this project, I viewed many of these T-shirts in diverse locales such as Vancouver, Toronto, New York, and Washington, DC. Some of the most common occasions to wear them are at political marches, Lesbian and Gay Pride Days (or weeks), and at gay social events such as parties.

The creation of political meaning may assume various other subversive forms. For example, during the fieldwork, I found one particular poster advertising safer sex which was publicly displayed in the Second Cup coffeeshop in the ghetto. It featured the following captions and accompanying photographs: "the Moral Majority," with a picture of several gay men jumping up with their arms raised in the air; "Family Values," with a picture of two barechested men embracing; and the third, "Right to Life," matched with the picture of a condom. As Hebdige (1979) points out, this technique of juxtaposing disparate, seemingly incongruous elements or stimulii involves *bricolage* and is a clever manner used to subvert conventional ideologies and create new ideological meanings which appear more liberating. One implicit message which may be semiotically read from this poster is that the authentic, truly moral people in society are gay men who engage in community, love one another, and most important (as the advertisement was developed by San Francisco's AIDS Committee), engage in safer sex. The advertisement is also an attack on the Christian fundamentalist right (the Moral Majority imposters) in the United States as led by public figures such as Pat Buchanan, Pat Robertson, and Ralph Reed. Another example of this type of subversion with a somewhat similar meaning (which is not quite as complex or difficult to interpret) involves the use of a particular T-shirt which I saw worn at a number of gay events. It stated, "The Christian right is neither." The data support the contention that subcultural consumer products with strong political content often bash back at organized religion, among other perceived institutions of compulsory heterosexuality, homophobia, and antigay intolerance.

In summary, across a number of informants and cases within the participant observation, I discovered that consumer goods and services were carriers of both consumer ideology (i.e., the way consumers believe a good should be used or consumed) and of political ideology describing how society should be in relation to gays and lesbians. Before someone comes out of the closet, these beliefs were generally either very negative and critical or neutral toward products such as gay bars, Doc Marten boots (also for the punk association with this product), red ribbons, and gay sartorial style, for instance. However, as described in the previous section on gay acculturation, these meanings eventually change and develop even beyond the coming out process. Unsurprisingly, these types of meanings are often angry, hostile, and political with regard to the heterosexual majority or dominant culture. This ideology of rage provides the raw materials and fuel for a process which a number of authors, including Hebdige (1979), label symbolic resistance—a basic function of the spectacular subculture—which is thought to provide "imaginary" solutions to "real" problems. However, for gays who have developed from states of self-loathing to self-acceptance and pride, the politics represented by products represent a shattering of the discourse of domination and a shift to a discourse of liberation. Can this truly be considered imaginary?

Consumer Stereotypes: Goods, Services, and Style

Can a product be "gay"? In *The Unofficial Gay Manual*, gay lifestyle is humorously satirized by presenting a number of meaningful consumption stereotypes of gay men. Interestingly (and perhaps alarmingly), the research here lends empirical support to some of these material stereotypes. Often, "buying in" literally does mean *buying in*. (Some readers may also form their own opinions that buying in often means "selling out," but that topic will be discussed further on when I discuss conformity and consumption in the gay community.)

Of course, one might argue that in the strictest, most objective sense, a product could not possibly be gay, for products as inanimate objects or processes do not possess sexual orientations. However, it must be stressed the paradigm underlying this work is largely a socially constructed, symbolic one. According to the symbolic interactionist perspective, people perceive their social worlds, interpret the meanings of people and things within them, and then choose to behave (Solomon 1983). Thus, if people believe and assert that a product is "gay"—it is gay.

Carl, a sixteen-year-old high school student, likes to shop at the Body Shop for various toiletry purchases. He maintains that shopping there is one of the giveaways that one is gay:

Carl, 16: When you have guys going to the Body Shop, people normally think that's gay. Because the Body Shop sells perfumes and things like that. I think it's something that shows you care. So once you do something at the Body Shop, people just assume that you care, and once you care, you're gay. If you're a guy. 'Cause guys don't care.

SK: Care?

C: Anything. They don't care. Stereotypically, men, they don't care. Stereotypically, society has men in the position where they don't care. If something happens, they don't care. And if they care, this is the sensitive type that we're talking about here. You're such a sensitive guy! [laughs] Or and then, if you're sensitive, you're gay! You're like, like . . . I get stuck with this all the time. People will go, "He's such a sweetheart. I'd love to out with him. He's so nice. He's gotta be gay!" And that's because it's at the Body Shop. That's why [they think] I'm gay. Um, yeah, so whenever I go to the Body Shop . . . I find that the only guys you ever see in the Body Shop, and there's one just right on the corner, because a lot of guys go . . . a lot of guys who go to the Body Shop are gay.

In this example, a retail establishment is given as an example of a stereotypically gay product or consumer experience. If the product demonstrates or symbolizes caring or concern, then it is considered gay. Implicitly, he is communicating the notion that certain products are gendered or directed toward one sex or the other. If consumer behavior is "inverted" or "gender inappropriate" (a term which he told me he hates), then this fact is a very probable indication of an individual being gay. From Carl's point of view, one can also discern the notion of an ideological duality: gay versus straight, caring versus indifference, good versus bad. Both heterosexual and gay men are being stereotyped by this informant, to an extent, and these traditional gender traits pour their cultural meanings into the Body Shop experience. Another informant, Cameron, asserted that while gay men are being associated with stereotypically feminine traits, he does not assign a negative valence to this observation.

Similarly, Jim interprets the social world such that certain products are stereotyped as gay:

Jim, 24: . . . a couple months ago, they were having this big party which I was considering going to, and it was called the White Party, and the idea being that you had to wear white clothing. So, I didn't really have like this, a nice white top, went out to get one, and there's . . . there's one top in kind of the style of it, I ended up buying it. I referred to it as my gay top. It's really tight, and has like the zipper from the neck, partway down. And just . . . I look at it and I think . . . it's one of those things you see on a guy, you automatically . . . even when you see it on a mannequin, you automatically think, "Fag!" Why? Just the style. I've only seen it worn by gay men. Pretty much, the only times I've only seen it worn, like once or twice on the street, but aside from that, it's always been in a gay club. I don't think I've even seen it advertised anywhere, and in terms of the stores that carried it. Again, for the vast majority of it, it was stores that were in the core downtown gay area."

SK: So, if you think . . . do you think um, most gay men seeing that style on other gay men would make the "Aha! Fag?"

J: I think most people seeing that style on another man would say, "Aha! Fag!"

SK: Even straights?

J: Yeah.

SK: Why?

J: Cause again, it's something that . . . it's not only that particular style but other things akin to that. I've only seen advertised or associated with gay personas. If anyone's been wearing it on TV, it's been a character that's been identified already as gay. Um, so I think that's . . . it's kinda . . . that's the closest thing I have to a shirt or something to big pink triangles on it or anything else.

Another informant, Jeff, a twenty-five-year-old former punk rocker, suggested during his interview a very interesting phenomenon related to the stereotyping process: the constant borrowing or appropriation of fashions from one subculture to another, implying the shifting and continual nature of stereotype creation. For instance, in Jeff's opinion, gays have appropriated kilts from punk subculture and tight jeans from rocker subculture. Appropriation also flows in the opposite direction, moreover. The dominant, mainstream culture (i.e., straight men, in Jeff's opinion) have appropriated the earring fashion from gay men. According to the few informants who spoke concerning the constant fashion appropriation process, there is a constant swapping of fashions back and forth between subcultures and dominant culture. However, one important element is *not* exchanged, and informants implicitly realize this fact: the original subcultural meanings invested in the good. This largely horizontal fashion diffusion process may be contrasted with McCracken's (1988) vertical, revised trickle-down theory in which subordinate social groups appropriate the fashions of their superiors (and thereby co-opt various powerful symbols); the latter then change the fashion in order to maintain the distinct symbolic representations of power. For example, Jeff recognizes that when heterosexual men wear earrings now, the original gay or feminine meanings have been stripped, sanitized, and virtually eliminated. Hebdige (1979), in his work on punks, illustrates this point when he asserts that the fashion system appropriates shocking apparel and accessories, tones them down, and strips them of any subversive power, rendering them virtually impotent. Mainstream appropriation of minority-oriented fashions also occurs across class lines. For example, denim jeans were originally marketed for working-class men in the last century. Now, they are considered a fashion for young people and designer jeans are marketed as hip, chic, and expensive fashion items.

Pat, a young participant who lived in the "ghetto," in his interview, suggested that the "frilly" shirts with string laces are very feminine and gay. While he does not condemn them for being so, he is not attracted to that kind of style as a matter of personal taste. He does suggest a very important associated belief with stereotyped products: a heterosexual would "never" wear it, in his view. It is tempting to speculate that during the time period when a fashion is very popular among gay men, heterosexual men would tend to avoid it. However, after a number of years when everyone wears or uses the fashion, it is considered safe for he-man consumption (in other words, they will not be labeled as fags for wearing something considered too outrageous, unusual, or risqué); the subversive sexual meanings have been stripped by clever marketers who position the product differently. It is most significant to remark here that in the minds of the informants, the very opposite is occurring. Gay men in the study believed certain products to be stereotypically gay because they possess a labeling capacity. The participants generally expected that heterosexual men would tend not to wear these types of products.

During the study, it was discovered that certain products, as illustrated above, were considered to be gay associated because they were considered to be the "in things" among gay men. While gay products are usually clothing and certain items of jewelry which display gay symbols, there are many other examples as well, as cited by various informants. For example, Jordan, a twenty-six-year-old Eurasian informant, believed that Evian water is gay because he has seen many gay men drinking it during physical exercise. While he recognized that heterosexuals use this brand of water, it is his personal impression that gay men would tend to use it more. Similarly, Ron believes that baseball caps are a very gay purchase because he has seen so many older gay men wearing them. Even music can assume a gay meaning, as Arnold asserts. While *Threesome* was a movie about two men and a woman engaged in a ménage à trois (in which one of the men is gay), *Haddaway* and *Working Girl* are examples of artistic mass culture which do not have even a historical association with gay subcultures or gay people. Another informant, A.J., possesses the stereotypic belief that because gay men are very concerned about personal appearance, that they use greater quantities of hair gel and mousse. Marshall noted that he has heard of some gay men's apartments decorated in "Early Penis," indicating the existence of gay furnishings and artistic phallic symbols. Jeff also talked about fancy gay food dishes.

Lennie, whose short biography was featured in the last chapter, makes a very relevant point about another feature of consumer stereotypes—the personal freedom associated with them:

Lennie, 32: Well, that's something that . . . it's one of the things I like about being gay is . . . you can do . . . things that straight men would um, be uh, um, needled for doing. Um, you know, um, you don't have to . . . all these . . . you don't have to put up a macho front, and you can uh, be a lot freer to express yourselves, so certain forms of expression . . . I would consider . . . not necessarily exclusively gay but . . . things that gay men are . . . tend to do more easily than straight men like dying their hair or buying um, you know, a dance CD or, I don't know, buying certain clothing I guess.

It should be noted that Lennie's hair turned prematurely grey before he turned thirty, and for a period, he did dye it back to his original black color. He believes that gay men are often freer of traditional taboos to which heterosexual men are subject. His sentiments are reminiscent of those of Pat and Jim, who spoke of Toto dogs and frilly shirts as consumer symbols which challenged the masculinity of the gay men who possessed them. As Carl, another of the informants, phrased it, "You're already in hell, so you might as well wear makeup too." Gay men, by coming out of the closet, have openly acknowledged that they have subverted their masculinity and their politically and socially dominant position in society as men. According to many of the informants, wearing makeup, dying one's hair, or wearing unusual or provocative clothing (just to name a few examples) are relatively unimportant breeches of societal norms. Thus, coming out of the closet, in a profound sense, sets one free to experiment with one's consumer activities and associate oneself with gay products, while it simultaneously and paradoxically stereotypes a gay man.

The existence of stereotyped products are the result of personal, historical, social, and arbitrary associations (Wilson 1993). As stated previously, there is no objective rule which irrevocably connects signifiers with the ideas they represent (Mick 1986; McCracken 1988a). According to the informants, gay men within the subculture have a particular look or style which they often display in public. Moreover, during the many consumption venues and other events I attended, I did become aware of an aspect of *homo*-geneity among various gay men there. It should be emphasized that the consumer behaviors described here by the informants are jointly enacted in that they depend upon the existence of an audience to reinforce the self; also they are combinations of various consumer behaviors to produce a holistic style. The style is also very public and its overall message is that the wearer is gay. In other words, the informants recognize that the simultaneous use and display of certain products, along with the manner in which they are used, indicate gay identity or the abstract concept of gay.

According to the informants, these stereotypes are very helpful to them as these "pictures in the head" of gay people assist them in identifying other gay men and thus, in making sense of their social worlds. One striking aspect of the stereotype is that being well presented (i.e., being well dressed and coiffed) implies being better presented than heterosexual men. Many of the study's participants communicated the stereotypic belief that gay men were better dressed, better groomed, and generally more interesting and sensitive as individuals than their heterosexual counterparts. Some qualified these beliefs by asserting that these qualities are neither a genetic result (the better-dressed gene, perhaps?) nor the result of anything so blatant as the immediate determination to dress more becomingly upon coming out. Rather, informants often expressed the idea that a change in sartorial beliefs occurred slowly as one became more familiar, comfortable, and accepting of other gay men and gay social occasions.

Gay sartorial style appears to be an important social aspect which is learned fairly early on in the gay coming out process. Three young teenagers—Sam, David, and Arnold—whom I interviewed all mentioned that they believed that gay men, as a whole, dressed very well. Moreover, the most closeted of the participants, François, was also educated in this belief; while he is fifty years of age, he is still relatively new to gay subculture and meeting gay men in social situations:

François, 50: It's . . . I guess being gay is a general attitude that's not only artifacts that you wear. But you see, meeting for the first time a gentleman forty years old who is too impeccable, too nice, too calm, too perfect, I say, "Ah Ah!" There is something that is not straight there. And after, nothing you can say. He has a suit, tie, jacket, perfect, nothing flashy, nothing flamboyant, but it's too nice, you know what I mean? You can be sure that he's careful and [sits] in order not to wrinkle the jacket, not to wrinkle the pants. That gives away, [in] my opinion, somebody who is gay, and in the old days and gays were not the way they are now, when gays were not wearing certain things which is accepted now, especially in North America, not in Europe. That's how you could think that you were meeting somebody gay as well. It's just too impeccable. That was one of the points that men would let another man know that I'm gay because he was impeccable.

SK: Impeccable?

F: Impeccable . . . nothing you could say . . . the French curve . . . the shirts too white . . . it was the right place . . . the neck of the jacket would be just too shorter than the curve . . . the shirt . . . the jacket . . . fine, fine . . . I've seen my father . . . I've seen my uncle

. . . [they] were gentlemen the way they dressed, but they never came too close to being dressed the way I am because I am too, when I get dressed, really, careful not to wrinkle my shirt, my jacket, my . . . it's not . . . it's not flamboyant, but it's a way to show, in my opinion, that we are not really straight.

François' rich and detailed description of gay style indicates how older gay men of his generation might identify one another during mixed social occasions. Also, even men over fifty who did come out previously, may not feel completely comfortable wearing some of the outrageous, sexually overt messages on T-shirts which I have noticed during the participant observation aspect of this research. One should also remark on the term François uses to identify this style: "not straight." In fact, he never used the word gay to describe it during our long interview together. Recall that François is very closeted and has extensive contacts with his ballroom dancing associates and friends who surround the French consulate. To them, he passes as a heterosexual man. Generally, his life is more centered around his straight world, which he "needs." Thus, in this informant's mind, the world might be divided more into "straight" and "not straight" because the concept of gay, with its often open and political connotations, is not something he has yet accepted: as he phrased it, "I am gay yet not gay."

Culturally stereotypic gay style goes beyond the belief of exaggerated care in dressing and grooming. Ordinary products such as shorts, T-shirts, socks, and boots are often put together in meaningful *ensembles* and subsequently assume gay meanings or style in the minds of the audience. Overwhelmingly, informants reported on the "new clone look" or style which they believe is quite pervasive in the gay community and, to a significant degree, symbolizes gay identity. The informants described possessions whose individual meanings define lifestyle or subculture. Moreover, they described possessions whose joint use (in various combinations) collectively denoted gay subculture or people:

Cameron, 22: ACT UP's [the AIDS activist group in the United States] demonstrations were also very . . . they came up with this urban combat mode of political T-shirts. That was a fashion statement as well. Um, political T-shirts, sunglasses, baseball caps. Shorts. And combat boots. That was the *uniform*. Um, bead chains with the whistles on them, um, the big silver chrome whistles that they'd carry and that reinterpreted itself back in the gay club scenes. You saw a lot of them . . . a lot of people wearing that. It was the new clone look. Clean-shaven, generally, sometimes all the [hair] shaven off, completely skinheaded.

One particular gay style or look which has evolved over the last five years was the "urban combat" look, as described above by Cameron. Most interestingly, he describes this sort of style or outfit as a "uniform," indicative of the level of perceived similarity among various "militant" gay individuals. The uniform is often described by informants as a composite of very short shorts (usually worn quite tightly above the thigh), white T-shirts, baseball cap, rolled socks, and "clunky" black Doc Marten boots. Pat confirms this observation, recalling an incident in which he was able to "tell" that someone was gay by sartorial style even though he was not within the geographical boundaries of the gay ghetto at the time (where it is usually assumed that if one is there, one is gay):

Pat, 23: I think um, the, okay, well the Body Body [clothing store] and the Calvin Klein wear, tight body-fitting bodysuits. Those I would label as gay as in . . . usually when I see someone—even, like, in the straight community, at work, wearing those things, it's, like, that looks very gay, I'm thinking in my mind, um, also the shorts that are very short, the cutoffs, they're not down to your knees which is the straight way of wearing it, which is kind of . . . if you ask me but up the . . . I guess . . . more than up the thigh, I guess, um, and I would say if you go out on the street in the summer and see the typical, I guess, like, gay male wearing two earrings, wearing a short haircut, um, the body-fitting bodysuits and T-shirts, cutoffs, and the short jean shorts, and Doc Martens, and usually one or two chains, necklaces. And you could say, they're pretty well gay . . . [laughs] That's really quite funny because other than . . . there are signs. Um, I just think there are. It's . . . there are a few things. One is eye contact, if you make eye contact with a person. One big thing was something a friend of mine did. We saw these two guys across the street, and they were wearing workboots with worksocks and they were nice, neatly rolled down, and short shorts, and they were both wearing cutoff shorts and they were like really short and very tight. And they were wearing a very skimpy top and little frilly stuff and they were wearing their little baseball caps and . . . and I just knew that they were gay as soon as I saw them. I just went, they're gay, and my friend goes, very sarcastically goes, "No! You're kidding!" And yeah! You can tell, by things like that, and as soon as they passed, they both like gave us eye contact and stuff, so it wasn't anything um, surprising that they were. Um . . .

SK: Where was this?

P: Near the Eaton Centre. So . . . so it wasn't necessarily in the gay community. So, uh, I guess that's . . . I didn't know uh, like you never know 100 percent sure but, unless you're in the community, and even then you're not 100 percent sure, but we were out of the community, and we saw these people, so they kind of stuck out, um like a sore thumb . . .

Another informant, Marshall, twenty-eight, who describes himself as a "furniture queen" due to his love of collecting it. During our interview at his apartment, he pointed out some of the acquisition history of some of his furniture pieces, including the white marble columns which appeared to dominate the entire living room. Although he lives quite close to the heart of the gay ghetto at Church and Wellesley, he considers his apartment as being situated "just on the edge of the ghetto" and correspondingly, does not view himself as what he calls "a subculture gay." Rather, he views himself as more "mainstream" because his life does not "revolve" around being gay. Nonetheless, he does understand the system of gay style outlined here, and as one can understand from his following comments, he sometimes participates in it personally. Marshall asserts that he can "tell if someone's gay" by the fashions they wear, especially if they are within the Church and Wellesley area of Toronto:

Marshall, 28: And clothes. Um, I don't have a lot of clothes. I have a couple typical fag outfits. The cutoff jean shorts and the black combat boots with the socks pulled down. I have a couple . . . one or two, of those. . . . All you have to do is walk down Church Street and you know the ones that are gay and the ones that are straight . . . by what they're wearing. Well, not all gay men dress that way, but those that do, you can tell they're gay.

SK: Okay, last time, you . . . can you give me an example, how would you do it?

M: By what they're wearing.

SK: Can you tell me in a bit more detail?

M: What I described earlier. By the Doc Martens, the worksocks that are rolled down just a certain way. You know, fashion's very important to these people. The short cutoff jean shorts. The wide belt, usually black. The T-shirt, white T-shirt. Uh, quite often a chain with the rainbow circles on it.

SK: Freedom rings?

M: Is that what they're called? Okay. Um, baseball hats. Mirrored sunglasses. Mirrored sunglasses seem to be for older gay men though.

I also found during the study that some informants believed that stereotypic gay styles have changed over the years. Antonio, who was thirty-eight, and Don, who was forty-five, during their respective research interviews, both came out in the 1970s. As noted previously, Antonio came out in the late seventies in Paris, France. Don, a Jewish real-estate agent who is heavily involved in AIDS-related charities, came out in the early part of that decade. Although originally from a Canadian Prairie province, he came out in Oregon when he attended a university there to study dance. Antonio and Don have the following comments about gay style about the early and late seventies, respectively:

SK: Can you describe it [the style in the 1970s]?

Don, 45: Yeah, sure. It was blue jeans. Blue jeans, different types of shoes or sandals or running shoes. It's not that different from now. And a lot of workshirts in Oregon. Oregon was very, very popular with workshirts and that was also . . . not just the straight but the young were very hippy. Into that lumberjack look because that was very . . . that was in Oregon, and Oregon's filled with trees, and we were all . . . we all wore our hippy sort of outfits and we were all very much what was . . . the workshirts were a real big thing for . . . plaid workshirts were very big for gay men.

Antonio, 38: Very colorful [laughs]. That was the style then! Very fluorescent, flamboyant colours. The things that straight men wouldn't wear. And uh, you know, I think it was more of a . . . the look was more stylish when I started going to bars and people actually used to dress up to go to bars, and it was a little more . . . it was closer to high fashion than it is now. Now, it's sort of the opposite. Now, you dress and you wear a lot of shorts and tanktops and tight T-shirts and cycling pants and things like that which is definitely . . . that's what I define as exercise wear. It seems to have become, um, the dominant theme in gay fashion now.

The idea of standardization or of the gay "uniform" was reported quite frequently by the informants. While one might reasonably claim that all gay men are unique individuals, it can also be argued that public display, word of mouth, advertising, and the fashion system conspire to create and diffuse popular cultural stereotypes which some individuals may adopt and many more others observe and remark upon. It should also be noted that I observed a number of different consumer gay "subsubcultures" within the gay area that I observed: leather, full drag, the above described short shorts and Doc Marten look, the preppy look, and the jock look (complete with skimpy tanktop, spandex, and a baseball cap)—all of which may be considered homologous styles.

In summary, the informants interviewed reported at length on particular gay looks or styles with which they were very familiar. Only some of them reported that they participated in these fashions from time to time. One significant style was the well-dressed, well-groomed gay man. The other style was really a grouping of somewhat similar styles which included the juxtaposition of various consumer items—shorts, Doc Marten boots, and plain T-shirts or T-shirts with explicit slogans on them, for example—which, when worn together, articulated a particular coherent meaning or ideology to informants.

One might express some objections to this controversial finding. After all, one might reasonably maintain that all gay men are unique individuals and this finding represents a form of extreme stereotyping. The gay movement has protested and argued for the last four decades that gay men and lesbians should be judged on their individual qualities and merits, not upon their sexual orientation. Moreover, it is the enemies of the gay movement who insist upon the existence of a gay lifestyle and agenda, and attempt to stereotype all gay men or lesbians as similar in significant matters. All political ideology notwithstanding, the stereotypic gay look or style was an overwhelmingly strong and pervasive emergent discovery from this piece of empirical research; at least within a consumer dimension, *gay men stereotype themselves* by choosing to wear fashions which they believe are similar to what others are wearing and by believing that other gay men wear these certain fashions. Moreover, they play with extreme sex-role stereotypes by wearing campy or butch uniforms. As one of the informants, Don, summed up his observations concerning the existence of gay style:

Don, 45: Well, gay men . . . well, you know, attention to detail, fastidiousness, well-groomed, um, I think most gay men are very aware of how they look. And I think uh, you know, they look at themselves as if . . . *somebody else would be looking at them.* And that's . . . they're doing it not necessarily for themselves as much as for somebody else.

Issues of impression management, self-concept, resistance (to the subculture itself as opposed to the dominant culture), and conformity—as they all relate to consumer behavior—are all strongly suggested by this finding, and they will all be addressed in depth further on. Yet, at this juncture, it is important to gain an understanding of the thoughts and feelings underlying this type of stereotyping. Informants communicated a number of significant reasons for their beliefs. First, some, such as Ron, believed that the gay dating scene to be very competitive, and the prospect of being alone for life was a very real, haunting specter for many gay men. Thus, gay men would tend to dress well and use many grooming products to maintain an image of youth, sexiness, and health.

There is another reason suggested by the informants which helps to understand the existence of consumer stereotypes. Gay men, upon coming out, begin to live uncharted lives. In other words, there are no set, predefined roles, societal expectations, scripts, or culturally accepted life programs communicated to them as there are for heterosexuals (i.e., find a compatible man/woman, get married, have children, work at a steady job to support the family, send the kids to college, retire, die, etc.). As some of the informants have agreed, figuring out who was to pay for the bill after a dinner date was a difficult issue. As Solomon (1983) maintains, consumer goods and services may be interpreted as social stimulii which can act as antecedents to later behaviors. Especially for gay novices who have no correct idea of how to behave within the new gay milieu, products may serve as important and useful cues to doing the right thing. During this period of the initial rite of passage into the gay subculture, the use of products (either wearing them or watching them for socially valuable information) may help neophytes by communicating the stereotypic set of role expectations until they have been socialized, have formed secure gay identities, and have acquired sufficient personal experience and knowledge which can serve them satisfactorily in gay social situations.

For stated reasons of in-group exclusivity, safety, and protection then, gay men upon entrance to the subculture (i.e., coming out to other gay men) learn a system of meanings (as outlined in this chapter) and also believe that this knowledge is almost virtually their own. There is another probable use of this type of language: the symbolic creation and maintenance of community (see Cohen 1985), using marker goods (Douglas and Isherwood 1979). Certain communities or subcultures must have particular boundaries (aside from the obvious geographic ones) in order to determine "who's in" and "who's out" and what kind of ideas, norms, and artifacts are part of the community or subculture. The construction and maintenance of gay community—which is often enacted ritualistically with consumer activities and possessions—is one of the topics which will be explored in depth in the ensuing chapters.

Chapter 4

Consumer Behavior
and the Construction of Gay Identities

Minorities, the oppressed and the marginalized almost always have a better understanding of the unconscious underpinnings of their society and culture than do the majority, the top dogs, and the insiders. To "pass," they must play a role consciously, whereas those in control usually can "pass" without conscious effort. Thus, listen to poets; look at unpopular art; seek out the malcontents and the deviants.

Dr. David Elkins
Political Scientist at the University of British Columbia
(*Globe and Mail*, October 4, 1995)

The previous chapter focused on the meanings and consumer acculturation of gay men explored during this study. The purpose of this chapter and those subsequent is to explore and present how informants *use* various meanings which they discovered within the gay men's subculture in relation to consumer goods and services. Thus, meanings as found within products and experience may be viewed as "raw materials" for further human activity. To echo consumer theorist Grant McCracken (1986), culture—the complex set of meanings as represented by beliefs, norms, values, traditions, and practices—is also a blueprint for human activity and helps shape what people do with their products and even the future meanings these products will assume. From the data, the finding emerged that goods and services were critical in the creation and maintenance of self-concept, politics, and community.

The relationship between consumption and self-concept has been well-documented in the consumer research and self psychology literatures (e.g., see James 1890; Cooley 1902; Mead 1934; Goffman 1959; Sirgy 1982; Wicklund and Gollwitzer 1982; Solomon 1983; Markus and Nurius 1986, 1987; Belk 1988; Schouten 1991). Taking a more humanistic or interactionist perspective, the symbolism of consumer goods and services (as usually employed or enacted within significant rituals) serve as "cues and clues" which may be interpreted by people in their roles as consumers and facilitate in the ongoing development of aspect of the self-concept. As I found during the study, consumer rituals play important functions in the formation, development, and maintenance of the different types of gay identities found commonly in gay ghettos: the closet queen, the out gay man, and the out and proud queer activist.

PASSING: CONSUMPTION PATTERNS OF THE CLOSET QUEEN

In Goffman's (1959, 1963) seminal works on the development and presentation of self within social contexts, he presents the notion of "passing," a concept which refers to the set of activities in which people with discreditable identities engage in order to conceal their socially awkward, deviant, or objectionable stigmata such as race, sexuality, or unemployment. Successful passing results in others believing that one is a "normal," in Goffman's parlance. The ritual construct as discussed by researchers within a variety of disciplines (e.g., Erikson 1959; Rook 1985; McCracken 1986) is helpful in promoting an understanding of many of these passing activities which are employed primarily to manipulate social meanings and others' impressions. Further, it is useful to distinguish between the *substance* versus the *structure* of public rituals in order to comprehend the significance of consumer rituals which aid in the concealment of the participants' sexual orientation in social situations. The substance of rituals, in Rook's conceptualization, refers to their intensity, formality, seriousness and the symbolic meanings attached to them. The structure refers to the scripts, artifacts, roles, and audiences which facilitate in their execution. Thus, with this understanding, hiding rituals (and all those which follow in the subsequent chapters) may be understood in a more conceptually rigorous manner.

Rituals of the Closet: Using Products and Services to Hide Gay Sexuality

Many of the informants found products to be very useful in deceiving others (and sometimes, even themselves) regarding their sexual identities. Note that with this form of impression management, the audience to be deceived may be specific but is often the generalized other. The informants assumed and often received supporting evidence from particular people that they were regarded as heterosexual.

The rituals which informants used to hide their stigma from others and from themselves were often very complex and involved sets of many kinds of rituals, performed for the manipulation of meaning for a specific or generalized audience. For example, Jeff, the former punk rocker who is now fully involved in the gay subculture, and Cody, who came out at twenty-four years of age after experiencing years of guilt and frustration, both became involved in very sophisticated scenes which involved ritualistic consumer behavior. Jeff became a punk rocker and dressed daily in his leather jacket, mohawk hairdo, and various other *accoutrements*. In contrast, Cody became involved in the Christian rock scene for a number of months:

Jeff, 25: If I dressed that way, I would think *that other people would think* I was nonconformist completely, and by doing that, I would give myself popularity in some ways. Other people would uh, also, be offended in the same way. I would not get harassed nearly as much because more people were afraid, and I wanted to cloak myself that way. You know, because of my sexuality, I knew a lot of people couldn't accept it, so I wanted to say . . . it was a statement of protection, I guess, in a way, more so, than anything else, not to mention the hair, the mohawk, I always wanted . . . but the clothes had a lot to do with protecting myself and saying, "I'm part of this crowd, you-can't-buy-me kind of thing. You can't put me down for the way I am or for whatever I think, I can do as I please." That's the bottom line. It's basically a statement that goes along with it. I do what I want, when I want, how I want, and if anyone bugs me about it, they get beat up, or whatever, right? [laughs] That kind of thing.

SK: [To Cody] Can you tell me a bit about Christian rock?

Cody, 31: [laughs] It was wild. Well, basically the Catholic faith has liberal theology and stuff, and I was exploring a more fundamental element to look for simplistic rules to avoid these sort of feelings I was having . . .

SK: About?

C: Sexuality, basically.

SK: You were insecure about it?

C: Yeah, about my sexuality.

SK: So, I don't want to put words in your mouth, but would you say that you became part of the Christian rock movement to . . .

C: Well, I was looking for a sort of a moral structure . . . like, I was afraid of being homosexual or gay would be immoral, so it was sort of looking for a moral structure to hide from that. So I kind of explored it, but then . . . and it was music too, basically I worked with a bunch of people in an outdoor recreation center that had . . . that were . . . into this, and it was basically through the music and I'm sort of . . . I thought well, you know, I basically realize I had these feelings, but I didn't know whether it was moral to follow them, so I decided not to follow them, and maybe some spiritual fulfilment would take the place of those needs or whatever, so I tried pursuing it that way, and got . . . and thought maybe if I had a mission or something, or through music ministry and stuff, so I got into the Christian rock scene, but I found it very fundamental and very narrow-minded, and it went against my religious upbringing which was pretty Catholic and [had a] liberal metaphor for spiritual interpretation. So . . . I mean, when I was hanging around with these literalists, it became too much to handle, so I got out of it. I also found some spiritual mentors that time in California. Matthew Fox, who's into the Catholic spirituality. So, he was Catholic, and he was very liberal, and that was eye-opening and stuff, a whole different take on things. I realized how the Bible had been kind of formed by this whole original sin concept which was a reason for a lot of homophobia in the Christian aspect of it.

SK: Christian rock movement? Is this appreciating music or is it creating it?

C: Well, it was *being involved in a whole scene.* It was um . . .

SK: What was the scene?

C: The scene is the performers . . . there's a bunch of performers, they're usually ex-rock musicians. A lot of them used to be famous songwriters. Like, Marlin Lefevre for a group called Broken Heart. Marlin Lefevre used to write songs for Elvis Presley and even did a couple for early Beatles. Another artist in the sixties who found Jesus and tours around, and they have these rock concerts and they try to recruit young people and they have Bible readings after the concert, and their songs are about God and his music ministry. And many . . . and there's all different types of music. A lot of its heavy metal which doesn't appeal to me. And uh, and some of its . . . some of its uh, I still have one guy I listen to who I think is really neat, he doesn't even mention the words God or Jesus in his music, but he has real cool songs, and his name is Steven somebody, I can't remember right now, but uh . . . So anyway, I was involved as a roadie. We stayed with this guy and we were involved in the sound technician equipment department 'cause this guy's whole living was going and doing the sound setup for these bands. So it was really an inside sort of track. Like I'm a musician too, and I played in the full choir of the Catholic church, but that was . . . I wasn't a Christian rock musician, but I was involved in it . . . more in the logistical end of it. My teacher friend David was very involved in the logistical . . . he was part of the Bible Belt North . . . that's what we call [a small Ontario city]. He was part of the . . . Canadian Christian music association. And they used to organize concerts and get them coordinated. He's a bass player too.

SK: Don't let me lead you anywhere here. Do you think you were trying to resolve your sexuality through this . . .

C: Just through basically finding a spiritual . . . intellectual, spiritual, vocation and mission, and sort of replace sensuality and human relationships with that kind of thing which a lot of Catholic people and Christian people who are celibate do. So, that's basically what priests are supposed to do.

It is remarkable to note how elaborate and involved these particular consumption rituals or sets of rituals can become. For months or even years (the latter in Jeff's case), informants seriously and intently performed rituals which allowed them to deceive others (and often themselves) and escape or deny their sexual orientations. Jeff was a punk since his mid-teens and wore variations of an elaborate punk costume which protected him from abuse. During the participant observation portion of the research, I had the occasion to see his punk garb, which consisted of full mohawk haircut, black leather jacket, chains, short kilt, Doc Marten boots, and eyeshadow—quite a startling, intimidating *ensemble*. This constellation of ritual consumer artifacts (Solomon 1983) provided a congruent level of symbolic meaning to the audiences for which it was intended. The study of punk garb offers a rich opportunity to observe the meticulous attention to ritual activity. Jeff reported that he spend literally hours preparing his hair and clothing, displaying key aspects of ritual substance: seriousness, intensity, and the investment of psychic energy. The careful preparation of the self through various elaborate grooming rituals (McCracken 1986) allowed Jeff to engage in a subsequent ritual: walking down the streets of Toronto with his friends in punk regalia for the "losers" (such as preppies, skinheads, and other normals) to gaze in surprise, fear, shock, or revulsion.

Cody, an avid music lover, became involved as both a consumer and as a producer of sorts (a roadie) in the Christian rock music scene. In contrast to Jeff, who was attempting to camouflage his sexuality and protect himself under layers of punk garb, Cody was hiding the implications of his sexuality from *himself*, primarily. He asserted that he was searching for a moral framework in which he could live his life without fear or guilt from his deviant sexuality. Ironically, it was his Catholic upbringing—a background which so many of the informants found to be a source of repression and bigotry—that "saved" him. Catholics, for the most part, interpret the Bible metaphorically whereas Christian fundamentalists do so quite literally (see O'Guinn and Belk 1989). This discovery inspired Cody to eventually reject the Christian rock scene and cope with his fear and rejection of his own sexuality.

One might compare Cody's self-immersion in the Christian rock scene to a religious ritual, rite of passage, or metaphorical pilgrimage (O'Guinn and Belk 1989). Cody, a schoolteacher from a middle-class family, assumed a supplicant, low-status role in the scene (that of roadie) in moving the heavy music equipment belonging to the religious leaders (the musicians). By assuming this role in his psychological pilgrimage toward a moral structure, he effectively diverted his own attention from his sexual issues by preoccupying himself with religious matters. He compares himself to a priest, and during his time with the movement, he even offered a significant and appropriate ritual sacrifice: he was celibate. Consistent with the concept of ritual structures and substance, Cody used various artifacts in his role as religious pilgrim in his search for self-knowledge. However, this particular quest had an unexpected ending. Rather than successfully incorporating the role of fundamentalist Christian, Cody came out of the closet and accepted his sexual orientation.

Cody was not the only informant who hid his sexuality from himself and others. Simon, currently in recovery from drugs and alcohol, experienced a stage during his adolescence in which, oddly enough, he hid his sexuality with the use of women's clothing, hairstyles, and makeup:

SK: Hiding yourself? What aspects of yourself were you trying to hide?

Simon, 25: Um, at that time, I was trying to take on another persona.

SK: Tell me about this persona.

S: Well, it was mixed in with eccentricity. Uh, dying the hair all different colors. I never knew what kind of haircut I'd show up with. Having like I said, full face on with weird makeup. Um, dressing in extremely baggy clothes with lots of layers. Trying to fade away.

SK: Don't let me put words in your mouth or lead you anywhere but I am wondering whether you were telling people something or yourself something, a message of some sort?

S: Um, basically I think it was more trying to hide any sort of message like everything was all right. Something was wrong but I didn't want to accept it, so I hid it. Under layers of clothing and under my persona of "everything was all right."

Simon was attempting to "fade away," using "lots" of clothes, making himself diminutive. If he could fade away, then perhaps this upsetting truth about his sexuality could also fade away. It is also interesting to note that substance abusers tend to use consumption behaviors to make the problems and the pain "go away" (Hirschman 1992). At first, Simon used layers of clothing and cosmetics as part of his "outrageous" grooming rituals" (see Rook 1985; McCracken 1986) in order to deal with the issues in his life, including the sexually-related ones. Simon used formal, distinctive rituals in order to incorporate a particular persona or false self. These activities included the elaborate and serious use of consumer artifacts such as foundation, eyeshadow, lipstick, face creams, colognes, and toners. The scripts also included the step of consulting friends on what products to buy in order to get the "right results." Once he had come out of the closet, he no longer needed the false self.

Lest Symbolism Betray Them:
Hiding Those Telltale Products

During various points in their lives, most of the informants gained some small measures of self-acceptance of their homosexuality while realizing that no one else would accept it. Usually, some part of the psyche internalizes the notion of "I am a gay person, like it or not." At this juncture, the beginnings of a gay identity are forming. During these periods in their lives, it was found that many of the informants purchased various products, usually of an informational nature: books, magazines, and newspapers of a gay nature, and often, film and print pornography.

Invariably, informants reported that it was a critical concern to hide these purchases lest they be found, and the symbolic power of the purchase inform significant others (such as parents, often) of their secret that they themselves have not fully accepted. As ever, the reports demonstrated great levels of creativity and inventiveness in the ritualistic hiding of their gay products. This degree of care and concern might seem surprising to many heterosexuals who might ignorantly scoff, "Oh, every teenaged boy hides his *Playboys* from his parents!" This may be true. Probably many teenaged boys do hide their pornography for fear of their developing sexual natures becoming public knowledge. Yet, the criticism is unfounded. First, this study does not purport to compare homosexual and heterosexual consumer behaviors and arrive at meaningful differences. Second, even if it were comparing the two forms of behavior, hiding one's *Playboys* is an effort to hide heterosexuality (because it might be considered embarrassing). Hiding one's *Blue Boy* or *Stud Puppy* is often a frightened effort to hide one's homosexuality (because it is considered offensive, immoral, and often illegal—in short, deviant). The difference is profound in not the actions but the symbolic *meanings* behind the actions. The need to manage impressions (i.e., maintain a false front) for the benefit of relevant audiences is both urgent and critical for the gay youth (or adult).

Sam, a sixteen-year-old high school student who began attending the youth group approximately six months before I met him, was still very much closeted to his parents. He has made many new gay friends at LGBYT and has told some of his heterosexual friends at school. His first purchase which had any gay association consisted of a book of gay short stories and some magazines at Glad Day Bookstore, Toronto's gay bookstore. He reported that he felt so nervous while driving to the store that he selected the wrong turnoff on the highway and drove to a distant Toronto suburb (Mississauga) rather than downtown (in the opposite direction). Finally, in a ritualistically scripted series of actions, he made the purchases quickly, ran to his car, and drove off lest anyone had followed him or had seen him, realizing his intentions. At home, he made a dedicated effort to keep his purchases a secret. His hiding rituals were facilitated by his grandfather's old desk (the artifact):

Sam, 16: I have a really big desk that I got from my grandfather. And there was one drawer, the top left-hand drawer, and it's really hard to open, and there's a trick to it. *So, I call that my gay drawer*, and all my books, and memos and magazines and newsletters, they all go in this drawer. And not that my mother is a person to go through my things to begin with because as far as I know, she doesn't, but as far as I know [laughs], so that's where I keep them . . . keep my purchases. I mean, if I want to buy a T-shirt or whatever, I don't know where I'd keep them. I suppose in a drawer, in my chest of drawer or something like that. I don't know.

SK: And now, what kind of stuff is in that drawer?

S: Right now, I have the books, the book I bought and the two magazines, and I joined also the Out and Out Club and every month I get a newsletter from them, so I keep that in there as well. And I have also in there . . . um, LGBYT newsletters and things. And I have a couple maps of Toronto, and that's pretty much it, the drawer's kind of full. I also have articles that I cut out of like, *Chatelaine* of k.d. lang. And also from *Playboy*, an interview with Larry Kramer. The *Chatelaine* I read, I guess it must have been in the summer sometime, and the Larry Kramer one, I just found that like in December or something.

Sam's hiding activities appear somewhat simplistic in comparison to those of Roger (who is from one of Canada's Maritime provinces). Roger is a graphic designer, and the creator of his own original comic strip which was briefly published in a major Toronto daily. He also exhibited great creativity when hiding his first pornographic purchases:

Roger, 26: Yes. I was fifteen. Um, there was a comic book store . . . and I went in there. I was just walking around the area. I saw it. I saw this whole shelf of gay magazines, and I thought, oh my God, so I left. I had like fifty bucks with me. The next time I went in there. I bought eleven magazines, straight magazines, and I took the one . . . I saw the shelf of magazines, I didn't even look at it, I just dragged the magazine, sandwiched it between two piles of straight magazines and went up the counter. One guy who was working there was saying to the other guy, "Oh, these fags who come in here buying magazines!" And I'm standing here, fifteen years old, going . . . [laughs], 'cause I knew eventually they'd get to the gay one. So I was really excited. I got home. I spent all my fifty bucks on these magazines. I got home. Took the straight magazines, threw them away, and I took out the one magazine I ever had and I was so excited about finally seeing pictures, and it wasn't . . . um . . . there weren't any photos, it was all literature, so I was totally, totally disappointed.

SK: Was it pornography?

R: It was written porn. And uh, and it had little tiny pictures in the back of things you could order. So I got a magnifying glass and was looking at those. And I went back a few months later and I bought my first magazine which I thought was *Mandate*, and I remember looking at that and thinking, wow, okay. And that's when I was fifteen. The first gay book I ever bought was *The Quirk* by Gordon Merrick.

SK: How old were you then?

R: I was around fifteen. Fourteen or fifteen.

SK: What did you do with them when you were not using them?

R: Well, the porno . . . what I did, was I had . . . in my room . . . my cat used to sleep in my room, so I had a litterbox in the room. So I figured the litterbox is the only thing in my room my mother won't sneak around. So what I did is I had a garbage bag under the litterbox. I used to put inside the garbage bag, I put the porns, folded over the flap, and put the litterbox on top of it, so I knew my mother wouldn't mess around. [laughs] And the Gordon Merrick books I had . . . I would . . . I remember when I bought *The Lord Won't Mind*, I was sitting in the living room reading it, in front of my mother. I had a Bible that I ripped off the cover, and I took off the cover of the Gordon Merrick book and I glued the Bible cover onto the thing and I told my mother I had to read the Bible for school. Meanwhile, it had a pink outer rim. Interesting Bible with a pink rim. It was all right, so my mother commented a couple times on how fascinated I was with reading the Bible. When I was done with my Bible, I would put it under my mattress and . . . if I wasn't reading it, I would hide it, and then I bought another one of his books, *Forth Into the Light,* which I found really boring, and I put another book by this German author, *The Girl in a Swing* . . .

SK: Oh, *The Girl in a Swing*, by Richard Adams.

R: What's that?

SK: *The Girl in a Swing*. Richard Adams.

R: But that was a German . . .

SK: A German character.

R: Okay, so I took the back cover, but unfortunately my stepsister was going through my closet one day, when I was out and saw that book, and she thought it would be interesting, and she opened it up, and there was a story of two guys sucking each other's cocks inside. It was gay porn, pretty explicit. She confronted me with it, but I told her that someone in school who didn't like me very much sent it to me as a mean joke. I don't know if she bought it or not.

SK: Your sister?

R: No, my stepsister, she found it, and um, actually, I think the first porn I ever bought was when I was fourteen. It was a magazine called . . . I was into photography. I used to buy *Photo Magazine* all the time. There was one issue where they had male nudes, and I bought that magazine, and I remember like looking at this guy who was really cute, posing nude, so that was quite . . . that was my first . . .

SK: Where did you read this stuff?

R: In my room. I wouldn't go to the kitchen table . . . [laughs] while everyone's eating.

SK: Did you lock the door?

R: Double bolted, yeah.

SK: Um, where did you put it?

R: I put that with the rest of my other photo magazines. I figured that would be pretty . . . if I had stuff like that hidden under my mattress, that would . . . kind of give me away, I think.

How many teenaged boys have done *that* with their *Playboys*?! This form of ritualistic behavior characterizes the serious, intent, involved, and intense nature of passing rituals to the consumers interviewed in the study. Note that Roger delineated special ritual times and places for his gay reading. It was done privately and away from his family. This ritual is a form of impression management which is intended to prevent rather than facilitate the communication of symbolically conveyed information. The consequences of being given away (and this sometimes occurred) were often perceived by informants as quite dire: public disgrace, rejection, and withdrawal of emotional and financial support by family (i.e., being kicked out of the house), or the loss of friends and other social connections.

In this section, I have noted one set of consumption rituals which the informants reported to me: using certain products or avoiding certain products to hide their sexuality, hiding gay products or products which would betray their sexuality and thereby creating a social double life. The reader might be struck by the elaborate, formal, and concentrated manner in which the informants perform these often detailed consumption related tasks. These were significant rituals in the participants' lives, as their primary purpose was to manipulate meanings as symbolized by various possessions and consumption events so that potentially hostile others were kept ignorant of their sexual orientations. These rituals are structurally characterized by special objects or places such as Barbie Dolls, bathhouses, gay bars, and magazines; by special scripts characterized by their furtiveness, clandestine nature, and investment of mental energy; by display of the scripts and artifacts to various audiences; and by the various social roles the informants assumed during the ritual enactment (usually that of a heterosexual). Substantively, these rituals all invoke and manipulate meanings of various products and consumer activities in order to manage the audiences' impressions of the actor. They are used to affirm a social status which the informants privately realized that they did not occupy.

This is only one form of impression management as described by Goffman (1959, 1963, 1963a) and demonstrated by the informants, performed for the attention of the external (and internalized) audience(s). At this stage of their identity development processes, the informants were careful to manage their discreditable identities so that they did not become discredited or spoiled. The results here also reinforce Goffman's (1963) conclusions that stigmatized people are very adept at managing information while pursuing the goal of passing; as shown vividly above, the informants here are very cautious in how, when, where, and *for whom* they use their stigma symbols. The next section, in contrast, will describe more public consumption rituals which characterize the more formal, disclosing nature of the coming out process.

COMING OUT: CONSUMER BEHAVIOR AND PUBLIC IDENTITY MANAGEMENT

Corey, 23: That sort of little strand of I'm gay and I'm proud. So . . . yeah, that's been a very interesting process and who do I tell? Who don't I tell? And if I wear a certain product, will I be revealing my identity? To whom am I revealing my identity and what are the implications of that?

The study identified a number of significant manners in which informants ritualistically managed their gay identities. The following important consumer rituals, all of which involved elements of identity management, were identified and will be expanded upon below: exploration of a gay possible identity, disclosure to gay others, disclosure to heterosexual others, and resistance rituals (i.e., not identifying with gay men).

As one might expect, performing these rituals involves a careful degree of audience segregation on the part of informants (Goffman 1959, 1963a). When the informants decided to come out in the sense of disclosure, they were very cautious about selecting the appropriate audience, at least early on in their developments—a key structural element of ritualistic behavior. Thus in the ensuing sections, consumer behaviors which render the stigmatized social identity increasingly more *public* (i.e., known to more and different kinds of people) will be discussed. There are some important substantive and structural differences between the rituals described in the previous chapter and the ones ensuing. First, different artifacts are involved in the more public consumer rituals. While the identity hiding rituals involved mainly books, pornography, and items which informants used when by themselves, the set of artifacts described in this chapter expands to include T-shirts, jewelry, various styles of clothing, and those items which may be used in front of others. Another structural difference is that the ritual audience has been expanded to include gay others and sometimes heterosexual others rather than only the self alone. Roles are also important elements of ritual. Identity hiding rituals, for the most part, are employed in order to deny and disguise the role of gay man from others. On the other hand, the public disclosure rituals below are consistent with the notion of a more public or out role, indicating to others that one is gay.

Exploration of the Gay Possible Identity

It was discovered in the data that all of the informants decided to confront the "awful truth" about their gay identities. They realized that they were attracted to members of their own sex, and they were faced with a quandary: how does one learn what it means to be gay or homosexual? What does gay mean, anyway? Many of them reported that they had learned and internalized the harmful myths and stereotypes involving AIDS, sexual molestation, pederasty, and uncontrolled promiscuity. Yet, they were presented with an interesting and hopeful contradiction: none of these stereotypes pertained to them personally. Generally, going to parents, doctors, teachers, and clergy to learn about homosexuality was not a viable option (except for a few informants). Thus, in order to learn, they engaged in various consumer behaviors.

Jacob, for instance, was in his early twenties when he decided that he had to do something about his same-sex attraction. During a trip to Europe, he visited a sex shop in Amsterdam's Red Light District, realizing that that no one would recognize him in this foreign location. At the store, he rented a gay pornographic video and a room where he could watch it in private. He reports that his motivations were more than sexual or hedonic. He needed to understand what it meant to feel attracted to a man and whether he would be turned on by the video. Essentially, he was curious and confused. After he finished watching the movie, his situation was somewhat clearer to him, for he had enjoyed the experience.

During another interview, one young informant, Sam, confided that he was deciding whether or not he should wear gay clothing during the approaching summer. So far, he had engaged in another example of private consumer behavior: he had admired queer-themed T-shirts, freedom rings, and gay fashions on others in the gay area:

Sam, 16: I just think . . . I think clothes, I guess, depending on the person but the way I see it at least . . . I think . . . I mean, it doesn't even have to be something gay, I mean, you know, if you like . . . if you're more of a flamboyant person, and you wear more colorful clothing, more off-the-wall type of clothing, or not mainstream clothing, I should say. I think that's wearing yourself . . . I think it gives people *a glimpse of your personality*, your clothing, things like that, pins or watches.

Sam was beginning to see himself—the gay portion of his identity—in clothing and other consumer items. Thus, at that point in his self-development, he was pondering whether he should start buying more T-shirts and wearing them within the confines of the gay and lesbian area. By doing so, he would be able to embrace and realize fully a more mature, possible gay self. During the time of the interview, he kept all of his gay books, magazines, and other printed material carefully segregated from his other possessions—in the locked "gay drawer" of his desk. Such a segregation is symbolically useful in at least two significant ways. First, since the drawer locked, he was able to keep his sexuality a secret from his parents. Second, the gay drawer reflected his own conflicting feelings about his identity at this time. Like the items in the drawer, his identity must be carefully contained and kept separate from other areas of his life. And like the many interesting articles and learning materials about gay culture that he had collected and placed in the drawer, the gay aspect of his overall social identity must be explored and learned about.

At the time of the interview, Sam was contemplating the purchase and subsequent display of gay-themed clothing. He told me that he would have to get dressed at his suburban home, put the new T-shirt in a gym bag, leave home, find a washroom on the subway, change into the new shirt, and then wear it in the downtown area. In so doing, he is being very selective about ritual audiences in his consumption, cautiously aware of all potential hostile audiences such as his parents or homophobic bigots on the subway. Implicitly, Sam is discovering that the contents of the gay drawer eventually overflow into other areas of the desk.

In the study, it was found that certain products were considered symbolically useful for the informants exploration and development of the new gay possible self: pornographic movies, nonpornographic movies, gay-themed novels or nonfiction and magazines which target a primarily gay audience (such as *Out, Xtra!,* or *The Advocate*). First, these kind of products provide useful information about safer sex, finding gay nightclubs or restaurants, and other consumption venues (which in turn suggest further opportunities for exploring gay subculture and the self). Second, these kinds of products, due to their sensory, hedonic nature, provide images of what gay men look like and do. Despite the fact that these images are usually of young, blond, hairless, muscular, white men, often these idealized images are an improvement over the dark, dangerous stereotypes to which many of the informants were previously conditioned. Often a form of emotional identification with the product was reported by informants: "Finally there's something for *me!*"

In summary, consumer products and experiences play an important role in facilitating the creation and maintenance of a new, gay possible self. In addition to their common utilitarian functions, products such as films, books, posters, art, and magazines possess a critical symbolic element. Many informants were able to find at least one institution—the consumer market—which did not consistently exclude them and their own needs. They were able to view goods and services as symbols of their own inclusion within society.

The above examples of consumer behavior demonstrate that many of the informants were contemplating the assumption of a gay role as part of their self-concepts. Certain consumer artifacts or activities have been invested with gay cultural meaning, and by cathecting these objects, gay men are ritualistically taking the meaning into their own lives (McCracken 1986, 1989) and realizing possible selves (Markus and Nurius 1986; Schouten 1991). Also, by viewing certain gay artifacts as part of their lives, informants are able to look at themselves as the object of inquiry in order to more effectively approach new aspects of the overall self-concept.

Schouten (1990), in his doctoral dissertation, suggests a very interesting theoretical question: does self-concept change play a role in the purchase and usage of low involvement products? It is suggested here that certain inexpensive, regularly purchased items such as reading and viewing materials may have a very valuable role to play in the overall development of new identities. However, perhaps it is more accurate to claim that by the very nature of self-concept change, any product that becomes associated with this transformation *becomes* high involvement through a process of subjective or cultural meaning transformation.

Disclosure to Gay Others

The informants frequently reported that there were times and situations during which they wished to communicate to gay others that they were gay themselves; consumer activities and their symbolic qualities were very valuable to them in this regard. While carefully selecting the venue and the gay audience involved, they were able to display certain products with culturally shared gay meanings and form the correct impression in the minds of these viewers.

It should be noted here that this is one of the social uses of the set of meanings as described in the previous chapter. Informants entered gay subculture and began to learn the meanings of various products and experiences, usually from watching others, word of mouth, or advertising. Once they were confident that they understood the cultural meanings attached to products and felt comfortable enough to display them in public, they had the opportunity to play with and participate in the cultural drama unfolding around them. In so doing, they reinforced their own developing self-concepts in front of other people.

Nelson is a nineteen-year-old informant whose family comes from the Caribbean. He worked as a dance instructor and as a go-go dancer in one of Toronto's gay bars. He initially experienced some difficulties in coming out due to his family's strong religious sentiments. Now, after almost two years of being in the youth group, he wanted to feel as if he were a part of something greater than himself, as he considers himself a very "spiritual" person. His involvement in activities and events in the gay community, is quite extensive, as they included his social life and his job. Moreover, during a political march which I attended on June 9, 1994 (the day on which very important same-sex rights legislation—Bill 167—was defeated by the provincial government), I accidentally met Nelson, who was also on his way to the march. He seemed as angry as I was over the bill's defeat, and both of us engaged in spontaneous "primal screams" right there on the sidewalk (it was not considered inappropriate at the time). Nelson has found something greater to become a part of: the gay and lesbian community. His awareness of the motivations inspiring his consumer behavior is quite impressive:

Nelson, 19: This is before I came out, I went to get [my ears] pierced. And I had two stones, so I started getting . . . I noticed a lot of um, gay men wearing silver. It was one of the first things I picked up on when I . . . I'm a very instinctual person, and I noticed a lot of gay men wearing a lot of silver. Not as a stereotype, I just noticed it. And so I went out and said, well, I'll get some earrings. And it looked and it balanced, and it just seemed to . . . suit the character.

SK: The character?

N: The character of a gay male. I was trying to fit myself into a stereotype so people would notice that.

SK: Where did you buy the earrings?

N: A downtown vendor out on the street. Nowhere special. I got the rainbow too.

SK: The rainbow flag. Where'd you get that?

N: On Church. At Out on the Street.

SK: What about the cap? Was the cap bought . . .

N: No, the cap was bought in a regular sports store, but um, and the combat boots I picked up because again I never wore combats before, and I noticed that every gay man has combat boots.

SK: Are they Doc Martens?

N: No, they're combat boots.

SK: Can you tell me about buying those?

N: Um, I went . . . it was pride day, again, that same week, and I just was thinking of getting um, everyone . . . was telling me that this was the year people were wearing combat boots, and socks and whatever, so I thought to myself, well, I can afford a pair of combat boots.

Nelson, at this stage of his personal growth, wished to fit the stereotype of a gay man, and he openly acknowledged this motivation during the interview. In so doing, he came out to other gay men wherever he was, implicitly delivering the message "I am one of you. I identify in a similar manner." In addition to the combat boots (large, black, clunky boots) and the silver earrings, Nelson also purchased a tight-fitting bodysuit especially for his first Lesbian and Gay Pride Day. His consumption of gay-related clothing and jewelry is quite extensive, as he reports. He told me that wherever he is, he desires to carry a piece of the gay community with him in the form of its common symbols or symbolic products.

Nelson's behavior and frank admission of attempting to conform to the stereotype of a gay man puzzled me for at least a year. I did not understand why he (or anyone) would wish to live up to a stereotype (in those exact words) when the word stereotype conjures up such negative connotations. Yet, upon further reflection and review of his interview, I believe I have arrived at some comprehension. Nelson is both black and gay. Not only has he suffered discrimination from strangers for being gay, but he has also suffered within his own religious family. Often, minority families or communities have the option of becoming very close-knit in order to provide support, particularly if they believe that they suffer discrimination in the wider culture. However, as Nelson is gay, he experiences life as an outsider also in the fundamentalist Christian family which should have provided him with a sense of pride and support. The gay community may act as the only real family he has had in terms of bolstering his self-esteem. Unlike Lance, another Black Caribbean informant, who found that the gay community was not the accepting utopia he had hoped it would be, Nelson has found a sufficient degree of tolerance, acceptance, and support. To indicate his allegiance to this community of people which provides him with very positive social and psychological benefits, he uses its products and symbolically draws upons its power and energy.

When informants decide to go public to some degree, the negotiation of the ritual boundary and audience becomes a critical concern. In effect, the world emerges as divided between the now "safe" gay space and the "dangerous" straight one. Interestingly, this cognitive division represents a reversal or inversion of previous conceptions in which gay objects and places were considered contaminating and deviant. In the youth group, Danny, who was then leader, noted that he wished to provide a "safe space" for the group. The Fraternity's meetings are advertised only in the gay press, and represent another safe gay space for many of its more closeted members, such as Tim or François. Thus, other gay men are empowered to participate in various consumption rituals (such as the appreciation of the public display of fashion) but heterosexuals are cautiously avoided. For many of the informants, the safe space at LGBYT or The Fraternity represented special ritual time spent in a ritual space. Once some of the members of The Fraternity walked out of the front door of the Toronto hotel where monthly meetings are held, the straight act in their normal (read: presumably heterosexual) lives begins yet again.

Most of the informants reported that they engaged in at least one consumption ritual which they knew—consciously—would communicate their gay statuses to other gay men, but not necessarily to heterosexuals, a form of selective consumption in term of audiences (Tepper 1994). They do this by wearing obviously gay products such as bodysuits and earrings (Nelson); creating the gay look of clunky boots, tight tanktops, and short shorts (Gareth); or by maintaining a very well-dressed, well-coiffed, and well-groomed overall appearance which is interpreted by other gay men as "the impeccable gay look" (such as Ian, Jordan, François, Don, Ron, and Sylvio). One very important observation is how *conscious* the informants are of subcultural codes of dress and grooming, of their own consumer behaviors, the symbolic meanings communicated by these material signifiers, and their own conformity to the standard. This cannot be labeled mindless behavior or habit as it represents symbolic, purposive, intentional, and serious (descriptives which characterize the substance of rituals) decisions made by the informants. Communication of meanings is performed both on a personal and collective level. Consistent with the previous literature (Rook 1985; McCracken 1986; Schouten 1991), these rituals facilitate important social processes such as the establishment of a new role and social bonds.

Disclosure to Heterosexual Others

Gay men, as asserted before, are not generally distinguishable from the rest of the population (Kinsey, Pomeroy, and Martin 1948; Wilson 1993). Thus, dress, grooming, coiffure, jewelry, general appearance, and other visible symbols which the marketplace provides are inordinately important in communicating one's gay social identity and other important aspects of the self. Some of the informants used consumer symbols and other activities to indicate their sexuality before an audience of presumed heterosexual others. As an impression management technique as described by Goffman (1959, 1963a), this may be considered as a socially high-risk activity, exposing the informants to insult, degradation, exposure, and even physical violence. It is the willful, conscious, and ritualistic assumption of classic stigma symbols.

Carl, who takes great interest in fashion and in exposing his sexuality, often uses clothing to communicate his sexual orientation to everyone: gays, heterosexuals, and even strangers on the street. Here he describes how he creates his own gay style, using clothes, accessories, and some particulars of wearing them:

Carl, 16: If you . . . certain things are just very, very, like they say its telltale. Like um, and then you could extend it into our . . . when you have a tendency to . . . people . . . gay people in this community sometimes go out and pick things that are purposely not gender appropriate as far as society is concerned. Um, just to titillate. And then to say, "Hey look, I don't have to follow your rules. I'm gay. I don't [pause] . . ."

SK: Do you do that?

C: I can, and I do sometimes. Um, my kilt, for example. 'Cause we're not in Scotland. Or so I've been told. And um, so men don't wear kilts here. But I do. Merely because I don't believe that I should be confined by my sexuality—by my sex. So because I wear a kilt, I'm gay. Um, which isn't necessarily the case, but as far as society is concerned, I am. Um, like when I wear . . . when I have this fitted velvet jacket and . . . I have this fitted velvet jacket and um, and these tights. They're black men's racing shirts. And they're very, very tight. And they're cotton. And when I wear them, and my docs [Doc Marten boots], I get labeled, because I look like a dancer.

SK: And that's faggy?

C: Yeah! Don't dance if you're a boy. Especially ballet, that's really gross. Yeah. It's faggy. Yeah, I'm just being sarcastic. And yes, so when I do that, people go, "Oh, my God! Look!" So when I get that, it's kind of like you feel the fire when they go, "Oh, my God, look!" Because, I remember my last school, somebody did that one day, and when I went into school with this big pink denim suit that I have. These big, actually awful, disgustingly ugly pants, but I like them because they're mine, right? And they come up to here. And they were purple and mostly pink, a really hot pink. And a hot pink vest, and I wore a black turtleneck underneath it. They go, "Oh, my God, he's a guy. He's wearing pink. He must be gay." So the next time I came in and I walked in . . . have you ever seen Blonde Ambition? Anything from . . .

SK: No.

C: Well, I walked into school and I had this jacket on with a turtle-neck and a jacket. I just looked like this guy out of an ad. And everybody went (mimics a shocked whisper), "Oh, my God, he looks like one of Madonna's dancers, he must be gay!"

SK: Is there anything you own or that you've seen around which says "gay?"

C: Um, I don't know. I think it's what I own . . . besides my kilt . . . my cloak, my Jesus stuff. I don't think it's what I wear, and I don't think it's as much what you wear as how you wear it. 'Cause I can wear . . . okay, here's something. This watch here, it's a pocket watch. I can wear my blue jeans, my jean jacket, this shirt, this white under-shirt, and walk around and look totally normal or totally heterosexual, the two being different things. Um, and then I can wear it and put a few accessories on it . . .

SK: Such as?

C: Such as, my earrings. My hoops (earrings). Um, I'll string a pair of sunglasses. I can pull them down lower, a different belt, a belt with a big metal buckle, steel silver. Um, and just like some keys or something like that hanging out . . . I can walk and I can swish my ass from side to side or basically sashay down the street and then it's like, "I'm gay! I'm gay! I'm gay!" And it's how you can wear the same thing and not say anything about yourself. It's how you wear it, not what you wear so much.

SK: And where would you do this?

C: I do it wherever I go. It just comes and goes with my moods. Um, because people sometimes . . . I'm walking with people and they'll walk up ahead, and they just look at me, and they go, "My God, it's a wonder you don't get picked up all the time," 'cause sometimes it's so obvious, and sometimes it's not at all.

SK: So you would do this in a totally straight suburban area?

C: I do it naturally. I do it at work. I do it everywhere. It's just the way I walk. It's something with my walk. Like if I'm in a bubbly mood, it shows through in my attitude and in my walk.

Carl, as one might surmise, is sometimes an exhibitionist. His consumer behavior in this regard is a curious mixture of the conscious and intentional selection of colorful, flamboyant, and provocative clothing combined with a natural, spontaneous flair or attitude which helps him create his own version of a gay style or look. Overall, he carefully maintains an impression of humorous and youthful gay exuberance. He also spoke of his subjective intentions and motivations behind this type of behavior. As he expresses it, he is *not* attempting to antagonize or provoke any hostility when he engages in his bubbly gay consumption style (at least not in this case). Moreover, he does not consider his style in any way an expression of identity politics or symbolic resistance. Rather, he is trying to be himself and fulfil his own aesthetic sense. However, Carl *does* sometimes attempt to antagonize or engage in straight baiting, but in a different consumer manner. For Carl, there are two very different ways of "flaunting it." The first, as described above, does not entail any intentional provocation of heterosexual others, but is a natural expression of his own upbeat personality. The second manner, by contrast, is decidedly an effort to offend and antagonize those heterosexuals who he considers stupid, ignorant, and prejudiced.

On the other hand, according to the stated motivations of many other informants, during many public situations, they expose their sexuality to heterosexual others neither to shock, antagonize, nor harass them, nor to flaunt weird sex or deviant sexuality in an in-your-face manner. Ironically, they do it to show how *normal* and everyday they and their sexualities are. By using gay styles and products in their everyday lives and in an open, almost unconcerned manner, some are attempting to *integrate* (not segregate) themselves and become a part of a society that is liable to reject them. Also, some informants such as Mario engage in such activities in order to test whether these activities will be accepted or challenged. From an etic point of view, one might claim that this is a very political act. On the other hand, these informants subjectively do not believe it so. As Russ so eloquently phrases it, he is not willing to be a "billboard for advertisers twenty-four hours a day!" These observations contradict other findings such as Wilson's (1993) which interpret openly gay fashion as symbolic resistance. Hebdige (1979) also interprets punks' consumer behaviors as a similar phenomenon. Lurie (1981), investigating from a psychoanalytical perspective, claims that punk rockers dress themselves like "unloved babies" which Wilson (1993) labels the usual "psychoanalytic put-down." However, it is notable that at least two of these researchers were working from Marxist or postmodern perspectives in which they performed "readings" of material culture as text. If they had simply *asked* members of the groups in question about their behaviors, perhaps they would have arrived at the observation which this study has: subjectively, informants display stigma symbols to live their everyday lives as normally as they can. In a paradoxical sense, these informants sometimes wish to showcase their identities as part of the diversity which one finds often occurring naturally in the mainstream, dominant culture. As Russ expresses it, it is "one world," and he too wishes to be a part of it. The nonpolitical, nonaggressive motivations as asserted by the informants are also consistent with prior literature such as Goode (1990) and Celsi, Rose, and Leigh (1993) in that these socially high-risk consumption rituals as described above become normalized in the subjective view of the informants; as they became habituated, the change in the self-concept is mirrored by a change in social interactions with other people, including people external to the gay subculture. This observation is not to suggest that some informants did not attempt to antagonistically flaunt their sexualities, using in-your-face consumption tactics. Some certainly did, according to their own reports. This phenomenon, however, will be described in Chapter 6.

Resistance and Avoidance Rituals: Not Identifying with Gay Men

During the data analysis and interpretation, it became evident that there was a great deal of evidence supporting the notion that the informants purchased and used public consumer items (and experiences) in order to intentionally identify with other gay men. These experiences, as recounted by informants, are related in the preceding sections of this chapter. However, negative case analysis identified another body of data which indicated that some informants sometimes or generally avoided products or services which would identify them with the gay community or gay men. Further, many of the informants who reported that they used products and services to identify with the gay community reported that there were times and places when they purposely did not do so. To complicate matters, most of these informants who avoided stereotypic "gay products" or the "gay look" (either all the time, sometimes, or at different life stages) were also very out and accepting of their sexualities (i.e., they were not trying to pass as straight). Thus, the hypothesis which might assert that as one becomes increasingly open about one's sexuality and accepting of it, one tends to consume more openly gay goods and services (which is true in some instances) is somewhat simplistic. The informants' lives are more complex than this proposition would indicate.

From the data, it was found that some informants often perform consumer rituals which help them to consciously resist what they perceive as the influence of gay subculture. This usually involves either purposely and intentionally avoiding certain forms of consumer experience or sometimes embracing other ones which they believe to be nongay. Note that these rituals are not subjectively thought of as resistance to the dominant, mainstream culture but to gay subculture itself.

Nigel, who recently completed teacher's college, thinks of himself as a "rebel" who never quite fit into the gay subculture. He possesses a certain stereotype of many young gay men who subscribe to a certain lifestyle of consumption:

SK: You use the word "queer" a lot.

Nigel, 28: Because I think I've become a lot more open-minded. Certainly, musically in the last few years than I was. I was quite narrow when I first came out in terms of like my musical tastes. Yeah, I have used the word queer a lot. I like that word because it's . . . kind of empowering. It takes back an epithet that was thrown at us, with such derision by so many people for so many years, um, and that I don't, I don't really consider myself . . . I prefer that word to gay because gay to me means you buy into the subculture whereas queer means you're a bit of a rebel to the . . . not only to like straight society, but also to the gay subculture which I do feel I am.

SK: You feel that?

N: Yeah.

SK: Can you tell me more about being a rebel? What does that mean?

N: Well, I don't listen to Madonna. I don't listen to Whitney Houston. I don't like the *Wizard of Oz*. Um, you know. I'm not gonna like something just because . . . you know, it's what the gay community likes. And you know what I mean? You know what I mean?

SK: No, I don't.

N: I'm not gonna . . . I'm not gonna like something just because it's got . . . a reputation of being liked by a lot of gays or a lot of gays do like it. For example, the *Wizard of Oz, Whatever Happened to Baby Jane* and the constant references to it which can drive me up the wall. Um, these things, the quote common culture that we have, which I don't particularly agree with . . .

SK: Agree with that there is a culture or agree with . . . the culture itself?

N: I don't buy into it. Let's say it that way.

SK: Um . . .

N: I don't, I don't particularly care for, for example, Madonna. I mean, a lot of gay people like Madonna and there's a certain attitude among a lot of gay people that if you don't like her, then you're not queer. Or how can you be gay and not like Madonna? I am gay and I don't like Madonna, and I refuse to be forced to like her just because I'm gay.

It may seem ironic that after considering oneself to be an outcast in relation to mainstream culture, some informants such as Nigel end up considering themselves as outcasts in relation to gay subculture as well. Yet, Nigel believes that there are a set of consumption norms embraced by gay subculture which he will not "buy into" because that would be selling out. To paraphrase the famous gay social commentator, Quentin Crisp, a lifetime of listening to Madonna is too great a price to pay for Nigel's sexual orientation. By rejecting popular gay icons such as Madonna or Judy Garland and other aspects of consumer culture, he is able to preserve something unique within his own identity. However, there is a cost to this rebelliousness. He often feels excluded or ostracized by others he

views as intolerant of his individuality. The rejection of certain
products is not idle contrariness or a cry for attention on Nigel's
part, moreover. Since he was a young teenager has always enjoyed
rock music and intends to do so. He finds the unwritten codes or
peer pressure exercised by other gay men and some marketers (such
as Benetton) to be an intrusive force in his life. Thus, he makes a
concerted effort not to buy them and to continue with his personal
interests. From the data, it appears that consumer rituals can both
help informants to approach a positive self and to avoid a negative
self (in Nigel's case, a stereotypical, Madonna⸴ obsessed, gay
clotheshorse). By placing mental energy into actively avoiding various activities, Nigel and Roger are fostering their own healthy
developments.

The Internal Struggle Between Conformity and Individuality

Underlying the resistance rituals is an internal conflict which
many of the informants have experienced: the existential struggle
between conformity and individuality within themselves, and manifested in the external circumstances of the gay men's subculture. In
effect, many informants ask themselves the following: how gay is
"too" gay? When do the norms and values—as expressed symbolically and sometimes enforced by social influence and consumer
experiences—violate the will and uniqueness of the individual,
becoming an alternative hegemonic structure? From the data, I
arrived at the following insight: many of the informants either con-
formed to standards (often knowingly and consciously), experienced some form of internal conflict, or both. What is truly interesting is that these informants were consciously aware of their
dilemmas and were even able to critique them. An understanding of
the psychological dynamics of conformity and individuality will
enhance understanding of the above described rituals of resistance
and avoidance.

Jordan was very cautious and deliberate when speaking of this
issue; he took great care and concern in speaking somewhat negatively of what he perceived to be gay consumption norms and their
perceived effect upon the individual:

Jordan, 26: It [the gay community] can be very . . . it can be a very welcoming place . . . *if you sort of follow the rules.* And I guess I'll go further and explain by what I mean by the rules. Um, I see it as there being . . . one of those . . . unwritten . . . there's a whole bunch of those *unwritten rules.* That you have to sort of . . . fit in with whatever clique that you decide to go . . . to run within the community, and that sort of involves *going to the right places*, knowing the right people. Um, *eating at the right* . . . you know, just the whole deal. Eating out, at the right places, going to the right parties, um, dressing the right way, things like that . . . Um, for example, I found that . . . um, listening to people talk and just hanging around and stuff, there's people that nobody associates with for various reasons, I couldn't give you particular whys or whatever. Um, 'cause they're . . . they're not, you know, trendy enough or they're not . . . they're not good-looking enough or they don't, you know, whatever. Like, there's a big sense of exclusivity. A lot of times in the community. Um, and that isn't necessarily a welcoming thing, but you learn to fit into um, the different patterns and the different groups that you hang around with.

SK: Can you, um . . . what does it mean to be trendy in this community?

J: To be trendy. To be . . . trendy is like um, knowing the top songs in the dance clubs, to be wearing the latest fashions or to just um, be hanging around with the right people in terms of the club crowd or however it might work in your group. That would be like trendy. Um, trendy can also be like . . . going on a politically correct, you know marches and stuff like that. That's another trend that I sort of noticed in the community. It's that people are becoming like more politically correct because it is . . . acceptable. More acceptable to be so now. After the defeat of the [same sex] bill. And during that.

Jordan asserts that the material uniform or consumption code is often an unstated set of criteria in the forming of cliques and social relationships. Clothes, jewelry, going out to the "right" bars and restaurants, and even marching in gay political rallies are transformed into very social fashion statements, according to him. From observing his own consumer behaviors, Jordan appears to be following the rules to a significant degree. He is in good physical condition, exercises, dresses impeccably, and eats and dances at some of the popular venues in the gay men's area. Yet, it would be reductionist and unfair to attribute his popularity within the youth group solely to conformity on the basis of social consumption rules. Jordan, as a youth facilitator, has demonstrated genuine patience and caring for people who join the group. He is also generally very outgoing and friendly.

Lance is also very aware of his overall consumption experience within the gay men's subculture and is able to achieve some critical distance from it:

Lance, 23: . . . and I guess I want to say something else about myself as well that's . . . 'cause I just don't feel comfortable wearing those like um, cutoff shorts, and the tanktop just because I just . . . 'cause I just . . . I've never been much of a conformist, but in some ways I conform . . . in *some* ways . . . I buy Doc Martens and these shorts, but if you go to what I call the extreme as in the tanktops and really short shorts and whatever, right? That are three sizes too small, it just looks stupid. I just don't feel comfortable wearing that, so I don't. So, even though like I recognize those things as um . . . It represents someone who is gay . . . [but] I don't feel comfortable wearing them, going to that extreme myself.

Within Lance's quote, one can interpret a form of internal conflict. On the one hand, he is involved in the gay community and has obtained a fair measure of acceptance and support from it. On the other hand, he is somewhat critical of its associated style. He realizes that he conforms in certain manners, but not in others in that he will not "go to the extreme." While Lance exercises, diets, and wears Doc Martens to appear attractive to other gay men and to identify with them, he will not wear what he believes is unbecoming, tight clothing. Like many of the informants, Lance accepts certain products and consumer experiences into his life, which he views as congruent to his overall self-concept, but rejects others which are not. In so doing, he continues a dialectical process (or internal tension) of maintaining individuality while conforming to some consumption norms.

Jeff, the former punk rocker, exemplifies a form of internal conflict or tension. Literally, there is no other participant in this study who reflects such a strong combination (and thus, internal conflict) of the will to individuality versus that to conformity, as evidenced by both his observed behaviors and long interviews:

Jeff, 25: Well, being gay now is no different [than being a punk rocker]. However, um, uh, the image portrayed is completely different because I've gone pretty much in extreme. I am more . . . I wouldn't say jock, but more I guess, preppy cleancut kind of whereas when I was a punk, I would always say preppies are the losers, you know, the enemies, the complete enemies, we always warn each other. But now, I mean, I've given up most of that because um, well, for simple reasons, mostly because *it's more difficult to find a man because people look at the way you dress. And um, the saying goes, judgment by its cover is not always a good thing, but that's the way it is.* That's also a part of life. *And so I had to change, right?* I couldn't get rid of things like my tattoos and you know, other things like this, but I could change the way I dress. I could grow my hair in, and uh, have it relatively normal. Sometimes I still dye it. Sometimes I go crazy for awhile, kind of thing, but I'm basically out of that so-called stage, I guess you might say. It was more than a stage, still only a stage, right? Because I left it. I chose that I wanted a lifestyle that would satisfy me and let me be happy. *You have to give a little in order to get anything.* You know, you have to give up a lot sometimes in order to get something [laughs]. That's why I changed my lifestyle now, like this lifestyle of dressing.

Now that Jeff is an openly gay man spending much of his time within the gay area, he is "giving a little." Some days, Jeff was dressed quite "punk" with many earrings, a nose ring, and dyed hair. Other days, he wore very "preppy" clothing including a university letter jacket. Within his two long interviews, he alternately claimed to conform to his interpretation of gay men's consumption norms and then to "fuck it" and do what he really wished to do (which was dress up punk, usually). Ironically, as a punk, he expressed his individuality by dressing up similarly to his punk friends, and together they formed a kind of homologous style. Now, as a gay man, he sometimes does the same, but occasionally, he breaks the norms and "goes crazy" in full mohawk, earrings, and chains—traditional punk garb.

While some informants genuinely experienced conflicts (and were aware of their conflicts) such as Lance and Jeff, others either accepted or rejected consumption norms consciously. Isaac, who lived in the northeastern United States for several years, describes how he became cognizant of the dominant gay style at his predominantly gay attended gym and what he subsequently did about it. From his report, it is apparent that his aerobics class was more than a simple exercise of one's body, but of fashion taste:

Isaac, 25: Their clothing that they wore there? Actually, that was very . . . *I think I was the most radical in terms of what I wore*, and I would be wearing a pair of Champion shorts and nondescript T-shirt. Um, which you know, the Metropolitan [gym] itself has its own clothing . . . like they've got Metropolitan shorts, tanktops, T-shirts, the whole paraphernalia, um, and some people would only wear that, and those who did aerobics, that's where the clothing gets very rigid and extreme. Um, there's a whole different code there. I tried one aerobics class and felt very out of place because again, I went with my Champion shorts and my nondescript T-shirt, and that was just unacceptable because . . .

SK: How did you know it was unacceptable? I don't understand.

I: [laughs] People just looked at you because you . . . everyone was in their spandex and tight-fitting stuff and there was a whole different code that operates with aerobics versus the people who worked out on the weights.

SK: How did you feel about it when you were with all these gay men who were wearing one thing and you were wearing . . . another?

I: Um, I couldn't care less, actually. It was a situation where I mean . . . I was very comfortable at that gym because I had been working out there for almost two years and knew most of the people there, so . . . it didn't bother me no matter what I wore. But yeah, I think there certainly is . . . obviously given that everyone else was wearing the required uniform, there's obviously some pressure to look a certain way when you're participating in certain athletic activities.

While recognizing the consumption norms at his gay gym and rejecting them, Isaac still felt "comfortable" (because he knew everyone) and yet "out of place" (due to the fact that he was dressed differently). Overall, the strategy he adapted is one of individuality (or resistance) as opposed to conformity. His overall attitude toward the issue of their conformity and his demonstrated individuality (or failure to fit in with consumption norms, as it could be viewed) is one of equanimity and detachment. Nigel and Roger, on the other hand, were much more involved in criticizing others' conformity and nurturing their own perceived struggle for uniqueness. Nigel described himself as a rebel fighting "the tyranny of fashion" within the gay community. Roger, on the other hand, considers his tastes to be somewhat "alternative" in terms of music (New Wave and rock from the 1980s) and dress (mostly black clothes). Roger believes that gay men are very materialistic and acquisitive in matters pertaining to dress, grooming, and furnishings, and he asserts that these kind of possessions do not interest him:

Nigel, 28: I'm not just the short hair model type, you know, very very thin . . . wearing . . . I think that's kind of outdated, but you know, it's like . . . it's not . . . there's not . . . a kind of . . . I'm trying to reject the kind of . . . um, maybe the tyranny of fashion that sometimes I feel in the gay community.

SK: Can you talk about that? What's the tyranny of fashion?

N: Well, that you have to conform to like a certain type that you have to be physically perfect with perfect teeth and a perfect body, and you have to wear the right clothes. Um, again though, I think a lot of people . . . I think especially a lot of younger people are rejecting that, whereas like, especially during the eighties, when everything was so yuppie, I think it was very *de rigeur*, if you weren't wearing something like with a crest on it, like Ralph Lauren or Calvin Klein shirt, then you were just like not accepted, if you didn't have the right precision haircut, if everything wasn't in place . . . then you were just like, you know, just what the hell do you know about being queer, whereas I think a lot of people reject that now. They're wearing much more grungy clothes. This goes along with the fashion trends. But as well, um, it seems to be since I've come out, I mean, the fashion seems to be a lot rougher than it was. It used to be very kind of refined and rich, and yuppie, and that was the whole eighties thing, and now it's kind of like underground, or you can feel the . . . the kind of like maybe the . . . frustration or rebelliousness that people feel now. Or despair maybe.

Roger, 26: To become part of . . . to conform into whatever, whatever, and it doesn't work on me, because it's not . . . this . . . to quote Sinead O'Connor, "These people are twisted and will never be, any influence on me." Um, so . . . it's not something to even consider. Maybe like a small child trying to get you to conform to something. You wouldn't conform 'cause a small child told you to. I look at people like that like small children. When they start . . . if they're doing it for themselves, it's one thing. But once they . . . if they're wearing leather because they like leather, I have a leather jacket. I wear it because I like it. If they're doing it because they . . . if it's a way of expressing themselves, it's wonderful, it's like a T-shirt, one of those in-your-face T-shirts. It's a mode of self-expression for them, but once they put so much weight on it, that kind of creates a false confidence in this identity that they have. And it's a store bought identity. And to me that's . . . that's, they're losing themselves in it.

Both Nigel and Roger (significantly, the two are very good friends) are fighting the "tyranny of fashion" by refusing to conform to perceived dress and consumption codes. As Roger asserts, he himself does not want the "false confidence" which a "store bought identity" provides. Both recognize that there is a struggle between modes of individuality and modes of conformity, and they have decided which side they are on. For these two informants, it is critical to manage their personal identities by not giving into fashion norms which they personally dislike for the sake of cohesion or identification with the subculture. Roger flatly asserts, moreover, that he does not identify at all with the gay men's subculture.

Yet, some of the informants do identify with the subculture and have knowingly decided to conform in various consumption modes. For example, Nelson, who came out within the last two years before I interviewed him, frankly admitted that he was trying to fit a consumption stereotype. In the passage below, he provides a further illustration of that. Similarly, Ian has decided to conform in various ways by dying his hair and wearing various items he would not ordinarily have worn if he had not been "influenced" by other gay men. In contrast to the outright and pervasive rejection of gay subculture asserted by Roger and Nigel above, these two informants have chosen to conform:

Nelson, 19: Well, that's interesting I thought, because it sort of ties in with the um . . . as part of my coming out experience. I sort of felt obliged to um, to boost up my standard of living, boost up my intellect, boost up . . . not the fact that I didn't have that there already, but it's just that I felt obligated to . . . so I didn't have to, but I would buy at Le Chateau and stuff like that and Priape and you know, Body Body, and I remember I bought a bodysuit at . . . 'cause I was . . . this was like when I realized that my body was half decent. I could go in a bodysuit, and it was Pride Day, and I bought myself a bodysuit, and it was just um, it was just the biggest thing at the time, because it's just . . . you know, just to have a body to fit in that and *it's like the personae that they want. So, it's what they're looking for.*

SK: Who's they?

N: I'm talking about people in the gay community. This is what they want. They want to see this sort of sexy male, *typecasted*, bodysuit, genitalia hanging out all over the place. Not to say that everybody's like that, but I'm just saying, this is general.

SK: Where did you get the bodysuit?

N: The bodysuit? Just um . . . I've seen friends who wear bodysuits and people always said that you know, I'd probably look good in a bodysuit, and I'd never given it much thought, because I've always been dancing, and I've always seen the bodysuit as a form of [artistic] expression, *not a form of advertisement.* But um, you know, it's . . . when they start saying I look good in a bodysuit, they tell me these things, you know . . . different videos and whatever, and I'll say to myself, I'll go get one. Um, well, when I was wearing it, I went to Pride Day in the parade [laughs]. Afterwards, there wasn't much of a bodysuit left on me!

SK: What happened to it?

N: It was just getting pulled and everything. I was drunk, and people were pulling it and it got ripped here, there, and it was still on me [laughs].

SK: So, I guess a lot of people looked at you . . .

N: Yeah, and it just sort of got wrecked.

Ian, 22: Um, I guess I'm influenced by people in the gay community, I guess. Um . . .

SK: Do you think so?

I: Probably, *but I think it's a conscious influence.* I mean, I could completely ignore it if I really wanted to, but um, *I choose* not to. I don't know. I know, I know . . . yeah, I think I consciously um, yeah. See what the norms are, I guess, in the gay community . . .

Frankly, as a researcher I did not know quite what to think about these very frank admissions of conformity to community norms. I first believed that I had led the informants, but upon review of the interviews and further informal discussions with the informants in question, they insisted upon the accuracy of their original assertions. It became evident that, unlike Roger and Nigel (and yes, I must confess—myself), they do not place a negative valence upon conforming to consumption norms. We all interpret behavior with slightly different value systems, biases, and cultural perspectives. The issue of conformity versus individuality is also presently settled for Ian and Nelson. They have *chosen*—actively and cognizantly—to manage their own gay identities by conforming to a significant degree in their purchases.

Yet, it would be irresponsible and false to claim that the dilemma of conformity and individuality is an all or nothing proposition or dichotomy for most of the informants. In at least one area of their consumption lives, most of the informants were experiencing some discomfort or conflict. Tom described himself as usually uncomfortable with anything which brought him "closer" to the gay community. Yet despite this discomfort, he cannot resist becoming involved in the "gay lifestyle" sometimes and placing importance upon his gay identity:

Tom, 32: I would say there is. There is a gay lifestyle.

SK: What is it?

T: The gay lifestyle is . . . living, you know, it's living separate from the straight world. I almost think sometimes that gay people separate themselves too much. I thought that the other day when I was coming out of one of the bars downtown, and I walked onto Yonge Street, and suddenly, it was straight! And I thought, oh my God! This is the way most of the world is. I'm just in this small, limited field. Like a field in a computer, like locked into this pattern of going to these certain bars and knowing only that, you know. You know, like people mention straight bars to me and I'll just think, it's like a straight bar. It's almost like a reverse prejudice. Sometimes I have that feeling that we perhaps . . . that we limit ourselves too much. But yes, I think the gay subculture exists. It's a . . . it's . . . the gay lifestyle exists. It's living in that narrow field, perhaps, you know, not allowing yourself to expand your boundaries. Yeah, beyond the . . . the gay lifestyle that you've channelled yourself into.

SK: Would you say that you're part of the gay subculture or gay lifestyle?

T: *I would say I'm on the cusp of it.*

SK: The cusp of it?

T: The cusp, the edge. The um, you know, just perched on the outside, on the brink. *Sometimes, you know, I'll take the dip, take a quick plunge, and then I'll come out and sit on the shore for awhile.*

SK: What is taking a plunge into the gay lifestyle?

T: Taking a plunge . . . well, participating in Pride Day, skipping arm in arm with seven gay men in the middle of Yonge Street, singing songs from the *Wizard of Oz.* Singing at a lesbian wedding, you know then accompanying the married lesbians down the street with . . . in a torchlike procession, holding a flag about their head, singing "going to the chapel, we're gonna get married" to them.

SK: When was this?

T: This was a couple weeks ago. It was either . . . it was after Pride Day. After Pride Day. Just after Pride Day. It was . . . it was a very special experience for me, and that for me, was . . . it was making a statement. Here I was proclaiming, I am a gay man in front of Maple Leaf Gardens, in front of all these people. We walked all the way down Church Street from Kawthra Park to the corner of Yonge and College.

Tom, like many of the informants, has discovered that he must manage his identity "perched on the cusp" of the gay community or subculture. His "dips" into it are sometimes judged as allowances to conformity—of "narrowing himself" too much and "living apart" from the rest of the world, issues which concern him about himself and other gay men. Even the most positive of consumption experiences such as Lesbian and Gay Pride Day and the lesbian wedding may be viewed as conforming too much to gay norms; going beyond the cusp, for Tom, may be going just beyond the Pale. It is a conflict or a tension, related to his gay identity, which he experiences and resolves daily.

Summary

Consumer products and rituals play important roles in the everyday fabric of the informants' lives as gay men. By taking care in deciding whether to communicate their sexual orientations to other gay men, to heterosexuals, or even to themselves (for purposes of personal growth and the maintenance of individuality) through consumer symbols, they are negotiating the meanings, centrality, and salience of their gay social identities. Recall that a gay identity is still considered by many to be a deviant one. By disclosing their gay identities to others, informants are taking a social risk. The potential cost of disclosure and identity development is the loss of valued human connections with significant others—family, friends, or co-workers. Thus, it is not surprising that the informants reported taking a great deal of care and thought in using consumer rituals in facilitating the management of their identities.

Informants, overall, reported that they experienced an interesting ethical dilemma (please see again Corey's quote at the beginning of this section). By disclosing their gay social identities to gay and heterosexual others through the use of consumer behavior (i.e., one of the forms of coming out of the closet), they are behaving as principled individuals who are true to themselves and their ethics. On the other hand, they risk social loss and even potential physical harm by doing so. On the other hand, if they keep silent, they may experience shame over being cowardly or unethical toward the self. This ethical dilemma is complicated even further by informants' perceptions of the subcultural tendency toward conformity in consumer matters (e.g., such as liking Madonna or wearing certain clothing). Some have chosen to conform in various manners, and they believe that they are indicating loyalty or allegiance to the subculture which has granted them a measure of acceptance; it is their oasis in the desert, so to speak. Other informants, however, have chosen to actively resist any force toward "homo"-genization, as this offends their inner sense of themselves or personal ethics. Either way, many informants live with a sense of conflict. Either one conforms and demonstrates allegiance through public material symbols (and sacrifices perhaps a measure of personal uniqueness and in some cases, self-esteem or self-respect), or one resists and suffers the potential of social ostracism (such as in the lives of Roger and Nigel). As with many of the informants, the social influences to identify oneself with similar others appears to compete with the private desire to develop and nurture a complex, unique, principled, and centered "core" of personal identity. Antonio, for example, found himself increasingly dissatisfied with "the same old, same old" within the gay ghetto and subjectively evolved and grew when he physically and psychologically achieved distance from it. For him, maintaining a healthy degree of consumer resistance to subcultural consumer forms helped him manage the many identities within his overall self-concept: Italian-Canadian, son, interpreter, gay man, and lover.

It should be emphasized that many of the choices are not usually either/or. Rather, the gay identity is socially negotiated continuously in many cultural contexts, creating a dynamic, inner dialectic within informants. The previous literature is, for the most part, consistent with the results in this section and even furthers the understanding of some of the informants' lives. For example, consistent with Goffman (1959, 1963a), Breakwell (1983, 1986), and Tepper (1994), these stigmatized informants take care in the disclosure of their identities and occasionally assume stigma symbols (consumer goods) to give visible expressions to cultural categories and principles. These may be considered interpersonal or intergroup strategies of identity management (Breakwell 1983, 1986). The younger informants such as Carl, Cameron, Sam, and Arnold—and even some of the older informants who have recently come out of the closet, such as Ben—find visible consumer behaviors useful as cues

for social interaction (see Solomon 1983). By viewing and subsequently interpreting the meanings of various consumer goods and
rituals, these neophytes are able to form stereotypic consumer ideals
which help them in negotiating future social consumer behavior and
the establishment of their gay social identities. Often, once the
newly out gay men here feel comfortable with their new social
worlds and with being gay, they make the decision to come out,
using blatantly gay consumer stigma symbols such as T-shirts (e.g.,
"I'm not gay but my boyfriend is") or pink triangles, for instance.
Goode's (1990) work, for example, is useful for understanding the
behavior of some gay men in that he maintains that certain activities' meanings are normalized and the change in the overall self-
concept incorporates an overall acceptance of the new, deviant gay
identity. The interpretation here is somewhat at odds with other
works such as Hebdige (1979), Willis (1993), and Wilson (1993)
who view public, outrageous consumer behaviors strictly as intentional acts of denial, defiance, or symbolic resistance. As some of
these informants clearly demonstrate, such is not *always* the case.

Chapter 5

Consumer Behavior
and the Construction of Gay Communities

In the previous chapter, I reported that many of the informants acknowledged that by the public purchase, display, and use of their gay-related products, they indicated an identification or bond with other gay men, demonstrating that they were a part of the gay men's community. This motivation on the part of informants provokes a critical observation. When affirming and reinforcing their gay, social identities in the company of like others, not only were they "making statements" about their own social identities, but also they were creating and maintaining a sense of gay community. Their actions may be meaningfully interpreted both as individual efforts at self-concept maintenance and as collective, conscious attempts to inform other gay men that there are similar others who share an important common bond.

Previously, I have used the term *subculture* to describe the gay social world studied in this work. Now, in order to avoid confusion and provide some conceptual distinction, it is necessary to more rigorously define and describe the concept of community, which emerged from the data as a very important theoretical consideration. Furthermore, I shall take this opportunity to distinguish a subculture from a community. Very basically, a community is a group of people who possess a common bond which distinguishes them from other people (Cohen 1985, p. 12). People within a community share a social relationship which is either face-to-face or anonymous and known among them. Significant to this study, community may also imply some sort of shared identity, such as within the gay community itself. Moreover, subculture, discussed previously, refers to a set of ideas, values, and norms which are somehow distinct from (and often critical of, particularly in the case of punk subculture or the hippies' counterculture) the mainstream or dominant culture; this ideology is embraced by certain individuals as demonstrated in various previous works such as Schouten and McAlexander's (1995) research on the Harley-Davidson motorcycle subculture, Stratton's (1985) research on youth subculture, and Hebdige's (1979) research on punks. Thus, as Gainer and Fischer (in review) suggest and these above works attest to, subculture is a special *form* of community. Thus, it would make sense to claim that every subculture is a community but every community is not necessarily a subculture. A review of the above works on spectacular subcultures would suggest that the key distinguishing characteristic of a subcultural form of community is a common bond reflected in different, strange, or "countercultural" beliefs, ideology, or behaviors. For example, the bikers in Schouten and McAlexander's (1995) work all share the extremely strong bond of commitment to Harley-Davidson use and ownership *and* devotion to a particular ethos.

One could argue that my discussion of the disclosure of sexual identity through public consumer rituals (in the last chapter) could just as validly have been discussed as or labeled as rituals of community. They could have been, and this observation inspires an important point. The notions of self-concept maintenance and community construction are linked because identity is not formed in a social vacuum, but in the company of real or even imagined others (James 1890; Cooley 1902; Mead 1934) who act as the audience, providing an important social and cultural context. In this study, many important consumer statements concerning the self may also be validly interpreted as symbolic statements communicating membership in or allegiance to a socially constructed community. Moreover, this view is consistent with that of the school of processual interactionism which strongly maintains the self and society interpenetrate (see Gecas 1982, p. 13).

Thus, where does the notion of identity end and the notion of community begin? The processual interactionist view would indicate that the boundaries are not clear; rather, they are permeable. In the symbolic interactionist perspective, self and other are considered interconnected (Blumer 1969). In a profound sense, many of the informants considered themselves to be members (or parts) of the gay community, to varying degrees. They also considered the gay community as part of their extended selves (the community as part of them) and sometimes even as a possession. Viewed holistically, consumer behaviors may be usefully and validly conceptualized as material expressions of self-relevant beliefs and feelings (i.e., subjectively experienced personal identity), and as cultural symbols of belonging to various communities or social identities, depending upon their contexts.

The bonds or ties which characterize a community may be formed in different ways, and these may involve the use of consumer products or services. Moreover, community may be subjectively experienced by informants with consumer rituals playing a significant part. From the data, the following community-related themes involving related consumer rituals were uncovered: purchase and use of products as community building, the international and transcendental quality of gay community and consumption, and feeling alienated from the gay community or the community's consumption practices. Each of these themes and related rituals will be discussed below in turn.

Purchase and Use of Products as Community Building

The purchase and use of products are often social, public acts. As such, they often have social utility, promoting the construction of symbolic bonds or connection associated with communities. Overwhelmingly, informants reported that they made special efforts to make purchases of goods and services from gay businesses, most of which are found within the geographic boundaries of the gay area of Toronto. Implicitly, informants recognized and understood that such goods or purchases had some special, communal meaning attached to them. For example, Antonio, before he moved out of the gay ghetto and decided to broaden his life and self-concept, was an avid consumer at gay shops and restaurants. He claims here that he has stopped this practice in the last number of years:

Antonio, 38: Clothes. Okay, I used to, uh, it's hard to say. I used to be more into clothes that I am now. Whenever I bought clothes, it was usually in shops that were run by gay people. I would go in there and buy clothes. Apart from that, I buy uh, what else? I used to go to gay restaurants, does that count?

SK: Sure.

A: Used to. Because that's sort of changed now. I don't really do that anymore. I think my consumer habits have changed. But certainly when I lived in the neighborhood. I lived just down the street from here. I used to . . . I used to make it a point to eat in the ghetto. Well, yeah, this was a period when I really felt that I was a member of the gay community, *and I wanted to be a member of the community, and so I would . . . I would say this was from 1983 to about 1988-89. And I really made it a point to only frequent gay businesses. For a number of reasons. I felt strongly about supporting gay people in the gay community. Financially and economically.* I felt that we were sort of um, a minority united, so I wanted to help them out. And also because, especially because it was a social establishment. It was a place to meet gay people, let's face it. You were out there with your own so there was a chance to meet people. You ran into people that you know, you'd meet people there, so. There was a social atmosphere that . . . you wouldn't find in other places. *I just felt that . . . people were part of my family.* I wanted to go to the stores and to the restaurants. Go to bars. A lot, in that period.

For Antonio, being part of the gay community was related to identity maintenance concerns. When he realized his gay social identity in the early 1980s, he often went to dinner at gay owned and operated restaurants. However, as he broadened his self-concept beyond the ghetto and beyond his gay identity, his experience of community and forming social bonds with others in a commercial mode changed as well. Thus, the community was considered an important part of Antonio's extended self while he was living and dining there, and a less important one at the time of the interview. Understandably, the social ties he feels toward the community are fewer and more tenuous.

Ben's ties, on the other hand, are still very strong with the local gay community, and he lives in the area (renting an apartment) and is another very loyal consumer at the "gay businesses" there:

Ben, 53: Well, most of the things I buy today or the last two or three years, I buy in the gay community because *I like to put my money where the gay people are*. People that advertise. Same as the books that come out, I'm sure you've seen it, Gay Pride week, they have a book out. And the advertisements in there, that's where my money will go. Because at least they're there, and they're not afraid of me going in and saying what I want or what I don't want. And I'm not necessarily talking about the streambaths or anything else. I'm talking about, it could be the lawyers, it could be bookshops, printshops. Like I get a lot of printing done at Ryerson's. They advertise. They're gay-orientated. And I guess what I want printed, I can have it done, and I don't have to do a lot of explaining on it. Like I said, I'm running the gay and lesbian caucus [at AA] this year in October, and a lot of material has to come out on that. I feel good about the people I deal with there . . .

Certain marketers such as the *Pink Pages Directory* and the *Lesbian and Gay Pride Day Souvenir Guide* have researched the gay market and issue annual or quarterly promotional booklets which feature many advertisements from local businesses within the gay area (and some large businesses such as Digital Equipment Company). Thus, publishers and marketers are attempting to form symbiotic commercial relationships with the gay community. Ben, like some of the other informants, is the kind of consumer who will "put his money where the gay people are," demonstrating his loyalty to his community through supporting those businesses which support it. In so doing, he forms social ties with both the proprietors and an abstract category of people.

One important observation which emerged from the data is that often, informants were not extremely satisfied with the quality, price, or selection of the goods and services they received, but they continued to frequent the same business regardless. Often, informants asserted that they liked to support businesses within the community despite their less than excellent level of satisfaction:

Chuck, 50: Now, I'm starting to tailor my purchases slightly towards the gay market more. Um, I will now eat in gay restaurants. *Not that they're particularly good, but I do it because they're gay,* although I like places like *Vaggara*. Um, I would consider going to a gay resort now. I've been to Key West. I would consider . . . I think that um, I would perhaps use a service that I knew was provided by a gay person deliberately.

SK: Any reasons for that?

C: I think it's time! I think that uh, the gay community has to stand up and start being looking after itself, so I think that yeah, we can be very strong. I think consumer dollars are very important.

Chuck was in a relationship with another man for almost twenty-five years and during this time, they entertained a small clique of gay friends within the house. During this period, Chuck did not "venture into the gay community much." However, now that Chuck is single, he makes more of an effort to try new gay experiences and "come out of the closet a little more," as he puts it. Significantly, he loves to be "pampered" at restaurants and hotels. Yet, he knowingly and repeatedly tolerates the subjectively viewed inferior quality at gay restaurants because he obtains a level of *social utility* from buying gay. Chuck feels that he is supporting some of his own people, forming links with them by commercial means.

Many of the informants felt that they benefited from some form of social utility by supporting the community. For one informant, this product benefit of "comfort" is one manifestation of this phenomenon:

Ian, 22: Food, I usually buy in . . . I enjoy buying it. I feel more comfortable that way, buying in the gay community.

Social utility is considered to be a product attribute which possesses a commercial value. The store or product may be inferior on some product attributes such as flavor, style, or selection, but if it is located or sold in the gay area, that product dimension alone may be perceived as valuable enough to compensate for other apparent weaknesses:

SK: [To Eilert] Do you buy underwear from Priape [a store in the community]?

Eilert, 32: Yeah, I only started recently doing that.

SK: Can you tell me a bit about that, how that came about?

E: I walked into Priape one day because I had nothing better to do on a Saturday afternoon, and I walked in and discovered that they had . . . they had um, a wide range of normal clothing, not just the glittery stuff or the leather stuff, so I decided to browse around.

SK: What do you mean by normal clothing?

E: Socks, underwear, jeans, stuff that any other store would carry. But now I find I buy all my stuff, where possible, you know, at Priape.

SK: At Priape? Can you tell me why?

E: *I don't mind spending the extra money to support the gay community*, and if they have the same kind of selection that Thrifty's might have or that um, Levi's might have, then I'll shop there, that's it. Now, unfortunately, Priape doesn't have the regular selection, and uh, most of what they stock is uh, just a bit too flashy for me. I like plain, simple things. Um, they moved to a new location, and I've been there once. And I think their selection has gotten worse and not better with the new location. They've stocked up on a lot of fancy things and they've cut down on a lot of the basics.

Significantly, in some instances, not only will the informants overlook some product weaknesses, but also they will pay more for the products and make special, ritualistic efforts to search out businesses within the community, as Eilert did. Thus, social utility gained from forming bonds with others may enhance a product's worth or benefit in the subjective view of gay consumers.

Forming social ties with stores and businesses is considered to be a critical commercial activity by some of the informants. For example, Tim, who considers himself to be "a very private person" does not have very much to do with the gay community for fear of losing his job as a public school teacher and makes an effort to support the businesses such as restaurants and travel agencies within the gay community, despite the fact that he lives rather far from the area itself and is rather closeted:

Tim, 34: I think . . . as a gay person, if you're comfortable with who you are and your homosexuality, then your consumer behavior is going to be affected that as it would if you weren't comfortable. I mean, if someone's not comfortable with who they, with being gay, then they might tend to avoid gay products, gay places, gay businesses, etc., etc. But if you are comfortable with it, you're more willing to support . . . and much more willing to frequent these establishments. Um, because I think the gay community is very small and because gay people certainly don't . . . appear in the numbers like straight people, then smaller becomes much more close knit, and therefore, people are much more willing to support each other. Especially in a society that's discriminatory. Therefore, *if you bond together as a group*, you have a greater strength. And therefore, I think people would support each other because of that. Unfortunately, I don't think it always happens. I mean, I've seen gay people being . . . not being very supportive to each other. And um, I think they have to be made aware that this is destructive.

In Tim's view, supporting gay products and the like are a way of showing that one is comfortable with being gay. He believes that one obtains a "strength" from "bonding together," and one of the ways to bond is to purchase from businesses in the gay area. Like many of the informants, Tim obtains a sense of comfort and even of strength from being able to demonstrate his support through commercial activities.

In summary, many of the informants place a special meaning on the simple act of buying goods and services from businesses which are considered part of the gay community. This act of buying is considered a form of social support for an abstract concept of community and for actual people one meets face to face (such as proprietors and salesclerks). However, this ritualistic form of activity—which often involves some search and evaluation of alternatives—is not considered a charitable act. Informants receive something extra which is valuable to them: the opportunity to create and maintain social ties, links, and bonds which constitute a gay community. These findings are not inconsistent with other consumer research. For example, Frenzen and Davis (1990) found that market embeddedness (i.e., deriving utility from both utilitarian and social product attributes; see also Granovetter [1985] on the topic) impacts the likelihood of purchase within home buying situations. Belk and Coon (1993) assert that gift-giving often has significant social or symbolic utility (aside from the economic worth of the gift) between two people in a dating relationship. Gainer (1992) found that social

ties between buyers impacted purchase likelihood in an artistic consumer context. These last two studies further suggest that the symbolic
value of various consumer behaviors has the capacity to create or
maintain the social ties which characterize communal orientation. The
informants in this study subjectively attributed their buying behaviors to their motivations of supporting gay businesses and in turn,
other gay people. In return, they received both the product's functional utilities and the social benefits of maintaining social links.

The discovery that informants regularly frequent gay owned and
operated businesses within the geographic confines of the gay area
is quite significant in that this form of symbolic, meaningful consumption allows them to establish bonds both to businesses and to
other gay men that they do not know personally. Some informants,
such as Don, Ben, and Godfrey, claimed that they had supported the
community in this manner for years. Thus, this form of community-
building activity must be differentiated from *communitas* (a temporary bonding or camaraderie which transcends existing social structures; see Turner [1969, 1982]) in that its duration is quite long-term
and repeated. Moreover, it is distinguished from communitas in
another important manner: while both concepts share the com-
monality of social reward, communitas implies a strong degree of
face-to-face, personal, intimate contact among presumably a known,
finite collection of people. Purchase and use of goods in building
community, on the other hand, involves the creation of a bond
between strangers. It is the predominant manner in which the gay
men interviewed in this study socially constructed and maintained
the elusive notion of gay community.

The International and Transcendental Quality
of Gay Community and Consumption

According to some of the informants, the concept of community
encompasses more than the local, geographic vicinity and people surrounding the corner of Church and Wellesley, and certain consumer
behaviors (travel in particular) help them to create, understand, and
appreciate this community bond. Once these individuals start coming
out of the closet, they realize that they share a tie with gay men and
lesbians everywhere, including those in other cities and countries.
Experiencing this social tie includes the realization that gay men are

similar on various dimensions (besides sexual orientation) and are united in a struggle against prejudice and hatred, a cause more important than themselves individually. Often, these bonds are reflected in consumer behavior rituals.

Roger, who considers himself somewhat apart from the material aspect of the gay community and does not do any traveling, considers the community to be a part of him, an aspect of his extended self. The sense of gay community which he has internalized has grown to encompass gay men and lesbians everywhere and furthermore, it has *even transcended the boundaries of sexual orientation itself.*

Roger, 26: So the community is a very broad term—very, very broad. And in fact, it's not just Toronto's gay community. I look at the gay community as an international thing, because you know, if there's something that goes on anywhere in the world, we, in a general community, will network together. Like for example, the [gaybashing] that went on in Montreal. I went out and marched for that a couple years ago. I think that was the birth of Queer Nation, which I was a member of. So . . . it's, I mean, k.d. lang [the country singer], for example, her coming out was uh, great for the community. Svend Robinson [one of Canada's two only "out" Members of federal Parliament], his coming out, was something positive for the community as well. I guess, community could probably be considered gay and straight. I'm not one of these people who will separate straight people from the gay community. So if somebody is gay positive and makes that attitude part of their lifestyle . . . If a woman is raising her child, and she's straight, and she's raising her child, telling them, that being gay is fine, don't hate homosexuals. I consider her part of the community. Because the whole idea of the community is teaching positive things about homosexuality. That's what the community is all about.

Roger considers himself part of the community—and the community as a part of him—in the broadest, most expansive sense of any of the informants. Roger has transformed the notion of community into an abstract concept which includes the principles of inclusivity and acceptance of *all* others. Like the other informants, Roger supports the community with his dollars and obtains a degree of social utility from his purchases. But more important, Roger has created a sense of community which transcends money, purchases, and even the mundane sexual differences between heterosexuals and homosexuals. For Roger, both social categories can be united in a quest and struggle for acceptance and equality. He supports the gay community with this vision.

Recent literature in the mainstream consumer behavior literature and in the sociological literature on subcultures has discussed what has been labeled "the subculture of consumption" which has been defined as "a distinctive subgroup of society that self-selects on the basis of a shared commitment to a particular product class, brand, or consumption activity . . . " (Schouten and McAlexander 1995, p. 43). It should be stressed that the gay subculture does not belong to this conceptual category *per se*; gays and lesbians *do* "self-select" in order to participate in activities typically (and sometimes stereotypically) associated with gay subculture such as going to gay bars, marching in the Lesbian and Gay Pride Day parade, or going on all-gay cruises. However, there is no definitive product class to which all gay men are devoted, and this latter characteristic is absolutely necessary to qualify as a subculture of consumption.

There are some subtle distinctions between the two categories in this regard. With subcultures of consumption, a form of consumption itself helps the individual to fulfil the need or solve a problem. With the gay subculture, the subculture itself (which extends beyond fashion or consumer behaviors), assists the individual in coping with social alienation and prejudice. Moreover, the gay subculture is not generally organized into a rigid, well-recognized hierarchy such as that which characterizes the Harley-Davidson biker or the punk worlds (see Fox 1987). Yet, this study has identified some commonalities between the gay subculture and the subculture of consumption. Like the Grateful Deadheads (Pearson 1987), various youth subcultures such as skinheads or surfies (Brake 1985; Stratton 1985), punks (Hebdige 1979; Fox 1987), Harley-Davidson enthusiasts (Schouten and McAlexander 1995), or bodybuilders (Klein 1985, 1986), gay subcultures do have an ethos or ideology as articulated in a coherent set of meanings (see Chapter 3) and a set of various unique, homologous sartorial styles such as leather, drag, jock, or prep. Similar also to the subculture of consumption, the gay community has a complex form of social organization and interaction. Consistent with the literature on deviant subcultures (Cohen 1955; Brake 1985; Rubington and Weinberg 1987), both the gay subculture and the subculture of consumption assist the individual in solving various problems which are related to the need for freedom, identity, affiliation with others, or uniqueness. Moreover, like the members of subcultures of consumption, the gay informants in this study did, to some degree, identify with gay men in other cities or countries. The shared bond of sexuality and oppression—as symbolized by various products and activities—was often seen to transcend personal, social, and cultural, and national boundaries. As Dirk claimed, "Gay people are still gay people, whatever language they speak, whatever nationality they come from."

Feeling Alienated from the Gay Community or the Community's Consumption Practices

Community possesses some very favorable connotations. Often associated with social connections or bonds are concepts such as concern for others, social support, tolerance, and acceptance of other people. Yet, the gay community has its dark side, often represented by a number of consumer behaviors in which some informants participated. Moreover, negative case analysis also identified some instances wherein informants felt very "apart from" or alienated by the community and consumption practices which informants believed were stereotypical of gay men. Two observations should be made here. First, informants often identified certain consumption practices, such as working out at the gym and going to bathhouses, with the gay community itself. The gay ghetto's various parts (the physical locale and businesses within) emerged as important symbols for the notion of the whole. Second, the issue of negative aspects associated with the gay community was often a very sensitive topic for many informants. When they eventually began to feel comfortable with critiquing their own experiences within the gay community, it was as if they were either cautiously criticizing a very powerful friend or strongly condemning a hated enemy. Some informants felt very conflicted about this issue; on the one hand, the gay community often afforded many of them the self-esteem, physical and psychological safety to be openly gay which they had never taken for granted in the past. On the other hand, the same informants were quite disparaging about various gay consumption practices and the tendency toward conformity which the close-knit gay community sometimes demanded. Therefore, a dialectic tension emerged within their lives. Many of the informants considered themselves to belong to the gay community while simultaneously experiencing a strong aversion or alienation from the community.

The feeling of alienation has many sources and assumed a variety of forms. Lance, for example, believed that his skin color and lack of a perfect body was an "issue" within the gay community. During his late teens and early twenties, he was quite overweight. Now that he has lost weight and toned his body, he still feels that he is not fully accepted by other gay men:

Lance, 24: . . . I don't know any person who can say they don't . . . I think that compared to the . . . like just talking and asking people about it, and they're more . . . women try not to be overweight, but the gay community is not just not overweight but is muscular and as in not bulgy muscular but very toned. And I think it's closer to the image of being fit so they can buy these tight bodysuits and the short shorts and show off their muscles and bodies, so it's like . . . my straight friends tend to say that gay males look better physically, and I think that's the image that's out there right now. They have to look a certain way . . . have the Calvin Klein loose-fitting jean model's body. And it's like anyone who does not fit that stereotype of having that type of body is um, is, is going to have a . . . I'm going to say, is going to have a tough time, like I personally, I was very fat in high school, and even in the first year of university when I came out, and I saw this image out there, it was still out there four years ago when I came out, it's still there now. That it's you have be slim and muscular and fit and I looked at myself and started having a very low self-confidence level and I still do in a lot of ways, and even right now like after today when I go home and work out to get that body, 'cause it's a pressure on everyone whether you're older or coming out, just to fit in and it's like um . . . I really applaud the people who are either skinny or a bit overweight who are happy with themselves because they have the . . . I see them as having the um, will and the character which I wish I had and I envy them for it to not trying to fit into stereotypes and just accept themselves for what they are and just to realize . . . and one person who really likes them for who they are and not for how big their chests are or how much ripples they can count on their stomachs. So . . . even though I do like I . . . I do try to buy in . . . I guess because I still have the fat mentality, like I still consider myself as out of shape and fat, right? That's it's like, I wish I didn't, but I do [laughs]. And . . . I don't know, maybe I won't feel like this in a year, it's just a lot of pressure on people coming out to just exercise and go to the gym and to look good. At least, good in their minds.

SK: That's more or less all I have here, unless there's something else you'd like to talk about . . .

L: Um, one thing I will say and it's sort of goes with the last question you asked me, one thing I noticed about um, the consumer behaviors and advertising and some people will go here goes Lance again tirading against this but um . . . one thing I notice is that in *Xtra!* or whatever, it's basically a lot of things that are geared to the white males of the community, right? And just like um, and you have to be like blond, blue-eyed, have the Calvin Klein body, and one thing I've noticed with people of minorities like myself are not really viewed as attractive. The best word that comes to mind is exotic which is not the same because it's like, it's with me, one view of me out there, I'm not exotic, but . . . to be attractive you have to be white, blond-haired, whatever. And um, yeah. So, it's like what I see . . . when I notice the advertisements being geared towards, toward looking like that. And toward having that kind of body as well, but for me no matter how much I work out, I'm not going to lighten my skin, nor do I have a wish to, right? And it's just um, it's just too bad because I think it . . . it has an effect two ways, that someone who is a person of color can't . . . and I went through this myself . . . tends not to see themselves as attractive, and to basically when you want to date, you tend to date someone who looks like that, like blond, white image, and you don't consider people of your race or any other race attractive at all. But only that type. And um, also, so it gives them, and also it makes them feel less attractive as well, right? And it's, it's really too bad that they don't see their beauty themselves. That's what out there, and it's taken me a while to stop buying into that and to . . . like I date anyone of any race but it seems like when I first came out, I didn't date . . . I dated among one race because I didn't see myself as attractive, so I dated the totally white males, and but now, if I do date somebody who's white or somebody's who's black, I'm doing it for the reason that just because I find them attractive as a person not because they're some race or color, whatever. And just to relate it more to what you're talking about, it's just um, when you see these things in *Xtra!* geared towards this um, one type of male, you tend to um, I guess, you tend to either want to look like that or buy stuff to look like that, or you tend to like, withdraw into yourself and just to like, okay, I'm never going to do it, and just withdraw. . . .

Lance does not fit the idealized image of gay men in two significant manners. First, his body is not perfect in terms of muscle development. Second, Lance is black in a community where blond, blue-eyed, young, muscular, and hairless men are valued for their appearances. Despite the fact that he is very involved in the youth group and has many friends who are gay, he sometimes feels like an outsider or second-class citizen in a community whose ideology ostensibly encompasses acceptance of differences. He is not alone in his feelings. Johnny, who is Chinese, confided to me that most white men either were not interested in him sexually while some other white men (the "rice queens") objectified him and expected him to be a quiet, passive, and submissive stereotype of a Chinese man. Both of these men claimed that they never saw their kind of beauty idealized in gay newspapers or magazines. Indeed, when I carefully read over one year of *Xtra!* publications, the vast majority of the models in the advertisements were young and white. (I found one ad which featured a man who looked to be of Hispanic origin.) Ironically, both Johnny and Lance were excluded from subcultural media for their respective races just as their sexualities were rejected within more mainstream media. For minority gay men, some gay men are considered a little more equal than others in a subculture which embraces equality as one of its ideological goals.

Tom also feels that there are certain consumer experiences that weaken the bonds of community and leave him feeling "cut off" from other gay men:

Tom, 32: Well, like the bathhouses, for one thing. I mean, I have been to the bathhouse, but I would never spend money on it now. I did . . .

I went once. I went with my old lover, Jim, and it was an experience I wouldn't want to repeat. A lot of people spend money on that. And of course, the bars, although, I can't say that I completely avoid the bars. I go to the bars. You know. I spend money there.

SK: I notice when I said negative things, you mention bars and bathhouses . . . do you mean that?

T: Yeah, I do mean that! I consider them negative things because. . . they make you feel . . . I have to speak personally . . . they make me feel less of a person and more of a . . . of this sordid . . . it's this sordid underbelly of the gay community. That's the way I think of it. You know, the . . . you go into the bars, and there's all the losers standing up against the bar, holding the beer bottle on their thigh, you know, kind of standing there, and I just think, "What am I doing here?" I'm just like these people. So, I have a negative association with the bars when I go by myself. If I go with other people, then I have a positive association. When I go with other people, then I just engage with the social aspect of gay life, men laughing, men joking about sex to the exclusion of all else, most of the time. And uh, and that's . . . and that brings a lot of . . . a lot of interesting things out . . . but going by yourself is a totally different experience. You're there to cruise, you're there to see if you're still attractive. And . . . "Do I still have what it takes? Would somebody still pick me up?" That's the question I ask myself. When I go to a bar. When I'm driven to go to a bar. Every once in awhile, I'll feel this drive . . . and I'll have to just go just to prove to myself that I'm still worthy, that I'm still attractive. To strangers. And that's sad. That's sad. That's why I say that's a negative context.

SK: Any other things?

T: The thing that I was just mentioning. Talking about sex to the exclusion of all else. Sometimes, the jokes are great because they allow the same kind of freedom you experience on pride day. WOW! I can finally joke about sex and all that stuff without having to worry about it. But after awhile, if you're in a roomful of gay men, that's all they talk about! Everybody, you know, they'll talk about . . . well, the same things straight people talk about, their jobs, stuff like that, but then they'll start all this stuff about sex. "Oh, well, my dear (archly), his cock was so huge!" . . . Like, all that kind of stuff!!! And that . . . what is that for? It just kind of grates on me after awhile, so I find that a downer sometimes. Sometimes, I pitch right in, don't even notice. I just join right into the conversation and think nothing of it! But other times, when I'm feeling a little down on myself, sure . . . kind of look at that. That's one thing. Perhaps the closed-mindedness of it. The reverse prejudice I was mentioning earlier where all of a sudden, "Oh God! I think that's a hetero place. You know, all those people, I think they're straight (in a stage whisper). Oh, really? They're straight? Is he straight? Oh, my God!" You'll get a lot of that! People will actually talk about that kind of thing. It's a reverse prejudice. So, I find that in the gay community.

SK: Any other things about gay consumption?

T: Gay consumption? Um, yeah, like going out to the strip bars, because that's such a lonely thing . . . although, with friends, again, it can be a really fun experience. But I was at a party a couple weeks ago, and these gay men were talking about this thing at Remington's. It's a jerk-off contest that's held every Monday night. And . . . and you know, men go in . . . and all the lights are lowered. And they sit there in the dark and watch models, strippers jerk off on stage. And I just think . . . that's kind of awful. It's kind of . . . it is seedy! It is sordid. It lowers the whole, the whole class, caste, of the gay community. You know, in my eyes.

For Tom, sexual freedom has its less attractive side. Like many gay men, he has "cruised" the bars in search of community and maybe a relationship. Instead, he meets "losers" with whom he feels he shares nothing in common and leaves feeling depressed. Additionally, instead of his identity becoming more expansive through connections with others, he finds that it narrows significantly through a preoccupation with gay subculture and becomes associated with "sordid" activities like public sex displays.

The most searing and powerful indictment of the gay community (or lack of it) belongs to Gareth. Recall that Gareth was undergoing a powerful transformation in his life. One of the changes he was experiencing was "becoming a fag" and becoming more connected to the gay men's community. Yet, as in most important rites of passage, not all of his feelings were positive. Approaching his mid-thirties, he believed that he would be considered a *persona non grata* once he was considered too old. While he felt that he was part of the gay community, he also felt repulsed by it and alienated from it. There are certain aspects of it which he believes are harmful and dysfunctional:

Gareth, 34: I think we consume too much alcohol. I think we consume too much drugs. I think we smoke too much. I think we're a culture full of bad habits. I think we're a culture of denial. I think we're a culture of self-hatred and self-doubt. Um . . .

SK: It's interesting that you're expressing a lot of your criticisms in terms of consumer behavior, which is good, don't get me wrong. I mean, it's your opinion. You're saying that in terms of bad habits, smoking and drinking, and drugs. You're saying that we overconsume?

G: We do. But we overconsume because . . . and there's no question we overconsume, but that's part of being the . . . I think that's part of being the . . . the . . . what's wrong with the community, there's this tremendous sense of . . . of not being real.

SK: Can you elaborate on that?

G: Well, that's where there's the . . . the um, I . . . there's this . . . I think that gay men in general don't know how to be intimate, and they don't know how to be real.

SK: What's being real?

G: Being real is being . . . emotional. Being in your feelings. Being um, um, not always being "on." Not always being perfect and beautiful and um, I think there's a tremendous amount of pain in the community. I think there's been so much . . . so many gay men have experienced rejection. From a consumer point of view, I think that we're a perfect target market. I mean, we really are because we're so busy avoiding our feelings that we buy, we buy, we buy! We spend. We . . . you know, we really do.

SK: I don't want to put words in your mouth, but I want to make an interpretation here. We're so . . . busy trying to become people who are really not, being not real, that we buy in order to become not real?

G: We're so busy running away from who we are and the pain of . . . okay, I'm generalizing, but the pain that it caused us to get to the point of just self-acceptance. And I don't know of many gay men, and I'm not saying that I'm there, but I know very, very few gay men that have a healthy foundation, a healthy sense of who they are. What they identify with. And I think that we escape. We escape into the bar scene, we escape into the drug scene, the bathhouse scene, the sex scene, whatever, and we consume. We eat out all the time, and I think that there's this um . . . there's this um, it's like a neverending . . . and we're so . . . we're so flexible and we're so trendsetting that we're . . . I think we're easy to manipulate which really makes me angry.

SK: Manipulated by whom?

G: Manipulated by . . . because the foundation isn't . . . I think, I don't know . . . Because it's never just . . . I mean, how we consume says so much about who we are, and . . . so . . . and I've learned to simplify my life a lot. Um, I'm very comfortable and I've learned to live with a lot less, and that's choice, but not always choice, but um, I think that . . . we're so . . . I mean, we look at . . . look what we're presented with. Look what we're told to buy into. And we're doing this to ourselves. I mean, the gay culture. The bodies that we work so hard to have because that's what we're presented with. This is what we're told is acceptable. Um, and I think because there's so much self-doubt, and there's so much self-hatred. Look at the level of addictions both sexual and substance in the community, alone.

SK: What kind of evidence do you see of that?

G: [sigh] Well, I don't counsel gay men with substance abuse, but I have . . . some of my peers do, and there's . . . there's a problem. There's also a high level of violence in the gay community amongst couples. Which we never discuss, ever discuss.

SK: Where do you hear about that?

G: Oh, people that I know that do community work. People who . . . I work, um, with an AIDS committee of Toronto as a . . . uh, I finished the counseling, not counseling, cofacilitating the support group for care partners. I mean, there's a tremendous . . . *I* went through a very violent relationship. I mean, there's so much that . . . I guess what I'm saying . . . let's get what . . . any consumer, anyone who wants a certain product wants to find out is what is behind the intentions of the mind of the gay man, the gay male, what is it that gets this person to buy a product? Is it that um . . . we're such a . . . I mean the prettier is . . . what am I saying? The more apt we are to buy. But I think that again, it comes back to . . . there're ghosts. There are ghosts behind ghosts. And what drives . . . and why do our bars sell more beer than almost any other bars in Toronto? Why do we consume in our community more beer or alcohol and . . . I was on the beach the other day, waiting for the boat, and there were about fifteen gay men, that I knew. I was the only one who wasn't smoking. I was the only nonsmoker. But there's um . . . there's a community that is . . . um, again, I think there's a lot of self-doubt. You can tell. The men here are very strange. I'm having a real hard time lowering my expectations of gay men, you know. It could be just my own. That's just what I'm experiencing right now. That gay men, they don't want . . .

SK: They don't want . . . ?

G: When they say call me, it means don't call me. You know? There's this . . . funny kind of thing that I'm experiencing that they're . . . there's this real fear of being intimate. There's this fear of um, and that translates into . . . because we all are creative and we . . . and so much of that creative energy goes into spending money. Working and spending. Working and spending. Gay men do that very, very well. And I think that's like a Band-aid. It's an aspirin, I think for . . . I don't know. For . . . um, I think, well why does anyone consume? Why do women have to look beautiful and pretty all the time? Why are they encouraged and socialized to be that way? Gay men are no different in that sense. We've created a gay culture that dictates what is and what is not acceptable.

Lack of intimacy, pain, alienation, and overconsumption are all wrapped up in Gareth's feelings of separation from the community. On the one hand, he wished to become a part of the subculture. On the other hand, he believed there to be a great deal of pain which gay men inflict upon themselves out of their sense of "not being real." The suffering goes deep, Gareth believes, and as a result, gay men acquire false identities—"ghosts"—from the possessions they acquire. Consumer behavior acts as both a buffer between gay men and real intimacy and as a "Band-aid" used to temporarily heal the injury and aid in an individual's escape from pain (see Hirschman 1992).

Gareth's sentiments, albeit to a lesser degree, were echoed by other informants. Corey, Don, and Roger, for example, sharply criticized both the "store-bought identities" which many gay men acquire in the place of serious introspection, and the acquisition of painfully won self-knowledge. Corey, as well, believes that he is being reduced to a market segment, a condition he finds personally unacceptable. Another informant, Cameron, notes that gay men see themselves in the things they buy to a great extent.

A number of cases from my personal experience and participant observation data reinforce the theme of alienation through consumer behavior presented here. First, a close reading of various gay magazines such as *The Advocate* and *Xtra!* corroborated the informants' claims that idealized images of young, white men are to be found in great numbers. Often, even I found myself feeling dissatisfied with my body and appearance after looking through or reading these magazines, so I can understand how some of the informants felt.

During the fall of 1993, an advertisement which read "Do You Know Where Your Boyfriend Goes?" was printed in *Xtra!* magazine. The advertiser was The Cellar which is a bathhouse at which there are no lights and which is famous for very anonymous sex. After a brief controversy during which many readers wrote in and complained, the advertisement was pulled. Readers in their letters felt that this particular promotion was objectifying, degrading to gay men, and stereotyped. As Tom related, his experience in the bathhouse made him feel like "less of a person"; this advertisement made many other gay men, evidently, feel somewhat the same way. I personally concur, and during my few trips to bathhouses, I also felt objectified—less of a person.

My participant observation has also led me to question the problematic relationship between consumption and community. During a Tuesday meeting of the youth group, I sat in on a talk featuring a woman involved with leather and S&M sex, and a man who did drag for a living. During her talk, Helga related her experience about "getting into" the leather scene and how all of her friends rejected her as a result of that. Then she proceeded to bash those gays and lesbians who lived relatively quiet lives in suburbia (which I interpret to be any physical or psychological space other than the openly gay one in the ghetto), implying that they were unsupportive of those on the front lines of the gay community. I felt quite uncomfortable by her talk, and it was not due to her predilection for wearing dead cowhides and engaging in "deviant" sex. When it came right down to it, she was doing the very same thing which had been ostensibly done to her: rejecting others perceived as different for their sexual, consumer, and political choices. Moreover, I believed her to be stereotyping suburbanites as necessarily closeted (some are not) and giving the gay youth a rather distorted message: to be truly gay, you have to be closely involved with the community (on the front lines) and live up to some sort of implied stereotype.

This brings up an interesting question: what are the litmus tests for being gay? Is anyone less gay for living a quiet life in the suburbs (the white picket fence dream) as opposed to one of aggressive political activism downtown in the ghetto?

The situation had some interesting implications for my level of involvement with the study. During the question period after Helga's talk, I wanted to offer my list of criticisms of her position, which I found intolerant and a little self-serving. But I kept silent, believing at the time that it was not my place as an older researcher to influence the group one way or the other. Fortunately, during the smoke break, some of the youth group members commented that they found Helga to be as closed-minded and intolerant as her own detractors. Strange! She should have gauged her audience a little better. Most of these kids were from the suburbs too.

In summary, this section has identified an important conflict in the lives of the informants. Consumer behaviors both play important roles in facilitating the building of community and social linkages, but they also seem to alienate gay men from the community with which they are attempting to identify. This is an important dialectical tension within the men's lives and indicates that the relationships which these gay men have with consumer products and accompanying rituals is complex and cannot be effectively understood within the context of the one positive dynamic of *communitas*. Communities may be the source of support, companionship, and resources, but they can also be the source of much personal conflict and pain.

Consistent with Douglas and Isherwood (1979) and with Rook 1985), the data in this study suggests that consumer possessions, ituals, or experiences are bestowed with social meanings which fa-ilitate the building of social relations and promote social cohesion r order (Cheal 1988) by stabilizing publicly expressed commitment o values. Also, the gay community uses goods and services to ommunicate among one another in the articulation of shared, cul-ural meanings and furthermore, by doing so, indicate the psycho-ogical boundaries of community (Cohen 1985, 1986)—who is con-idered an insider versus who is not. Moreover, consistent with nuch literature in the consumer field such as Belk (1988), Belk, Vallendorf, and Sherry (1989), Belk and Coon (1993), Hill (1991), Iill and Stamey (1990), Mehta and Belk (1991), Frenzen and Davis 1990), and Wallendorf and Arnould (1988), this study indicates hat some goods or consumer experiences are valued not only for heir utilitarian or exchange values but also for the social benefits vhich they provide to the buyers. Moreover, the data go beyond the indings of say, Arnould and Price (1993) or Celsi, Rose, and Leigh 1993); in these two studies, the bonds of community were often ound in transient feelings of camaraderie. In this study, the partici-ants appear to be forging much more permanent ties of community vhen they ritualistically purchase from gay businesses within the ommunity and develop an ongoing form of loyalty toward them.

Yet, the above researchers in their work did not focus on what night be termed the "dark side" of consumer behavior and commu-ity, which is suggested by social critics such as Lasch (1979) or by onsumer researchers such as Gainer and Fischer (in review); the atter two researchers suggest a very valuable proposition: is con-umption destroying communities? In other words, does consumer iehavior have the capacity to break down the ties of community? This study lends some empirical evidence to Gainer and Fischer's onjectures that consumer behavior can facilitate both in the build-ng and destruction of social connections which characterize com-nunities. It was found from the data that many of the informants felt ioth inspired and alienated by various consumer behaviors, creating i dialectic in which informants must continually negotiate their legree of commitment to a gay identity and community.

Chapter 6

Consumer Behavior as Political Protest

The outrageous or shocking nature of dress and fashion of various subcultural minorities has been well-documented in various sources (e.g., see Hebdige 1979; Wilson 1993). Subcultural fashion has been meaningfully interpreted as protest and challenge to sexual or class *status quo* and as subversion of existing hegemonic structures. This finding has been confirmed and reinforced by the research of this study; some informants had developed a revolutionary consciousness and sometimes or often engaged in tactics geared to shock the sensibilities of heterosexuals. Yet, this research goes further than previous studies and has observed new behaviors in relation to the politics of consumption. First, the rituals described below actively employ and play with the political meanings of goods and services as described in Chapter 3. Moreover, they do so in a new and innovative manner, co-opting the ideology of family values so often used against gays and lesbians by antigay bigots such as Ralph Reed, Pat Robertson, and Pat Buchanan. Second, the awareness of market legitimation has prompted a new form of consumer activism among informants, stimulating brand loyalty to those companies supportive (or seemingly so) of the gay political agenda, and boycott or punishment of those organizations (such as Coors) who support the efforts of the religious right or fire gay and lesbian employees. Companies should take heed: the majority of the informants asserted that they regularly or often ascertained the moral actions of the organizations from which they buy and made concerted and vigorous efforts to reward gay-positive businesses and punish homophobic ones. Below, I shall discuss the politics of consumer protest in more depth.

Offending the Hets:
Open Protest and Consumer Symbolism

In contrast to the public disclosure of sexuality discussed in Chapter 4, many of the shock tactics described below may be interpreted as forms of symbolic inversion (Abrahams and Bauman 1978; Babcock 1978) which challenge, negate, and ridicule the established, conventional order. Nigel, now living in Montreal with his lover, claims that he used to be a very quiet and shy child who "felt absolutely mortified" when he attracted any sort of attention to himself or stood out in any way. However, over the past years, he has gained confidence to protest his political beliefs through consumer display:

Nigel, 28: Well, I had this campaign during the spring at my classes. One of my profs, I was pretty sure was gay, so the day I had that class, I'd always wear a gay-themed shirt. It was like, "come out, come out! I know you're one. You know I'm one. It's a safe environment, so you can come out. You can make, you know, more allusions to your sexuality," and you know, it's funny that . . . Surprise! surprise! I saw him in a gay bar a few weeks ago. So, I guess my campaign worked.

SK: Is that important to you?

N: Well, in a way. It's kind of like . . . I felt like I made a difference. As well, I like being in environments where I am the only gay male, because it gives me a sense of identity. It's like, I'm different from you, and it's like, I'm here, you have to tolerate me. In a way, I like to shock. That's a central part of my personality, and to a certain extent, I think you can still shock by saying, I'm gay. Not as much as you used to be able to, but . . . certainly in very homophobic environments. And I like being able to do that.

Before Nigel left Toronto for Montreal in order to complete his Bachelor of Education degree, he considered himself very out, as he had informed most of his family and friends and marched several times in Toronto's Lesbian and Gay Pride Parade. In Montreal, however, he assumed a more empowering "queer" identity, wearing queer-themed shirts to his classes and constantly asking his professors, "What about lesbians and gay students?" in relation to academic issues. Nigel asserts that he was trying to shock heterosexual (and in this case, homosexual) others into tolerance, if not acceptance. He passionately believed in increasing gay and lesbian visibility. Also, by challenging his professor in this manner, Nigel was also reversing the traditional power relationship between student and instructor. By wearing his T-shirt in class, he was attempting to influence the behavior of someone who had some influence over him, one instance of symbolic inversion.

Carl, who is sixteen and still in high school, takes great pleasure in being different and asserting his gay identity at the expense of the "fish," his fellow high school students:

Carl, 16: I want, okay because I'm a mind tease, um, I like to fuck closed-minded people's minds around just so they go, "What?" I want to get this shirt which says "dyke" on it 'cause that just drives everybody mad. 'Cause they'll go, "Is he gay or . . . does he know what that means?" 'Cause they do that.

SK: Who would say this?

C: A lot of people at my school. Straight people. Confused people. My school is like the biggest closet case. Most of them aren't straight anyway. Just people in general. Closed-minded people.

SK: Gay people?

C: I don't think so, not as much. I think they'd find it more of a joke.

SK: What would it mean to these people when you would wear this shirt?

C: That's what I want to know, I want to know what it means to them. What it means to me is I want to screw around with your mind, *so I want to get a conversation going.* But what it means to them . . .

SK: A conversation going about what?

C: About sexuality . . . and why people are so closed-minded. I do go around. . . . me and my friends we go around, people will say some closed-minded statements, and you go, "What makes you think that?"

SK: Closed-minded statements like?

C: Like, um, "Fags just want to get in bed with you." Or, "If I had a best friend who turned out to be gay, I'd dump him immediately." We'd cut them up, and then we'd get the teachers to come over and cut them up too.

SK: Your teachers would do this?

C: Yeah! The teachers at my school cut them up.

SK: So, would you label this a political statement?

C: Yeah, I don't make many of them.

SK: Tell me about those you do make.

C: Um, when people tease and call me "fag, fag, fag, fag," then I'll go into school, I'll wear something absolutely flaming, like I'll come in with a bright pink shirt and tight jeans and keys or something like that . . .

Carl claims that he feels deep contempt for his classmates due to their bigotry and closed-mindedness toward sexuality. His stated goal is to make them look foolish and yet begin a dialogue about sexuality and perhaps change their "silly" minds. Interestingly, Carl's sexuality and modes of openly expressing it almost constitute a form of "reversed status symbol" in his school. His tactics of displaying sexual ideology gain him attention from others, and he is able to express his difference publicly. Carl has transformed political symbolic resistance into a form of play. He openly admits that he and his bisexual following at school take great pleasure in "mind-fucking the school of fish" for whom he feels so much contempt. By maintaining this distance from them, moreover, he is able to achieve a sense of superiority. "Flaunting it" allows Carl to invert the social hierarchy in his high school, and is yet another example of how openly branding oneself as a deviant symbolically inverts the "natural" order of social structure.

Recently, family ideology has been adopted (or rather, *co-opted*) by lesbians and gays in their cultural war against their homophobic persecutors. Some of the informants report that they too wear T-shirts similar to the ones Jeff, Corey, and Jordan have described: "Hate is not a Family Value" or "The Pink Sheep of the Family." Moreover, on a broader, more subcultural level, lesbians and gays are continually reminded that they are valued members as well. In Toronto's gay periodical *Xtra!* magazine, for example, there are two very popular comic strips—one gay- and one lesbian-oriented—which often employ related themes. The first, *Doc and Raider,* by Sean Martin, is a continuing one-frame vignette about the lives of two gay men in a long-term relationship. One of the men is HIV positive, and occasionally, the strip features continuing stories of how the two cope with this information. The second popular strip, *The Chosen,* by Noreen Stevens, describes the life of a single lesbian woman, Kenneth-Marie and her many scrapes and adventures with friends and lovers, her chosen family. Ideologically, gays and lesbians have assumed the concept of the chosen family to describe their intimate social structures and assert the worth of them.

Marketers who routinely advertise in the gay press have also embraced the ideology of gay pride and the chosen family. Manline, a telephone chat line for gay men, started a new series of advertisements in the spring of 1994 when the same-sex bill was being debated in the Ontario Parliament. Usually, Manline advertisements were very sexual and advocated immediate gratification and casual encounters. The new ads, however, featured continuing pictorial vignettes of two clean-cut men who met for coffee, kissed while fixing a motorcycle (this was the most sexual of all of the ads), met Mom, got married, and brought up baby, distinctly family-oriented themes. This company has identified the strong theme which began during the 1992 presidential campaign in the United States, and has continued to use this ideology within its promotions into the present time.

Another more mainstream, international brand, Absolut Vodka, has also been advertised in *Xtra! West,* Vancouver's gay and lesbian biweekly. The two ads feature the bottle's silhouette with the following captions and designs: the first ad, called "Absolutly Out," features the typical, silhouetted bottle in the shape of an open closet; the second ad, called "Absolut Pride," depicts the bottle silhouette painted with the colors of the rainbow flag, the international symbol of gay and lesbian liberation. Both Manline and Absolut reflect the identity politics of gay liberation, using them in order to connect and identify with their market niches, rendering their products as the appropriate "gay brands." Thus, gay consumers are reminded of the ideologies, even in commercial settings.

In summary, it was found from the data that many of the informants made special efforts to assert their identities and community allegiance by displaying their "gay apparel" in front of heterosexuals. They did so for very political reasons. They openly acknowledged that perceived power was a strong motivation for what they were doing. They wished to empower themselves, empower gay others, and "bash back" at heterosexual targets, taking some of their hegemonic power away. One may ask, "But where is the drag and leather?" Some of the informants did state that they wore drag and "a little bit" of leather occasionally, and other informants such as Lance, Marshall, and Gareth (who is becoming a fag) told me that they had a few "fag outfits" (the gay style of Doc Marten boots, short shorts, and rolled-up socks) which they would wear with the political T-shirts as "accessories."

It is interesting to note that it was the political T-shirts which allowed many informants to make unmistakably political, antagonistic statements to heterosexuals. As one informant, Marshall, stated, in some areas downtown, *"everyone"* wears a leather jacket; the style is not conspicuously gay. Thus, the context is not conducive to making a political statement which is clearly understood. Wilson (1993) writes of how some lesbians and gays "make a queer appearance" using fashion such as flambuoyant colors or the 1970s "clone look," concealing or flaunting sexual orientation. Hebdige (1979), Fox (1987), and Brake (1985) all studied punk or other youth cultures and interpreted the outrageous and extreme antiaesthetics involved as signifying symbolic resistance and rage against the status quo. However, with the relatively new T-shirts with the slogans on them, making an extreme gendered, effeminate, or even a stereotypically butch appearance is no longer necessary to make a political statement. The T-shirts are not as heavily coded as these forms of dress are. All one must do to effectively communicate a clear, angry message against homophobia is to purchase and wear an Out on the Street T-shirt. Gottdiener (1995) discusses the difference between systems of signification versus systems of communication. Outrageous clothing worn by some informants might be considered an example of the former but not the latter because of the polysemous nature of fashion: it is highly prone to misinterpretation. In contrast, wearing coded T-shirts from Out on the Street may be considered an example of communication. According to Gottdiener (1995), communication occurs only when "intentionality, like-mindedness, social context, and the various functions of the sender-message-receiver model are performed adequately . . ." (p. 62). Thus, it may be interpreted from this passage that "queer" communication occurs only when the receiver unmistakably "gets the message."

Market Legitimation and Company Loyalty

In the past five years or so, gay men have been invariably portrayed and stereotyped as a dream market niche of sorts: well-off, well-educated, and eager to consume luxury items. Informants in this study were generally aware of this type of media coverage and had developed a sense of themselves as a market segment of "gay consumers." To an extent, they reacted favorably to this type of portrayal, as it afforded them with a degree of legitimation or validation (see also Peñaloza 1996) and perceived market power. Yet, they were also wary and cautious of companies' motivations and marketing efforts, realizing that they were not purely altruistic:

Jordan, 26: Well, I think they're cashing in on a good thing. I think a lot of people have to remember, you know, that . . . you have to a lot of time, people tend to look at, you know, why people, why companies do things altruistically, like are they doing this for the good of society or whatever, but you have to remember they're businesses. They're out there to make money. Um, and they're probably out there just to do it to make money, and you can't, I don't think you can do them on that, because that's what they're there for. They're there to sell product. So a lot of times, the argument, "I don't think it's an appropriate sponsor because of whatever or . . . stuff or they don't support gay rights or whatever." I think you have to be realistic and remember that these people are out there to make money. That's their goal. Their goal is not necessarily to be socially conscious. Um, yeah. So, you know. So, you're seeing a lot more mainstream advertising in gay literature, and you're also seeing a lot of gay themes outside of gay literature in the mainstream. Like the movies that are coming out. Stuff like that.

SK: Do you feel that you want to support these companies that help the cause, so to speak?

J: In my own way, yes, *sometimes* yes. Because I would think that, again, it goes back to if they advertise in gay media, they must be gay positive. It's the sort of thing that you automatically associate. So I tend to go, "Maybe I'll buy Absolut." Besides the fact that I usually do anyway. But it's something that yeah, Absolut advertises in *Genre* [a gay magazine published in the United States], so whatever. I think with the Paseo ad, for example, being recognized as would probably have drawn a lot of gay men to buying Toyota products. They might not . . . they might be the most homophobic company out there, but by putting that in their ad copy, they've attracted a huge market. And again, they might be the most homophobic company, but they're there to make money, and if this is a market that they want to expand into, it's a market. You know, they don't look at morals when they look at their markets. They look at the dollar value.

Jordan is aware that he and other gay men may be exploited by "homophobic" companies which, in fact, do not care about gay men but simply wish to generate sales and profits. Jordan is suspicious of some companies' motives, but he will tend to buy or examine certain products if they advertise in the gay media. He states that he "automatically" associates gay-positive motivations to those companies that do so, but upon sober second thought, he wonders whether or not the company really wishes to assist gays and lesbians in their quest for equal rights. However, he will buy Absolut vodka, he maintains, because he understands that they have supported the gay community "for years" and he himself has seen and admired their promotions. Thus, for Jordan and some other informants, consistent behavior on the part of business organizations is important.

Corey was also somewhat suspicious of the motives of companies who advertise or market to the gay men's market, but he recognized that he gains some benefit from them. He learns market information from these advertisements and believes that he is then more informed to make a better decision. Yet, any kind of obvious, mercenary intention on the part of a company repels him:

Corey, 23: So, those . . . seeing those trends makes me aware of where I want to shop, where I want to live, what kind of purchasing power . . . it's almost like, I realize . . . I pay attention to what companies are doing now so when I do have marketing power, I will um, reward companies who have been good to us. You know, and that's where I'll do my shopping. And if I go . . . like we're going to New York this summer . . . I'm getting some services done through the travel agencies in the community. Little products like bathroom products I'll buy at the Body Shop at Church and Wellesley 'cause that's where it is . . . The gay marketing strategy works . . . I don't even know what company produces Pride Beer, and I don't even know if they're still producing Pride Beer. It's a beer bottle with a big pink triangle on it, and it's clearly marketed to gay men. And it's not very creative, it's not very imaginative. It's just so blatantly . . . it's so blatantly geared towards me, and trying to get me to drink it. But I wouldn't. They're sticking a huge . . . they're almost . . . there's an element of segregation to that kind of marketing. You know . . . this beer is for gay men. And that idea, I find really offensive. But I'm just trying to think of . . . the most obvious example of a company doing something for gay people, has made me become a customer is probably Sears. I normally shop . . . Sears is not my kind of store, but they are one of the few companies to have benefits for same-sex couples. And that has made me a customer, so I will go in there, and I will buy um, stuff that I think Sears is reliable . . . appliances . . .

Corey perceives that the Body Shop is generally very supportive of the gay community, and he does make a special effort to buy toiletry articles from there when he needs them. Yet, Pride Beer turned him "off" as it was a very "blatant" effort to make money from gay men. He felt that this company attempted to take a concept important to gay men (Gay Pride) and commodify it by naming their beer after it. This market behavior was unacceptable to him. However, Sears (which is a company he would not ordinarily frequent as it is not his "kind" of store) granted their gay and lesbian employees same-sex benefits, and he views this act as a more altruistic, important one because it benefits gays and lesbians in principle by recognizing their relationships. Thus, when he moves out from his mother's apartment, he plans to go to Sears in order to buy smaller appliances.

Chuck, who was in a relationship for almost a quarter of a century, was not in the habit of supporting businesses in the gay community or seeking out gay-positive businesses. However, once his relationship ended, he decided to come out a little more and experiment with his gay identity. He now reads more articles in the gay press and makes an effort to buy from companies which take a progay stance:

Chuck, 50: Well, I wear Levi's and Levi's are pro-gay. In fact, the religious right are boycotting Levi's and their sales are going up because of it [laughs]. I guess that's one example. I got these on Saturday. That's pretty close.

SK: I heard about Levi's. So you heard about Levi's from . . .?

C: I'm not sure where I heard about it. But apparently the religious right don't like Levi's advertising, and they have told people to boycott Levi's. And presumably, the gay community is striking back because Levi's products are doing very well . . .

Levi's had, traditionally, manufactured the uniforms for the Boy Scouts of America. When the Boy Scouts announced its homophobic and bigoted policy of denying gay men the opportunity to be Scoutmasters, Levi's canceled its highly lucrative contract with them. Following this announcement, members of the religious right in the United States organized a boycott of Levi's products. Levi-Strauss then reported an increase in sales. Chuck has psychologically aligned himself with an organization that has demonstrated opposition to one of the gay and lesbian movement's most outspoken enemies. He feels very positive about his purchase of this brand of jeans because he likes the clothing and admires the company's firm position in opposition to the right-wing fascists.

According to some of the informants' perspectives, a variety of companies have shown admirable market behavior by advertising in the gay media—even a tuna fish company. Lennie, who informed me that he usually seeks out companies that have a reputation for fair and courageous behavior, was surprised to discover that one of his minor purchases was unexpectedly reaffirmed:

Lennie, 32: Um, I uh, if I see a product advertised in a gay magazine, I will try and buy that product over . . . a competing brand if I'm in the market for that product. Um, I know I saw a Cloverleaf advertised in the *Capital Xtra!*, Ottawa's *Xtra!*, and uh, Cloverleaf tuna, salmon. They have like a half-page ad in there, and I thought to myself, "Wow! This is great!" And I actually had tuna for lunch today, and I looked at the can and it was Cloverleaf, and I thought to myself, "Well, I'm gonna make sure that from now on, I'm gonna buy Cloverleaf because they advertised in *Capital Xtra!*."

Overall, informants spoke very positively (with a few exceptions) about companies who had "shown the courage" to advertise in gay media or grant their employees spousal benefits. They further believed that they could exert their own personal market power by devoting time and money resources to these companies, demonstrating to other organizations and society at large that their "money was as good as anyone else's" and that they could wield influence in the form of market rewards. Yet, it should also be remarked that a few informants were somewhat cautious in regard to relationships with marketers. While they appreciated the attention which some marketers demonstrated, they questioned whether the nature of this relationship was entirely altruistic. Many informants recognized that companies' goals were to earn profits, but at the same time, they would rather support a gay-positive company rather than a homophobic or neutral one when purchasing items which they stated they would acquire *anyway*. Looking at it from this perspective, the informants obtained both the utilitarian and symbolic benefits of their purchases in addition to the social utility derived from knowing that they had exercised a degree of buyer power and were supporting organizations which had formally recognized (and perhaps validated) their existences and worth as gay human beings in some manner.

While some businesses perceived as gay positive and supportive of the gay rights have been rewarded with gay brand loyalty and repeat sales in return for market legitimation, others have been punished through organized and personal boycotts for perceived homophobic or antigay sentiments or behaviors. Russ experienced what he perceived to be personal homophobia when he dealt with Sears. After successfully suing his ex-lover who had illegally used all of his credit cards, he attempted to get reinstated with Sears, who would not allow him to take out a new card and treated him "horribly":

Russ, 29: Oh, definitely!!! Definitely! For the record, the one organization I absolutely hate the most and I am not a person of hate. Believe me, there's very few things I hate in this world and I avoid with a passion, but one of them is Sears! And the reason for it is because . . . I have been with Sears for seven years, I have racked up over 7500 Sears points which means that I spent over 7500 dollars since the point system began, and I did that in approximately three years. Uh, I always shopped at Sears, whether it be for Christmas gifts, clothes or whatever. Well, as it turned out, I was living with someone at the time who was my lover, and we were together for about four months. He used my credit cards, and when I say that, I do mean the Sears credit card as well as emptying out my bank account and uh, writing checks on my account, so to speak. How Sears handled that case was . . . now, I won in court. He has to pay restitution to me, and I in turn, am to pay Sears for that. Sears treated me so horribly, and I just . . . I couldn't believe it. I tried to justify it, 'cause I also had life insurance with them for seven years. So when you think about it, seven years of every month, I paid at least the minimum balance, and usually paid fifty to a hundred dollars, I'm a credit cardaholic, so believe me they had lots of business from me. Um, I never ever once bounced a check to them, I . . . was very, very supportive of many locations. It wasn't as if it was one particular location. The only thing that I could think of was the gay issue.

After years of demonstrating a high degree of customer loyalty to Sears, Russ will no longer "set foot" into Sears after his negative experience with the company. From now on, he will not buy from them, and he has communicated the circumstances of the rude treatment toward him to his other gay friends. It is interesting to note that Corey, on the other hand, feels quite positively toward Sears due to his belief that they have a same-sex benefit policy. However, Corey despises another company infamous for its poor treatment of gay (and other) employees—the Adolph Coors Company:

Corey, 23: I choose my beer by whatever advertisement I think is best. 'Cause I think all beer is the same, so I just . . . like the look of . . . whenever a clever ad comes out, I'll start, you know to buy that beer. Um, and also, I mean, there are certain, I mean, the big Coors scandal, saying something homophobic. I mean, I mean I . . . I never buy Coors products anymore. I just refuse after . . . if a product or a company has a blatantly homophobic stance or position on something, I won't . . . I won't purchase the . . . their stuff. And sometimes, I don't like blatant . . . I don't like to be marketed to.

SK: Okay, the Coors scandal . . . can you tell me about it?

C: This is a long time ago. Right? Um, I can't . . . I even forget most of the details. Um, my perception was that Coors produced a lot of beer . . . I think the details were that they wouldn't hire anyone who was openly gay. I think they took a blatant stance like that. I'm not exactly sure. And so we just . . . we just decided to stop buying their beer. Forget it.

There actually was an organized boycott of Coors products during the late 1970s after the company allegedly performed polygraph tests on employees, asking about sexual orientation (Baker, Strub, and Henning 1995). Since then, Coors has added sexual orientation to its antidiscrimation policy. However, it should be noted that despite the company's aggessive marketing to women's groups and to gays and lesbians, the company is still controlled by the Coors family who are extremely conservative German Americans. Several members of this family are prominent funders of far-right organizations such as the Heritage Foundation, a driving force behind the "new right" (Baker, Strub, and Henning 1995). The Heritage Foundation advocates mandatory HIV testing for all public employees. Members of the Coors family also fund the Free Congress Foundation (FCF) which produces virulently homophobic literature which claims that gays and lesbians are a dire threat to Americans and their families. But the Coors company still buys advertising space in gay and lesbian publications. Brendan also personally boycotts Coors:

Brendan, 28: I'll go out of my way to not buy a product if I know that one, either uh, is . . . the company is . . . homophobic. No. I think homophobic is the wrong term. Bigoted is a better term. Um, Coors, for example. I think it's the classic example of a product that the gay community has boycotted, and I don't know any people that don't follow that boycott, and I personally believe in using economic clout to support and/or punish people that don't, you know, support us and our agenda, and just are bigots, and you know, you shouldn't be putting money in their pockets . . . if I knew . . . if I knew of a business being bigoted, I wouldn't go there and/or like you know, I remember once, I was walking down the street, and I don't know if this is an example of consumer behavior, but uh, someone from the Salvation Army asked me for a donation, and I said, "I'm sorry, I can't donate to you because you know, the people that run the Salvation Army support legal challenges to my basic human rights," and sort of walked off, feeling very, very good about myself. And it was like, you know, and if someone asked me, you know, when they wouldn't let them use Nathan Philips Square when the city prevented the Salvation Army from using it because uh, one of the gay counselors had complained that their actions discriminated . . . like I was totally for that. Um, anything, anything that I'm aware of . . . I'll use that knowledge to dictate my spending behavior, so if there's a product I normally buy and I find out that that company discriminates against gay people, I won't buy that product anymore.

Like Brendan, many informants report feeling very "good about themselves" when they exercised their market power to punish homophobic or bigoted organization like Coors or the Salvation Army. Having done this myself, I can identify with the "rush" of righteous anger and satisfaction which occurred when I got the chance to "get even" with corporate bigots by denying them my patronage. Brendan himself reads often and scans the newspapers for any gay- or lesbian-related news. If he learns of a nonsupportive organization, he allows this knowledge to "dictate" how he will buy in the future. Like Brendan and Russ, informants, for the most part, do not take part in organized collective boycotts. Rather, they find out information on their own from various and mainstream sources, disseminate it informally to others, and then withhold their dollars in the future from organizations they view as bigoted.

In summary, this chapter has described the various ritualistic ways by which the informants expressed political, symbolic consumer resistance against institutions or people they believe to be homophobic oppressors. By doing so, they strongly assert their identities as gay men and even develop them further. Many of the informants stated that they feel better or prouder of themselves for publicly coming out in these manners and defending their commu-

nity. The informants consume in manners which communicate important social values which are very important to their self-concepts.
Additionally, the informants maintain the ties of community by
engaging in such actions. By flaunting their sexuality in public,
boycotting bigoted companies, and supporting gay-positive ones,
they are symbolically demonstrating their allegiance with a community which is important to them. They feel a bond with other gay
men who they believe often do the same actions. Also, particularly
by using shock tactics in the form of "ghetto wear" or provocative
T-shirts, they are publicly establishing the psychological boundaries
of community (Douglas and Isherwood 1979; Cohen 1985, 1986),
indicating that gays are welcome and valued but heterosexuals are
generally not included.

Thus, the rituals of consumer resistance described above serve
very important functions in the cultural lives of the informants.
Consistent with the notion of identity politics, these rituals are ones
that stress the importance of sexual boundaries within society and
the identities and communities which form around these boundaries.
They are also often very public actions which may be interpreted as
the sometimes antagonistic, symbolic tactics of social struggle of a
marginalized subculture in relation to an oppressive dominant one
(Phelan 1989; Eriksen 1993; Wilson 1993).

One important theoretical questions remains, nevertheless. Are
these rituals a form of meaningful rebellion or resistance to the
status quo or are they "only" empty rituals which serve to reinforce
and perpetuate it? Those who accept Gluckman's (1954, 1959) conceptualization of rituals of rebellion might opt for the latter, arguing
that the above rituals of symbolic resistance or protest are instances
of politically impotent venting and ranting. Yet, there are some
underlying problems with Gluckman's work. First, Gluckman has
been criticized for limiting his work to seasonal rituals. The second
criticism is paradigmatic. By assuming that such rituals constitute a
"structural steam valve" which allow harmless, transient disorder,
Gluckman presupposes a thoroughly functionalist perspective
which assumes that all social institutions serve to promote continuity and social survival (see also Burrell and Morgan 1979; Pearce
1995). Underlying order is simply assumed to exist. Yet, rituals have
their bases mostly in *conflict* (Rook 1985; Cheal 1988; Turner

1982). An interpretation more grounded in a radical perspective might suggest that many rituals are in fact indicative of the basic conflictual nature of society or culture.

More to the point here, rituals of symbolic resistance are not meaningless venting. The last two rituals discussed—supporting gay-positive businesses and products, and boycotting businesses perceived to be bigoted—may be interpreted as evidence of a "revolutionary consciousness" bent on changing certain aspects of culture; they may even have real economic consequences upon the businesses involved. For example, it is generally believed that Absolut vodka has benefited greatly in terms of brand loyalty and sales to gay men (Lukenbill 1995). On the other hand, after the Adolph Coors Company's employment policies became known, no gay bar in the United States would sell their products (Lukenbill 1995). Ritualistically supporting gay-positive businesses and boycotting the homophobic ones rewards the good and punishes the wicked, respectively.

Moreover, intentional, meaningful, and ritualistic public display of certain products often constitutes a form of symbolic inversion (Babcock 1978) which challenges the dominant heteropatriarchy. One might be tempted to label this behavior a classic example of "venting" or empty "ritual of rebellion." But on a further examination, such is not really the case. These inversions challenge the "natural" assumption of heterosexual predominance and superiority and are blatant evidence of the same consciousness discussed above. Belk (1994) notes that rituals of rebellion usually are effective only when people accept that their social situation cannot be changed. Yet, the gay movement is predicated upon the assumption that civil rights *can* be obtained through peaceful (and sometimes not so peaceful) protest. While a political consciousness of gay oppression and pride is no guarantee of subsequent, real social improvement (such as the general change of attitudes and legislation), it is reasonable to assert that *no change can result without it.* Thus, the outrageous clothing and T-shirts worn in Toronto are indicative and symbolic both of the transformation of gay shame to gay pride and of all the real political activities which do promote actual progress such as lobbying, rioting, and marching.

It can be convincingly argued that all of the rituals described above share elements of symbolic inversion. Turner (1969, 1982) asserts that there exists a certain "sacred power of the weak" (who are usually liminal people undergoing rite of passage) found in preindustrial societies. To apply this notion here, one might assert that when the informants openly brand themselves as social deviants in the above various manners, they symbolically resist, invert, and subvert the conventional order and grant themselves a form of social power. In effect, they have "beat society to the punch" by branding *themselves* as deviants. The implicit message might be construed as "Yes, I am a deviant! And I'm proud of it! So go fuck yourselves!"

These rituals have a significant role in the lives of the informants which suggests that they are closer to real rebellion than simply the rituals of rebellion found in various other sources (Gluckman 1954, 1959; Hebdige 1979; Belk 1994; Kugelmass 1994). They are expressions of the hope and struggle for human freedom; they represent the ritual enactment of new ideologies and the collective overthrow of ones which previously influenced in the formation of the self-concept (Leonard 1984; Breakwell 1986). Berlin (1969) asserts that there are two kinds of liberty: freedom *from* (the negative kind) and freedom *to* (the positive kind); in the recent consumer behavior literature, Schouten and McAlexander (1995) discuss these concepts in the context of Harley-Davidson use. The former is to be rid of coercion or prevention of any kind in an area in which one could otherwise act—noninterference. To possess positive freedom (or license), on the other hand, is to be a doer and to become someone who directs his or her own actions through independent will. In a very profound sense, the informants are expressing their desire for both types of liberty by engaging in various forms of consumer rituals. By boycotting bigoted organizations, they are exerting a will toward freedom *from* oppression, *from* violence and gaybashing, *from* persecution by the instruments of the state, and *from* the efforts of organized religion such as the Catholic Church and the right-wing Christian fundamentalist movement. By supporting companies that target them and sometimes validate their human existences, and by flaunting their sexualities in the faces of heterosexuals, they are demonstrating their will toward freedom *to* engage in sexual relations with members of the same sex, *to* live with a partner of one's preference, *to* have children, *to* hold one's partner's hand in public, and *to* enjoy all the privileges currently restricted to members of society who engage in opposite-sex relationships. It is this great human desire and will toward liberty which is fundamentally expressed by symbolic, political consumer resistance tactics. Beyond the antagonism and the rage lies the alternative ideology and the "critical imagination" which dares to speak its name and dream of a better, free world.

Chapter 7

Consumer Behavior, Gay Community, and Identity

The original purpose of this research was to explore the deep meanings of goods and services within the context of forty-four gay men's lives. In so doing, relationships among consumer behavior and gay identity, gay community, and gay politics have been articulated in the previous chapters. To a significant extent, the informants share important symbolic meanings which are associated with the ritual acts of buying, displaying, and using their purchases. In gay subculture, consumption has emerged as a key activity in the creation, maintenance, destruction, and recreation of the principles and categories comprising the culturally constituted world (McCracken 1986, 1988a). Consumer researchers now better understand the complex relationships among constructs involved in consumer acculturation: deviant consumer behavior, self-transformation, and progressive subcultural identification. Informants formed subject-object relationships with various goods and consumer experiences (previously considered stigmatized and taboo) which helped them to establish and anchor their new social identities as gay men within the context of a new small world, subculture, or gemeinschaft, a phenomenon not too different from the Indian immigrants described in Mehta and Belk (1991), for example. In contrast, however, the Indians in their study attempted to retain aspects of their past identities, as symbolized by certain possessions. The purchase and use of certain products often assist in the establishment of various important psychological and social phenomena which consumer researchers have studied in relation to the discipline: the importance of consumer rituals in facilitating acculturation to subcultural norms and social stability in the forms of gay identity, the boundaries and bonds associated with gay community, and even the internalization and outward symbolic expression of political ideology. Below, I shall discuss various insights which emerged from the study and have relevance to both consumer research and gay and lesbian studies.

Generational Differences and Consumer Subculturation

One interesting discovery which I uncovered in the data was a relationship between the process of consumer acculturation and generational differences. Originally, I endeavoured to find informants from as many age categories as possible in order to provide a diversity of views which would both reinforce and challenge interpretation.

One discovery which emerged from the data is that those "baby bust" informants born well after the Stonewall Riots of June 1969—Carl, Sam, Nelson, Danny, Arnold, and David—who are all under twenty years of age, experienced less fear, shame, and other difficulties than those informants of previous generations. Moreover, they disclosed the knowledge of their sexual orientations at an earlier age and consumed in a somewhat different manner than the older gay men in that they were more public, sooner in their lives. By contrast, baby boomers such as Cody, Tom, Antonio, A.J., Eilert, Gareth, Paul, Tim, Lennie, and myself are all in our thirties, born before the Stonewall Riots. We all experienced a significant degree of difficulty in coming out. Cody and Gareth experienced much religious conflict. Lennie became a drug addict for a significant portion of his closeted youth. One of these informants attempted suicide. All of them experienced major hesitations about becoming more public in expressing their orientations, and this fear was reflected in their various consumer choices. Nelson and Danny, for example, have few qualms concerning the public disclosure of their orientations through fashion or other forms of consumer behavior. On the other hand, Antonio waited until his late twenties to participate more fully and openly in Toronto's gay community and started wearing more colorful, flamboyant clothing during that time. Paul, in his late thirties, considers himself quite conservative in this respect. He generally never "flaunts" his sexuality in this matter, and he has some significant reservations about attending events such as Lesbian and Gay Pride Day.

François may be considered an extreme case who provides an excellent example of the generation gap uncovered. At the time of the interview, he was fifty years old, born in Europe during World War II. He is the only informant who actually disagrees with many ideological aspects of gay liberation. He voted for the right-wing conservative Reform Party of Canada which is considered virulently antigay. He believes that gay men are "not sick" but are "not a part of the community." He accepts the status quo and his own marginal status. He also disagrees with same-sex domestic benefits. It is not surprising that he is very guarded and careful about his personal appearance, taking care that all of his gay products are well hidden when his heterosexual friends visit and that he is never seen in public with any telltale stigma symbols exposed. By contrast, Chuck, who is also fifty, has spent the last twenty-five years of his life quietly living with his lover. Now that he is "single again," he has decided to frequent gay restaurants and other businesses more often and become somewhat "more out" than he has ever been. Thus, while the older men in this group were generally more conservative and reticent to disclose their sexual orientations to others, this is not a foregone conclusion. Still, they did not embrace visibility with the breezy alacrity which characterized the actions of some younger informants.

This latter group tended to spend more time in the gay community, buy a greater variety of gay products, and thus, their accculturation processes proceeded faster and was more all-encompassing than the older men. Danny, for example, visited LGBYT for the first time when he was eighteen and within less than one year, was leading the youth group, had come out to his parents and grandmother, and was stamping all of his money with a "gay dollar" stamp. By contrast, both Antonio and Paul, both in their late thirties, have yet to tell their parents. Paul would never entertain the idea of stamping his money with such a stamp.

As the younger, post-Stonewall generation of gay youth continue to embrace the ideology of visibility, and as mainstream culture appropriates subcultural products for their own uses, it is likely that they will need new and innovative ways to communicate their invisible stigmas. Thus, public consumer behavior involving T-shirts, buttons, makeup, various fashions, and jewelry will become increas ingly important to them. Certainly, there was evidence of this phenomenon from the study's data. The younger generation of gay consumers were the only informants to wear *avant garde* products such as makeup, kilts, and other more newly unisex fashions (see Gottdiener 1995).

Consumer Rituals and the Imperfect Chronology of Gay Identity Development

In the gay subculture, consumer rituals serve at least four important roles in the gay men's lives: to hide one's sexual orientation, to manage one's gay identity, to form the bonds of gay community in various ways, and to express rage and opposition to the dominant heterosexual culture; in so doing, they promote social stability over time. After an analysis, comparison, and interpretation of the interviews of informants who appear to be at different stages of the coming out process and of individual retrospective self-reports in a longitudinal manner, a chronological order of the rituals—which roughly mirrors the coming out process—emerged from the data. By using various forms of ritualistic consumer behavior to manage impressions over the long term, informants were enabled to negotiate the ongoing formation of gay identity, consistent with their existing experiences of agency (i.e., the will to act), self-esteem, and consistency over a number of situations (Stryker 1980; Gecas 1982; Solomon 1983). The order is as follows:

1. Hiding rituals
2. Exploration of gay possible identity
3. Disclosure rituals to other gays (selective disclosure) and grooming rituals
4. Disclosure to heterosexuals
5. Rituals of symbolic resistance (optional)
6. Identity synthesis—often avoiding consumer behavior which identifies with gay men

Please see Appendix 4. According to the informants' self-reports, I have listed them by name under the dominant type of ritual stage which most appropriately describes many of their consumer activities, according to their own self-reports. I have been able to determine this classification by the following methods:

1. I carefully reread the interviews and paid particular attention to what the informants said they did;
2. I read about how they felt about this type of ritual, focusing on how comfortable they stated they were doing these types of activities (e.g., marching in Lesbian and Gay Pride Day or wearing political slogans on their T-shirts);
3. And finally, I used the participant observation data. This proved very valuable because during the study, I often bumped into the research informants who were also attending various consumer events and functions. During these occasions, I sought more data which reinforced or contradicted their long interviews.

It should be noted that this is not a stage model in the conventional sense (e.g., see Troiden 1989; Tepper 1994). Thus, some informants have actually skipped the symbolic resistance stage, especially if they viewed themselves as "nonpolitical." As an example, Antonio has experienced each stage except the symbolic resistance one. He never dressed in any gay, subcultural style in order to flaunt it in front of heterosexuals in order to offend them. Yet, now that he is older and has become bored of the "same old things," he has entered a ritualistic stage of identity integration wherein he is trying to develop "other parts of himself" by going to restaurants outside of the gay ghetto (i.e., *not* supporting the community as much as he used to), not going to gay bars as often, going to straight bars with heterosexual friends, and staying home and entertaining more often. In so doing, he is practicing rituals geared to achieving a synthesis among his many different identities. For Antonio, being gay is no longer a master status.

It should be further emphasized that these stages are not necessarily mutually exclusive. They may be looked upon as a chronological continuum or spectrum rather than as a series of discrete categories. One can be in two ritual stages at once. For example, A.J.—who considers himself quite nonpolitical—does march in Pride Day, wearing a rainbow *yarmulke*, in order to express his disdain for homophobia and for anti-Semitism. His actions indicate that he uses rituals of symbolic resistance in some of his consumer behaviors. However, over the last few years, he has come to value his Jewish identity even more. Thus, he must manage or juggle both important identities so none achieves ascendancy or dominance. Like Antonio, he has reached a stage of identity synthesis where he feels balanced. It should be noted that A.J. is demonstrating behavior which is unusual for him here, as he himself acknowledges. He will wear openly gay, political T-shirts and flaunt his homosexuality on Lesbian and Gay Pride Day. Generally, he considers himself to be more subdued.

François is still very much in the hiding ritual stage, as evidenced by elaborate and extensive rituals to hide all gay-related materials from heterosexual visitors. Yet, even he will occasionally wear freedom rings and a more colorful choice of shirt when he is with his gay friends—but only when he is absolutely sure that none of his heterosexual friends will see and recognize him. It could be that François is passing from one stage to another; he may be experiencing a liminal period wherein he is reconsidering his closeted existence and contemplating being more out. During this transitional time, he could be vacillating between a closeted actual gay self and a more gay possible self.

Sam hides all of his publications in his "gay drawer" but is contemplating buying some T-shirts with gay slogans on them, indicating that he may soon be ready to enter the stage of public identity management. (Indeed, when I checked back with him a year later, this had occurred.) During our interview, Sam had expressed his interest in wearing T-shirts from Out on the Street and making his sexuality more generally known. This is indicative of his wish to embrace a different kind of gay possible self and progress to a new stage of identity. During Sam's liminal period, he experienced some confusion and misgivings, some days wearing the T-shirts and other days questioning his choice. Eventually, however, he decided to come out a little more and realize a more public gay identity.

Some informants reported that they were very comfortable when publically disclosing their sexual orientations through consumer goods to heterosexuals (e.g., Danny and his gay money stamp, or Jordan and his "Family tree stops here" T-shirt) as long as it was in a dignified, nonconfrontational, and nonpolitical manner. At the same time, they would never presume to offend heterosexuals' delicate sensibilities with T-shirts such as "Cocksucking faggot" or "My face leaves in ten minutes. Be on it." These informants do not feel comfortable in being more political and aggressive toward heterosexuals, generally.

In contrast, Carl, Isaac, Lennie, and Eilert are all involved in the gay political movement to varying degrees and often use or wear products in front of heterosexuals in order to make political statements. Eilert, for example, complained in front of his colleagues and to Dairydale golf club's management about Dairydale's policy of not buying Molson beer. Dairydale's management considered Molson to be "antifamily" because the latter company had sponsored Toronto's Lesbian and Gay Pride Day. At the time of the interview, he had committed himself to coming out to "everyone" by the end of the year. Corey, a "real fan" of and "believer" in "T-shirt philosophy," wears political ones often, and has even designed a shirt of his own which he sold to others attending the Washington, DC March in April 1993 and the Stonewall Anniversary in June 1994.

Russ, Sylvio, Alex, Jacob, and A.J., however, indicated very little interest in politically expressing their gay identities (or any form of identities) on a regular basis (except for A.J. who will do so only on Pride Day). At the present periods of their lives, these informants would rather avoid gay styles, not to pass as straight, but in order to cultivate other areas of their self-concepts. For example, Jim does not wear tight shorts and political T-shirts because he does not wish to be reduced to a stereotype. Russ sometimes wears a "small" "fag" T-shirt ("fag" written in very small letters, significantly) because he considers his sexuality to be a very little part of himself. Moreover, he does not wish the meaning of these kinds of symbols to be reduced to fashion statements.

Interestingly, a few of the informants have never engaged in many consumer rituals which directly involved other gay men. Chretien, for example, is out to his family and does not particularly care who knows that he is gay. Yet, he will not buy any gay styles or symbols of alliance as he considers this act as an infringement upon his agency and sense of who he is. Similarly, Jacob maintains that he has not changed his consumer habits in the least since he has come out of the closet. Characteristic of those informants who employ rituals of identity synthesis, he performs consumer behaviors (or more accurately, he avoids certain consumer behaviors) in order to allow his gay identity a limited amount of importance in order to cultivate other areas of his self-concept.

Overall, it should be noted that the data from this research calls into question the appropriateness of linear, stage development models such as presented by Troiden (1989) or by Tepper (1993). One important contribution which this work makes is that it introduces the notion of a more cyclical pattern or spiral of consumer development. The observations that first, informants may actually go back from one more "advanced" type of consumer ritual to the one which preceded it, and second, that informants may engage in different types of rituals during the same periods in their lives, suggests that a conscious and cautious learning process is occurring. Rehearsal of rituals or experimentation is a significant dimension of this evolutionary consumer acculturation process.

The Problematic Role of Consumer Behavior Within the Informants' Lives

Corey, 23: I think it's really neat we're making the connection between representing our identity through product consumption. Under that, there's sort of a . . . once we start going through that process, what does this do to our identity? And I'm . . . I'm not sure what it does. To me, it just commercializes my identity. And well, if this becomes the dominant way of expressing my identity through product consumption, then . . . then my identity just becomes subsumed into a market force, and that's not what it is. You know, I'm not . . . and if that's what it becomes, I'd probably withdraw from this market equation, and not buy into it. I mean, *being gay to me has so much more, so many other layers of signification.* While . . . my relationships with people, I mean, if I wanted to like, demonstrate what being gay was to anyone, I think I'd invite them to my house for dinner and let them know my . . . let them know . . . not even invite them over to dinner. I'd probably put them behind a wall with a one-way mirror, and let them observe my interaction with my friends.

The McCracken model (1986) is very useful in helping us to understand the relationships between subculture, products, self-concept development, and meaning acquisition and flow. Yet, despite its advantages, it does not illuminate all of the data collected here. During the period of data analysis and interpretation, one of my students in a senior undergraduate marketing class remarked after reading McCracken's 1986 work, "This is a good model, but it fails to take into consideration a more critical perspective. Sometimes marketers coerce consumers and influence them negatively!" After recovering from being taken so aback at this insightful, mature observation and critique, I contemplated what she had said and questioned the model's appropriateness to this work. It should be noted that the McCracken theory is interpretive and humanistic, and as such it describes relationships between constructs of importance to marketers without engaging in critical debate. As it is situated within the humanistic or interpretive paradigm (Burrell and Morgan 1979; Hirschman 1986), it does not account for a more radical interpretation of consumer culture which critical theory or theories of a more Marxist bent might demand. To my discomfort, it became apparent that this student's criticism had relevance to my own relationship with much of the data. Unexpectedly, the data indicated that a significant minority of the informants had become "social critics" of the gay community, and of various forms of consumer behavior which they labeled gay, and had achieved a distance in relation to their own consumer experiences. On the one hand, these informants were living their lives within the realm of their own experiences, and at the same time, they were objectively critiquing this lived experience of life in the gay community—self as doer and self as object of inquiry. This powerful minority voice of the informants communicated various and serious doubts concerning the problematic relationship they had with the gay community, issues of conformity and resistance to the community, and the problematic role of marketers and some products in their lives.

On the one hand, many informants expressed positive feelings and thoughts about the legitimation which marketers bestowed upon a previously neglected and marginalized subculture. In this respect, the relationship between gay men and marketers might be considered as one of symbiosis, described by Schouten and McAlexander (1995) in their exploration of the Harley-Davidson motorcyle subculture of consumption. Yet, this work goes beyond that of these researchers in that it explores another issue which did not arise in their work. That is, is this relationship viewed strictly as symbiosis by informants, or could it be more fairly described as *parasitism*, extending the same biological metaphor whereby one entity exploits and harms another? Corey's quote which opened this section fairly sums up many of the informants' sentiments of ambivalence and conflict concerning the role of marketers in their lives and community: "it's neat *but*. . . ." To paraphrase British gay activist, Quentin Crisp, some informants find that a lifetime of listening to disco music (or wearing Calvin Klein or Doc Martens or living a lifestyle of conspicuous consumption) is too high a price to pay for honoring their sexual orientations.

The Hegemonic Perspective

On a more serious note, a critical look at marketing to the gay communities as advocated by Peñaloza (1996) is warranted here. Traditional American Marxists, for example, might argue that gay men have exchanged one type of hegemonic false consciousness (see Gottdiener 1985; Hirschman 1993)—the belief that they are unworthy, immoral, or sick—for another one: that their existences must be validated externally by market forces and activities. One might ask the following: have gay men bought out of a cultural system which oppresses them for their sexuality only to buy into a commercialized form of identity and community which values them only for their consumption patterns? Consistent with Brake (1985) and Hebdige (1979), it might be argued that the market acts as a hegemonic process which co-opts subcultural fashions for the mainstream, stripping them of their original subversive meanings (i.e., a process of cultural sanitization). Thus, consumer behaviors act as sources of false consciousness which provide imaginary solutions (Brake 1985) to the the community's real social problems. As McCracken (1988a) remarks in *Culture and Consumption*, "[object code as encoded within goods] helps social groups establish alternative ways of seeing themselves that are outside of and contrary to existing cultural definitions. But it also serves to help a society incorporate these changes into the existing cultural framework and to diffuse their destabilizing potential" (p. 137). For McCracken, the ideological meanings as symbolized by goods may assist marginalized subcultures such as gays and lesbians in understanding themselves as worthwhile human beings by contradicting "existing cultural definitions" (i.e., gays as sick, perverted, offensive, and immoral). However, because the dominant culture is able to understand these codes, "the act of protest is an act of participation in a set of shared symbols and meanings; the act of protest becomes an act of rhetorical conformity . . . [there is the] unintended effect of finding them a place in the larger cultural system" (McCracken 1988a, p. 134). This pronouncement echoes Fuss' (1991) observation that to be out is really to be in the cultural system. As a result, subcultural forms of consumer behavior lose the power of symbolic resistance and are even co-opted by the mainstream as fashion statements. One might conclude then, that establishing community symbols and consumer rituals—which also serve to protest various conditions of society—reduces them either to the meaningless imaginary solutions which Brake (1985) describes, or to a new form of consumer false consciousness fostered by the gay subculture. Willis (1993) strongly echoes this pervasive view when she asserts that "subcultural groups may appropriate, use, recycle, and redefine cultural commodities, but their practices don't change capitalism as a mode of production" (p. 366); instead, radical and subversive subcultural artifacts are "reabsorbed and reified by the fetishistic quality of spectacle in a commodified society" (p. 365). Marketing practices are viewed as mechanisms which ultimately reinforce the existing status quo (e.g., Costa 1996).

Incorporating Human Agency and Subjectivity: An Alternative Perspective

Nonetheless, the above Marxist hegemonic viewpoint is not the only perspective which critically examines the effects of culture. One might observe that the gay consumers here are practicing a form of repressive desublimation (Weeks 1985), or "unfreedom," in which they protest oppression, but in fact they are ultimately being oppressed by the same capitalistic system with its emphasis on heterosexuality and the nuclear family. Are they the naïve victims of an exploitative, false consciousness as might be argued by the advocates of the above arguments? Have their personal, social, and political experiences of identity construction and community building been "commercialized" in the Marxist sense whereby "something human is taken from us and is returned in the form of a commodity . . ." (Blair 1993; p. 24)?

I assert here that the false consciousness/hegemonic argument must be challenged, in light of both the data and the previous literature. It is an incomplete and unsophisticated perspective which fails to take into account the critical power of consciousness itself (Gottdiener 1985). If in fact systems of thought imposed by the dominant culture (in this case, large corporations and the media) create untrue beliefs regarding social reality, permeating almost every area of life (i.e., the false consciousness which results from hegemonic processes; see Gottdiener 1985; Blair 1993; Hirschman 1993), then how is that the false consciousness advocates were able to identify such a phenomenon and label it so? If false consciousness is so pervasive and influential, what divine insight allows so many academics to rise above it? How is it that various societies overcame their forms of oppression, advocating new forms of thought: the French and American Revolutions, to take a couple of examples? To use the media and marketers as one important example of compatible hegemonic process, how is it that very expensive, well-researched new product launches by internationally-known, global organizations with exceptionally high levels of brand recognition and likability often fail to generate sales and profits (the New Coke affair of 1985 would be a powerful illustration instance of this failure)? One might argue that the hundreds of millions of dollars spent by large corporations on marketing research, planning, and media advertising can buy a lot of false consciousness! Yet, often these campaigns fail. How can this be so, given the assumed omnipotence of the elite groups? Obviously then, there is a serious flaw in the traditional false consciousness argument.

Thus, the Marxist interpretation has serious limitations; Gottdiener (1985) and Blair (1993) offer a new perspective on this topic which helps to illuminate the data here. The previous argument takes for granted that organizational practices generally transform psychological variables, achieving a form of cultural control—false consciousness—through media. Gottdiener (1985) notes that this is a very simplistic view which does not take into account human subjectivity and agency as described by various other theorists and researchers (Altman 1982; Giddens 1991). These are the premises of Gottdiener's (1985) semiotic approach, which theorizes a three-way relationship among cultural objects (i.e., goods and services), marketers, and subcultures. In the first stage, marketers produce goods and services which are purchased for their use value. Second, consumers in subcultures buy and use these products in various ways, transfunctionalizing them into various symbols which are thought to possess great personal and social meanings (what Gottdiener calls second order meanings). At the third stage, the marketers themselves adapt these meanings and sell them to consumers, sanitizing the more radical meanings so that they are palatable to a greater variety of people who are not members of the subculture (see also Hebdige 1979). Yet, Gottdiener argues that at any time during this cycle, values counter to the status quo may seep in. While marketers may make an effort to manipulate purchases and their meanings, consciousness can never be fully controlled, and consumers are free to use these goods in contexts which the marketers never expected, producing meanings deviating from the intended ones.

The Emergent Perspective: Creation of Subcultural Meanings in the Gay Community

There is considerable support for Gottdiener's theory which emerges from the data. First, as discussed in the previous chapters, the gay consumers recognize and often participate in a complex, meaningful semiotic system which includes native gay meanings. Brands and organizations such as the Body Shop, Doc Martens, freedom rings, Absolut vodka, and Calvin Klein underwear have been idealized and reified as gay products which, when used in the correct manners, form coherent constellations of meaning and communicate messages involving identity, political ideology, and community membership. It should be noted that while some of the above organizations advertise in gay media or locate within gay ghettos of major cities, it is a dubious proposition to assume that they ever intended to become the gay brand. I invite the reader to speculate upon the extreme implications of such an occurrence. For example, Molson beer has advertised for years in various gay publications (such as the *Lesbian and Gay Pride Day Souvenir Guide*). One might reasonably predict that if the vast majority of heterosexual Molson drinkers discovered that one of the significant meanings attached to their beer was that it was commonly considered to be "the number one choice of gay men everywhere," some might be

very tempted to switch in order to protect their frail masculine egos
Thus, members of subcultures such as the gay men here are free tc
create very subculturally specific, native meanings for certain products which "straights don't get." Thus it is reasonable to expect thai
the *un*sanitized community meanings attached to various products
usually to do not generally diffuse widely beyond the subculture
itself.

Conformity and Consumer Behavior

Second, congruent with the Marxist view, if marketing organizations and the media effectively manipulate consumer consciousness,
one might reasonably expect that the majority of gay consumers
would unquestionably and uncritically accept what they perceive to
be an inflexible dress code or set of consumer rules and subsequently conform to it. In other words, we should expect to find that
social influence and adherence to normative reference groups are
extremely strong. Again, the data do not support this contention.
While it is true that some gay men interviewed here (such as Nelson
who is trying to realize the gay male stereotype, or Ian who watches
gay men in coffeeshops to copy what they are wearing) do appear to
conform in important consumer respects, a significant minority of
the interviewees vehemently challenged what they considered to
appear to be consumption norms in the gay community. For example, Gareth, who in his own words is "becoming a fag," dresses in
the stereotypical gay uniform while questioning the health and
worth of many forms of gay consumption. This type of strong inner
conflict is evidence of a critical imagination hard at work.

Instead, the data strongly support the contention that different participants develop several consumption strategies in order to cope with the
issues related to subcultural conformity versus individuality, media
influence, and peer pressure. (Please see Appendix 5.) According to
their own self-reports, I have listed four consumer strategies and those
informants who appear to employ them in order to cope with social
influence (see Solomon 1994 for this typology): conformity, anticonformity, independence, and 'mixed' (which includes elements of
the previous three).

Conformists such as Simon, Nelson, Martin, and Ian reported to
me that they feel very much a part of the gay community and

significantly, make an effort in public to follow the rules, explicitly changing beliefs and actions in accordance with subjectively experienced social pressure. Nelson's efforts to make himself into a gay male stereotype through the bodysuit and Doc Martens powerfully illustrates this phenomenon.

Roger, Don, and Nigel describe themselves very much as *anticonformists,* on the other hand, and are much more defiant than any of the other informants—Roger and Nigel vehemently so, and Don in his quiet, assertive manner. Don notes that if everyone in the gay community wore white T-shirts, he would wear black ones, just to be different. Even in San Francisco during the early 1970s, he made a point of buying only "parts" of "the gay uniform," demonstrating his gay identity was only a part of his overall self-concept. This group of consumers actively resist and go out of their way to avoid what they perceive to be subcultural consumer patterns.

Chretien, Arnold, and Corey may be considered *independents.* Chretien, for instance, reported that he does not feel that he is a part of the gay subculture, that the gay subculture is not part of him or his life, and much of what happened in it was of little interest to him. Similarly, Arnold, an avid science-fiction reader with little interest in clothes or fashions, insists on "marching to his own drummer."

By far, the most common consumer coping strategy was a *"mixed"* one which explicitly incorporated elements of the above three. Study participants such as Cameron, Lance, and Russ seem to be negotiating a compromise between the social expectations of the gay community and their own interests and desires. Russ, for example, wears subculturally associated T-shirts and clothing in order to show a degree of allegiance and solidarity with the community, but on the other hand, he is cautious in ensuring that these expressions do not become "fashion statements" and that they retain a level of symbolism with is personally compelling and meaningful.

Summary

From the data, a perspective emerges which makes an interesting and unexpected contribution to our knowledge in the field. In the consumer behavior literature, there exists a well-developed and extensive stream of work investigating the effects of social influence (in the form of reference groups and the strength of social ties) on consumption patterns (Bearden and Etzel 1982; Reingen et al. 1984; Johnson-Brown and Reingen 1987; Bearden, Netemeyer, and Teel 1989; Bearden and Rose 1990; Frenzen and Davis 1990; Ward and Reingen 1990; Childers and Rao 1992; Netemeyer, Bearden, and Teel 1992; Rose, Bearden, and Teel 1992), which relies heavily upon quantitative, positivistic market research techniques (but need not necessarily rely on them). Much of the sociological literature, on the other hand, has focused more on social critique of the influence of mass culture and subculture as a response to hegemonic domination (e.g., Seabrook 1976; Hebdige 1979; Lasch 1979; Altman 1982; Kinsey 1982; Gottdiener 1985; Weeks 1985; Fox 1987; Blair 1993; Willis 1993), usually from an interpretive or radical perspective (Burrell and Morgan 1979). This latter stream of work, in contrast to the mainstream consumer behavior literature, relies (with some notable exceptions) upon the authors' "armchair" observations and interpretations with no grounded work being performed. This study on gay consumers is, to my knowledge, the only study which fills in a gap which arises when one contemplates these two seemingly incommensurate streams of research: from a grounded theory perspective, we understand better how consumers use symbolic rituals in order to cope with subcultural, normative social influence, and the pressure to conform. In contrast to Peñaloza and Price's (1992) nascent conceptual work on consumer resistance, this study provides a richer understanding of these social rituals or strategies grounded in qualititative data.

In light of these findings, we may conclude that these informants, for the most part, are not the passive, deceived creatures which traditional Marxist theory might contend. Rather, their consumer choices reflect different kinds of strategies and the meanings which the subculture produces in spite of (or perhaps, more accurately, in concurrence with) advertising and the media. One might also observe that Gottdiener's (1985) model is very like McCracken's (1986) but with a radical spin. Yet, I would argue that the former's theory has important theoretical implications for the latter. McCracken, in his description of the fashion system, discusses the role of product designers and journalists and yet he recognizes that ". . . the consumer good will leave the designer's hands and enter any context the consumer chooses. Product design is the means a designer has to convince the consumer that a specific object possesses a certain cultural meaning" (p. 77). However, McCracken (1986), also acknowledges that the intended meanings which are transmitted through advertising and product design may meet an unexpected fate due to the fashion system's capacity for the "radical reform of cultural meaning" via groups "existing at the margins of society, e.g. . . . *gays*" (p. 76; my italics). In other words, *the expected and intended meanings may not associate themselves with the products at all.* McCracken should have elaborated on this problematic aspect of the fashion system (which this research has done) because it is of considerable theoretical and managerial importance. Its major implication is that the activities of any subcultural group with a strong set of coherent ideologies and common symbols might have the inadvertent capability of *co-opting and subverting the entire meaning movement process* and spoiling the intended effects of marketing strategies (such as positioning, product design, and advertising) assuming that Gottdiener (1985) is accurate in claiming that "at each stage of semiosis, values counter to the *status quo* can seep in because cultural creation is a process and not a schematically controlled product" (p. 997). So mainstream marketers beware!

Chapter 8

Managerial Implications of the Study

There is the potential for various entrepreneurial individuals and organizations, using some of the findings of this report, to make a whole lotta money. Given the results of this study, I believe that the important issue is not so much whether an organization will profit from targeting the gay men's market segment (if they target it intelligently, they can reasonably expect to do well, given some of the previous marketing research studies), but rather how to do it ethically and responsibly; this observation is further substantiated by recent market research by the Yankelovich study (Lukenbill 1995). Frankly, some of the informants here are "fruits just ripe for the picking."

Thus, the following discussion will be premised upon the practice of relationship marketing. That is, I am assuming that the best approach to targeting the gay and lesbian communities is to cultivate long-term, mutually beneficial, commercial relationships with gay consumers. These relationships should be built upon trust, fairness, and an understanding of the special issues, conditions, and problems which gays and lesbians experience. I am further assuming that businesses interested in the gay and lesbian communities are not, for the most part, interested in "the quick buck." Rather, marketers must recognize that many gay and lesbian consumers are either cynical or cautiously enthusiastic about marketing efforts directed toward their communities. Thus, relationship marketing with its primary focus upon obtaining and keeping repeat customers (i.e., retention) through superior quality and mass customerized product offerings is preferable to a transactional marketing approach with its much more expensive focus upon acquiring new customers through advertising.

Other researchers in recent works studying the gay and lesbian communities (e.g., Bhat 1996; DeLozier and Rodrigue 1996; Peñaloza 1996) have also commented that this market has considerable potential for corporations. The following discussion will focus on two related topics: how to market to gay men, and the ethical pitfalls involved in doing so.

Market Segmentation?

There has been evidence that—with the help of corporations' efforts at market segmentation—various markets are fragmenting and have been diffentiating themselves over the last few decades (Solomon 1994). Economic, aesthetic, and political changes have resulted in the postmodern phenomenon of smaller market segments or taste cultures developing, many of which whose members self-select, to an extent: gays and lesbians and subcultures of consumption (e.g., Schouten and McAlexander 1995; Peñaloza 1996). Others minorities, through the processes involved with identity politics, also view themselves as distinct market groups: the Quebecois Francophones, Hispanics, and Blacks to name just a few (see Hirschman 1985; Peñaloza 1994; Solomon 1994). Gays and lesbians, through historical and market processes also, to an extent, view themselves as members of a distinct minority group (Weeks 1985).

Obviously, gays and lesbians consume much of the same products as heterosexuals do. However, the whats of consumption are not the only issue here. Rather, marketers might focus on other issues of interest: how much they consume and the meanings of that which is consumed. Fugate (1993) maintains that those who subscribe to the gay "lifestyle" would be concerned only with various products which relate to that lifestyle: products which have to do with gay sex, primarily. This assertion represents the heterosexist and paradigmatic error which many individuals, corporations, and too many marketing academicians make: that the only difference between gays and heterosexuals is one of sexual orientation. This error may in fact reflect a well-meaning liberal bias to be more tolerant. Nevertheless, the upshot of this perspective is the same as if these academics were right-wing, fire-breathing, religious fundamentalists: in a positivistic and reductionist manner, it degrades the sophistication of gay subculture—a complex set of rituals and meanings, as I have demonstrated herein—to the problematic status of a lifestyle which is unhealthily preoccupied with just one thing—sex. It is strange how heterosexuals are considered to have lives (which might be considered sophisticated composites of many lifestyles with some individual quirkiness thrown into the mix), while gays and lesbians are slotted into one stereotypical lifestyle. The humanist perspective, on the other hand, focuses more upon the meanings of consumption and has the potential to yield some useful insights regarding marketing practice, such as the following.

Should Companies Target Gay and Lesbian Communities?

One could argue that large organizations are prudent to hesitate to market to the gay and lesbian communities. Levis, Toyota, Wells Fargo, Disney, and BankAmerica were all boycotted by the American religious right when they were found to be somewhat gay-friendly (either through marketing or business policies). The religious right in the United States is gaining momentum, is very well-funded, and can be depended upon to monitor each gay publication in North America in order to develop a blacklist of those corporations which advertise in the gay press. Thus any large, public corporation which contemplates targeting the gay men's market must do two things. First, it should conduct marketing research of the gay market in the cities where it is considering the development of a separate marketing strategy. Second, it should perform demographic and psychographic analyses of its existing customers in order to determine some of their key social characteristics. If a company's sales and profits depend predominantly upon customers who hold very traditional gender-role attitudes toward women and gays, then perhaps it should consider carefully whether it should market directly to gay men. On the one hand, it should be remembered that large, public corporations have legal, fiduciary, and moral obligations to many stakeholders: shareholders, employees, and existing customers. From a thoroughly business-oriented perspective, threatening sales by inviting potential boycotts and negative publicity could be construed as an irresponsible, imprudent course of action. And perhaps it is unrealistic to expect corporations to be the leaders of social change in our society.

On the other hand, would many modern marketers refrain from advertising in *Ebony* or *Jet* (popular magazines targeted at African Americans) for fear of offending racists?! Perhaps the threat of a successful boycott is more imagined than real. Levi's, Disney, and BankAmerica are still thriving companies, in spite of (or perhaps because of) the fundamentalist boycotts. Second, according to Lukenbill (1995), only a minority of Americans (41 percent) would prefer "not to be around gay people." A *Maclean's* magazine survey performed by the Angus Reid Group of Winnipeg, Canada determined that the majority of Americans and Canadians (64 percent and 66 percent respectively) supported the notion that "gays should have the same rights as others . . ." (*Maclean's*, November 4, 1996, p. 38). So, what's all the fuss about? It is significant to note that a substantial *minority* (say, approximately 30 to 40 percent) of Americans and Canadians are homophobic, antigay bigots. In creating its strategies and plans, do business enterprises generally cater to the prejudices of such people? This is the moral and pragmatic question which businesses must answer before they openly targets the gay and lesbian communities.

If the answer is yes, then perhaps corporations in question should contemplate the following conundrum: are they willing to cater to the competing and (often) changing political whims of *every* special interest group: feminists, environmentalists, gun owners, senior citizens, right-wing militia members, vegetarians, animal-rights activists, the disabled, gays and lesbians, the religious right, the cultural left, Christians, Jews, Catholics . . . the list could go on and on!

The marketing concept may be of some value in resolving such a problem. If a company's data on its customers and products indicates that the products might serve the needs of gays or lesbians exceptionally well, ethically, profitably, and better than those of its competition, then it should seriously consider a dedicated marketing strategy and mix targeted at the gay and lesbian communities. For those businesses which do decide to proceed with developing strategic marketing plans for developing the gay market, this study has some relevance to them. First, segmentation is a critical, strategic concern. It cannot be determined presently exactly how large the gay and lesbian market is. Kinsey, Pomeroy, and Martin (1948) found that 10 percent of their sample engaged in homosexual behaviors to varying degrees, but it is reasonable to expect that only a portion of that percentage would be out and have a relationship with the gay subculture. Lukenbill (1995) maintains that 6 percent of those surveyed in the United States self-identify as gay or lesbian. Even if only 3 percent of individuals are out and self-acknowledge to a significant extent, then almost eight million Americans and one million Canadians comprise the gay and lesbian market. In an urban area, these percentages would reasonably be considered higher due to the migration of gays and lesbians during the last fifty years (Weeks 1985; Lukenbill 1995). Thus, for the sake of economics, marketing efforts are advised to be targeted toward large- and medium-sized American and Canadian cities.

Such a small market may not economically justify a separate campaign. Companies should be cautioned of the perils of excessive micromarketing: a proliferation of brands, sizes, colors, flavors, and varieties and increased production costs. Further, while some marketing research organizations have found that gays and lesbians earn more and are more highly educated, the following factors should be taken into account. First, previous surveys (with the exception of Lukenbill's [1995] work which is based on the Yankelovich data) are quite flawed and unreliable for marketers, as they are usually based upon biased samples of gay magazine readers, a relatively wealthy, educated lot generally unrepresentative of the gay and lesbian population. Also, gay men and lesbians may be culturally and economically divided. Lesbians may earn less. In Canada, for example, women still earn only 72 percent of what men earn (*Globe and Mail*, August 10, 1995). Politically, many out lesbians may identify with various branches of the feminist movement and may be quite suspicious of organizations attempting to exploit them (Peñaloza 1996). On the other hand, gay men as a market segment are quite diverse on critical marketing criteria. Contrary to the new stereotype of the gay male as well-off, educated, culturally sophisticated, and hungry for the very best of everything, many of the informants in this study were of rather modest means and did not care to buy the best. AIDS is still very much a tragic reality for the gay men's community. It should be noted that this disease usually strikes during the prime earning years between twenty-five and fifty, during which time most gay men have not accumulated the savings, retirement savings plans, and pensions upon which older people may rely if they become chronically ill. In other words, gay men living with AIDS may expect to be poor. Therefore, businesses should keep in mind that the gay men's community is not "homo"-geneous in many ways of interest to marketers.

Yet, businesses should not let the diversity of the gay men's communities discourage them. There are a number of compelling business and economic reasons why campaigns have the potential to be quite successful. First, according to Lukenbill (1995), gay men and lesbians are, on the average, more educated than the heterosexual population. Second, according to the data in this study, many gay men are willing to become brand loyal to companies which demonstrate some integrity and ethics toward them and their issues. Finally, despite that gay men do not earn significantly more (or less; yet another stereotype shattered) than other people, two employed and cohabiting gay men do have potentially higher disposable incomes. As one informant, Chuck, phrased it, when he was in a relationship for twenty-five years, one of their incomes became "fun money." During his interview, he often alluded to the fact that he was now "broke" and spoke nostalgically of the days when he had lots of money—when he was together with his partner, enjoying the good life. This insight implies good news for the marketers of luxury goods and some services: food, hotels, cruises, travel, fine wines, entertainment, financial products such as mutual funds, magazines, compact disks, and books. It is amazing what two people in a conjugal relationship are financial able to purchase when they do not have to worry about funding their offspring's college tuition or paying for diapers, baby cribs, or clothes and food for children! Marketers should ponder this important point.

Positioning

Positioning of the product—i.e., the communication of its central benefit(s) or social meaning(s) in relation to competing brands— is an important issue which should always be contemplated before targeting the gay market. As discussed previously, one of the meaning categories discovered in this study was one of stereotypically gay products or brands. This meaning category is also an interesting type of positioning for products. It may provide an important psychological benefit within the overall brand image of a good or service: "this is the product for gay men relative to other competitors." Some products such as Absolut vodka and Doc Marten boots have achieved such high brand awareness and loyalty among gay men that they are viewed commonly as gay brands.

However, marketers should be cautious about this type of branding approach. While it may be useful and beneficial for gay men to view a product as the gay brand, other heterosexual segments may avoid the product for the very same reason. As discussed previously, the meaning movement process may be subverted such that intended meanings do not successfully attach themselves in the expected ways. "Seepages" of meaning may occur from gemeinshaft (the smaller, gay social world) to gesellschaft (the larger, cultural world) since they both coexist and overlap to a significant extent. As one informant, Eilert, described, one particular golf club he visited banned Molson products because this beer company had advertised in the *Lesbian and Gay Pride Day Souvenir Guide*. Obviously, at least one bigoted heterosexual had read this gay media vehicle and had concluded that this particular Molson brand meaning was "not in accordance with family values"—a positioning many businesses may wish to avoid with its greater public!

One possible solution to this problem is the use of heavily coded advertisements. As demonstrated by this research, many gay men have developed a particular "consumer consciousness" (see also Lukenbill 1995) through their different perspective of the cultural world. Thus, the the very same marketing communication, if carefully constructed, may carry different messages, semiotically, to gays than to heterosexuals. For example, the Calvin Klein underwear ads which featured Marky Mark appealed to both heterosexual women (who presumably bought underwear for their special men) and to gay men, with no one much the wiser. Why? Due to consumer acculturation and the process of learning new gay product meanings discussed previously, many gay men are able to "pick up" on such semiotic ambiguities through a sensitivity commonly known as gaydar (i.e., gay radar).

Ultimately, promising and consistently delivering high quality goods and services is the best positioning for many products. Yet, quality may mean different things to gay men. The data yielded some interesting observations in this regard. For some of the informants, the comfort and connectiveness they experienced using some goods and services was a key aspect of superior quality. For example, some informants such as Chuck noted they went to gay restaurants because of the comfort they felt being in the company of other gay men and because they believed they were supporting their communities by doing so. Interestingly, they also mentioned that the food at many of these restaurants was not particularly all that good. Two points should be noted here. First, social capital can be created by businesses by treating gay customers well; correspondingly, gay men may receive a form of social utility by choosing goods or services by gay-positive businesses. Second, consider how successful a gay restaurant located in the gay ghetto could be if it had good food!

Thus, some effective tactics may be recommended. Businesses located in the gay area or those targeting the gay community should provide both social utility and economic utility. Hiring openly gay and lesbian employees (and treating them well), donating to gay and lesbian charities, providing a friendly, gay ambiance in service locations, and maintaining a high profile, trustworthy market presence in gay and lesbian communities, along with providing a high quality core product, are all advisable tactics capable of reinforcing a favorable positioning.

Advertising

Those companies which develop successful market niche strategies may consider advertising in gay media in order to attract gay consumers. This could be a very effective marketing tactic for a number of reasons. First, media costs for specialized media may be very economical per capita, given that gay media reaches fewer absolute numbers of consumers but almost all of them are within the targeted subculture (plus some enlightened, curious heterosexuals and a few fire-breathing Christian fundamentalists looking for evidence of the "gay lifestyle's" perverse nature). Second, when mainstream organizations advertise in the gay press, gays and lesbians often feel that their existences are recognized and validated, as this study has suggested and as Peñaloza (1996) has observed. Thus, advertising in gay media may be interpreted as meaning that the sponsoring organization is gay positive and its products are worth a more involved and extensive search and evaluation. Such a process may, over time, result in higher brand awareness and brand loyalty.

Advertising may be only the start of a marketer's relationship with the gay men's community. No marketing academic would ever claim that, in general, one single ad or series of related ads cause consumers to buy a product. Ideally, over the longterm, effective, creative advertising creates brand awareness, eventually leading to a viable positioning and brand image for a product. Moreover, advertisements when combined with the process of word of mouth may be critical in achieving success (Solomon 1994). Given that many gay men gain a sense of validation from those mainstream advertisers who do so, if a company decides to advertise in the gay media and does it well, it is likely that gay consumers will tell their friends within the closely-knit community social system. This powerful word-of-mouth effect may result in extensive diffusion of positive brand information.

Other Promotions

There are other promotional tactics which marketers might employ in order to persuade gay consumers to buy their products. Some of the informants were rather wary of the motives of various organizations who advertised in the gay media. Advertising was viewed as only one mode of commitment and support of the gay community. Those successful niche players who wish to gain long-term brand loyalty might consider donating to various gay charities or not-for-profit organizations. Even if some organizations did not want to be perceived as political, they could donate to AIDS hospices or organizations and appear to be very humanitarian. Moreover, since AIDS is not a disease restricted to gay men, supporting AIDS-related organizations would appear to be an overall humanitarian act which might be perceived as generous and good corporate citizenship by gays and heterosexuals alike. Other worthwhile marketing tactics entail the inclusion of sexual orientation under a company's nondiscrimination policy or the granting of spousal or domestic partner benefits to employees, acts which might signal that a company is truly supportive and committed to attaining social justice within the workplace itself.

Blatant attempts to market to the gay men's market might be considered cynical and opportunistic. Thus, it is important for marketers to be cautious in this regard. The co-opting of gay symbols such as the rainbow flag, the word pride, or the pink triangle is a problematic tactic. On the one hand, it does indicate that a marketer recognizes and acknowledges its gay customers. On the other hand, if a large organization, new to targeting gays, made such a move, gay consumers might consider such co-optation as exploitative and inappropriate: a gauche juxtaposition of the sacred and the profane. It should be noted that Absolut vodka used the open closet and the rainbow flag as prominent signs in their Summer 1995 advertisements in *Xtra! West* magazine, and there was no media outcry from readers. However, it should be noted that Absolut has been advertising within the gay press since the late 1970s and perhaps, as a gay brand itself, has "earned the right" to co-opt such symbols. Thus, as culturally constituted symbols considered within the realm of the gay world, the levels of meaning of Absolut and the symbols it used appeared congruent and appropriate. Thus, neophyte marketers might assume a more humble approach, until their status as outsiders is transformed over a number of years, in a process analogous to a commercial rite of passage.

Ethical Issues

The above point leads the discussion to the issue of ethical treatment of gay consumers, a critical concern for marketers. Lukenbill (1995), for example, argues that gay men and lesbians are more suspicious of large corporations than are heterosexuals. Thus, it is critical that corporations earn and maintain a high level of trust in relation to the gay and lesbian communities. Trust is the foundation upon which social capital is developed. And without the necessary connectiveness and bonding which such social capital can often yield, long-term sales and profits may not be possible, given the overall cautiousness and sophistication which the informants demonstrated during interviews. Thus, I offer one word of caution to marketers: do not try to fake it with gay consumers; some of them have some of the best bullshit detectors around.

Moreover, some of the informants in this study had experienced the problems commonly associated with oppression: alcoholism, drug addiction, escapism of different varieties, anorexia nervosa, low self-esteem, depression, ideations of suicide, and alienation from family or other significant others. One informant confessed to having attempted suicide. Some gay men may be very vulnerable to the strategies and tactics employed by marketers and open to the somewhat questionable benefits they sometimes proclaim. Even advertisements in the gay press featuring gay men in positive social settings may be construed as a possible panacea to feelings of alienation—if one buys the product. The following (admittedly normative) guidelines may be very useful to marketers in order to ensure ethical business behaviors:

1. Marketers of alcoholic beverages may wish to consider not marketing at all. However, this option is probably unrealistic, given that some of the large organizations who sponsor Pride Day are purveyors of these products. The advertisements themselves may mention behaviors such as moderate drinking and a refusal to drink and drive. Further, it has been suggested that alcohol consumption is an important part of the gay sub-culture (Weinberg 1986) and has an impact upon love relationships. Most important, marketers of alcoholic beverages must recognize the possible link between alcohol consumption and unsafe sex practices. Thus, in order to behave ethically, marketers may wish to initiate campaigns stressing the dangers of having sex while intoxicated, encouraging gay consumers not to do so.

2. The overuse of idealized images of young, muscular, blond, hairless young men should be eschewed. Gay men are disproportionately the victims of anorexia and those who are not may feel excluded or alienated by such images. Such images also reinforce the all too prevalent attitude that the only people worth socializing with or loving are the perfect, the young, and the beautiful. Naomi Wolf (1989) in her book, *The Beauty Myth*, has suggested a more useful, socially beneficial approach: expand the notion of beauty. Advertisements should consider using members of different ethnic groups and races, of different age categories, and of different body types. Such an approach may actually have the commercially beneficial consequence of inspiring consumers who do not fit the ideal mold to consider the product as well. This approach is not just

politically correct. It is good business as well. Like their heterosexual counterparts, many gay men are baby boomers, between the ages of thirty and fifty. While some of them may appreciate the constant use of idealized male images in advertising, many more may prefer to see attractive men their *own* age (warts and all) featured in ads for cosmetics, clothes, or health products, to take some examples.

And why not? Contrary to what many advertisers may think, many gay men healthily identify as older, mature individuals and have distanced themselves from their longings for a departed youth. Youth, after all, is wasted upon the young!

3. Advertising may be avoided completely. The Body Shop is considered to be hugely successful and has never advertised. Instead, every franchisee is expected to get involved in community events (Brown, Martenfeld, and Gould 1990). For example, the Body Shop at the corner of Church and Wellesley distributes safer sex and AIDS information. Creative promotions such as these can often be very proactive, ethical promotions.

4. Organizations should avoid the co-optation of important gay symbols in their advertisements. Unless it has a highly publicized history of support in the form of donations or public promotions, such a tactic may have the consequence of "sanitizing" powerful and meaningful symbols, degrading them into fashion statements. Benetton is famous for using this type of tactic, but it should be noted that its advertisement featuring HIV-positive branding and a dying person with AIDS were used as shock tactics directed at general audiences. While these advertisements were considered hugely offensive by some, they did have the social benefit of spreading AIDS awareness.

It should be remarked upon that no set of guidelines can ensure that an organization "does the right thing" in every moral dilemma or set of circumstances. Effective and ethical marketers who decide to market to gay consumers should become knowledgeable about the market *and* nonmarket aspects of gay men's lives and subculture in order to ensure that the ethical dimension is taken into consideration during each phase of the determination of the marketing mix. Ultimately, what is required are perspectives of the gay men's market, not simply prescriptions.

Chapter 9

Conclusion

This research study has provided an in-depth understanding of certain subcultural, defining consumption patterns of a social category of consumers (gay men) who have been neglected in the research literature up until this point. Primarily through semi-structured long interviews and participant observation, data was collected, analyzed, and interpreted in order to develop findings presented previously. This concluding chapter has three objectives: first, it will address the limitations of the study's findings. Second, it will briefly summarize the findings which this study has contributed to the consumer behavior literature. Third and finally, directions for future academic research in the marketing and consumer research disciplines will be identified and developed.

Limitations of This Study

Only forty-four men were interviewed, and participant observation was performed primarily in the city of Toronto. As Peñaloza (1994) has noted, citing Belk (1993), "it is the framework, not the findings, that are generalizable in ethnographic research" (p. 52). Thus, it is likely that gay consumers in New York City, Houston, or any large city undergo a similar consumer acculturation process, learn a set of cultural categories, and enact a set of meaningful rituals in order to create subculture wherein symbolic consumption figures prominently. For example, the stereotypical gay products in New York City or San Francisco may not be Doc Martens, Absolut vodka, bodysuits, or rolled-down socks. However, it is likely that other gay communities do have products which are considered gay by gay consumers. Moreover, this research is also specific to a certain time—the early to mid-1990s. One might speculate that as fashion changes and as greater numbers of people progress in their understanding, this research will be obsolete. Actually, this is my hope. The robustness of the theoretical framework here may be determined by how well it is supported when future research is undertaken. It should be noted that these findings may have no applicability to gay men in rural areas or small towns due to the level of oppression they may encounter.

Another limitation of this study arises from the fact that many of the informants were from Caucasian backgrounds. While a concerted effort was made to include men from other races and ethnicities, it is likely that black, Asian, or Hispanic gay men—to name just a few—have a different sort of coming out experience in that they must experience prejudice from both their families and from the gay community due to their differences. Thus, the consumer implications may be somewhat unique as well. Future research could explore this question in greater depth.

Contributions to the Consumer Behavior Literature

The theoretical contributions of this study have been developed and discussed in the previous chapter. Thus, they will not be dwelled upon in too much depth or volume herein. Overall, I found that the informants interviewed experienced a consumer acculturation process during which their view of the self and of the external world changed, focusing more upon meanings and things associated with the gay subculture. In other words, their cultural lenses experienced considerable change and development. A host of important meaning categories were identified which are associated with goods and services. Further, I identified a constellation of consumer rituals which were related to and seem to progress over the overall coming out process: hiding rituals, identity management rituals, community rituals, and rituals of political protest. I do acknowledge that perhaps I have created a false impression by strictly separating the discussion of the meaning categories from that of the rituals. However, I did so for some very compelling reasons. First, the data amounted to almost 2000 pages of transcripts and notes and it was necessary to organize it in some coherent manner. Second, from a common sense point of view, one cannot play with and manipulate meanings—as one does when engaging in ritualistic behavior—until one learns of them. Thus, Chapter 3 dealt primarily with the raw materials of consumer-related meanings of which the informants were ignorant before coming out of the closet (i.e., gradually acquiring a certain cultural perspective as lens), and the subsequent chapters discussed how they used meanings during the stages of coming out (i.e., enacting culture through a blueprint). Taken holistically, the meanings and rituals help us to understand how a constellation of meaningful, jointly enacted, and increasingly public acts of consumption plays an important function in deviant identity development and the construction of subculture and community.

The study also made some unexpected contributions which emerged from the data set. First, the data provided an interesting perspective on how consumers use and avoid various forms of symbolic consumer behaviors to negotiate conformity versus anticonformity in their lives. Combining diverse streams of literature from Marxist sociology and the traditional, mainstream consumer behavior field, this study provides a richer understanding of consumers as conformist and resisting, active agents who assertively construct culture through meaning creation, as opposed to the more traditional view of consumers who are influenced and oppressed by the agents of culture such as media and large organizations. In contrast to one branch of problematic identity politics, these consumers are not necessarily the victims of false consciousness.

Directions for Future Research

The consumer behavior literature, like every cultural domain, is both heterosexually oriented and heterosexist. Almost every important concept or theoretical framework—group decision making, the family lifecycle, and joint decision making, to name just a few— were developed by heterosexuals, by interviewing heterosexuals, and with a heterosexual bias in mind. Every important study that I have ever read has either ignored the implications of same-sex attraction or relationships or has implicitly assumed that there would be no meaningful differences between gays and heterosexuals. Perhaps in many areas there *are* no differences, but isn't it about time we found out? Thus, there are several productive directions which future research could take. Below, I shall outline some of them.

First, a study of the lesbian communities and consumer behavior could be initiated. Is the framework developed in this study transferable? Are the meanings of products similar?

Second, every conceptual framework in marketing and consumer behavior could be revisited and rethought as to its applicability to various ethnic groups, gays, lesbians, and in the globalizing and fragmenting world. For example, when gay men make a major joint purchase when they cohabit, do they exhibit stereotypical gender roles? Is the process more egalitarian? Is the process a result of the display of influence or consideration of the other's wishes? Or is the purchase made in a way that has not been conceptualized as of yet? How do some gay men ritualistically celebrate various holidays such as Thanksgiving and Christmas, given that some are alienated from their families of origin? Does the notion of "chosen" family have any bearing upon gift selection? Are there different levels of family with interesting consumer implications for each one? Are the conventional ideologies of various holidays altered in various ways?

Gay men are an interesting choice of study because their stigma is primarily invisible. One could explore whether the results of this study transfer to other stigmatized or deviant minorities. Do people who possess conspicuous stigmatizing features experience similar meaning tranformations and enact their own consumer rituals? In Goffman's (1963) terms, perhaps there is a difference in the consumption patterns of those with spoiled or discredited identities versus those with discreditable ones.

Another area of research could focus on how the lack of legal status for gay relationships impacts upon consumer behaviors. For example, when a gay man dies, how do the surviving partner and the friends cope with the loss and distribute tokens of remembrance? What are the problematic legal implications? What are the meanings of communal possessions such as Toronto's AIDS memorial and the international AIDS quilt? Given that AIDS is a constant, uninvited guest in gay men's communities, this study might have particular, immediate relevance.

Work on Lesbian and Gay Pride Day would be of great theoretical significance. As acceptance of gays and lesbians increases along with visibility and mainstreaming of the movement, will the festival become co-opted by hegemonic interests? Longitudinal studies over the next ten to twenty years studying many international variations of the festival will provide some interesting contrasts and observations.

The ground is fertile for future academic work and for more practical concerns of marketing practitioners. Will more organizations target the gay and lesbian markets in the future? If so, will their efforts be welcomed or rejected by gay and lesbian consumers? How will these companies ensure that their marketing strategies are ethical?

I would like to leave readers with one more perplexing loose end to ponder. Many more related questions have yet to be answered, and even posed. This fascinating group of consumers has overcome one type of ideology and hegemony—that of compulsory heterosexuality—largely with the symbolic and creative use of agents of the capitalistic market system. The gay and lesbian movement represents a problematic alignment of political activism and commercialism. Perhaps some may argue that in doing so, gay men and lesbians have become trapped within a destructive type of market hegemony or confining cultural discourse. This may be the the ironic and paradoxical price of liberation and license in Western, market society. It is my hope that future work, largely from critical perspectives, may address this troubling issue in greater depth.

Appendix 1:
Open-Ended Questionnaire

Inform participant: Absolute confidentiality.

Privacy.

Tapes will be destroyed or returned to you, your option.

Topic: Gay men's lives, gay men's consumer behavior.

No right or wrong answers, just tell me how you see things.

Don't worry about rambling or going on at length, just relax and feel free to talk about you, your life, your experiences.

1. Please tell me about yourself: friends, interests, family, important experiences, hobbies.

2. Please tell me about the gay world in Toronto.

3. Please tell me about your coming-out experience.

4. Please tell me about your experiences of being gay, with other gay people, in the gay world?

5. Could we talk about purchases and using products? (i.e., shopping, vacations, what you would like to buy, going to bars, where you like to spend money, whatever you like)

Appendix 2:
Specific Probing Questions

1. How old are you? (Usually asked near end of interview if participant seems uncomfortable at first.)

2. What do you do? (Again, this is sometimes asked near end.)

3. Can you tell me a bit about your background/yourself/family/friends?

4. Can you tell me about your "coming-out" experience—when you felt you might be gay, when you tried to do something about it—when you told other people? (NOTE: Keep going back to this question. Look at it in different ways. Get stages/sequence of telling others.)

5. Tell me about some of your social experiences with other gay men.

6. Tell me about some of the products/services you've bought/used/consumed which are your favorites. Tell me about the experiences involved.

7. Were any of them purchased in stores in the "gay ghetto"? (NOTE: Try to get to the theme of product/brand loyalty.)

8. Are there any purchases/consumption experiences which you would label gay for some reason?

9. Where do you show/wear/display/use this product or these products? (NOTE: Emphasize different audiences—self, gay, straight, both?)

10. Are the kinds of things you do/things you buy now which are different from before you accepted that you are gay?

11. Have you ever participated in Lesbian and Gay Pride Day? Can you tell me about these experiences, if so? (NOTE: Find out when. Feelings on Pride Day? Is it a party? Politics? Both?)

12. Can you tell if someone is gay? Outward, visible signs? (NOTE: Emphasize audience dimension.)

13. What is camp?

14. What is "gay community"? Gay subculture?

15. Can you tell me about some things you've bought or experienced when dating another man?

16. Have you seen movies with gay characters depicted or with gay themes? How would you describe them?

17. Do you work out at a gym? How did that come about?

18. What is this term "attitude" which people seem to use a lot?

19. Have you ever taken a vacation with a bunch of gay men?

20. Do you ever go to gay bars? Can you tell me about your first time there?

21. Can you tell me something about going to gay bathhouses? (NOTE: This may be sensitive; don't ask if they go, initially; they may not want to admit it at first or at all.)

22. Do you go to art or cultural events such as opera, ballet, symphony, other?

23. Do you ever go to see drag artists? (Try to get at camp themes.)

24. Are there certain products you would buy or consume only with other gay men around?

25. Are there certain products you would use/wear/display in front of people who are not gay?

26. Do you use pornographic magazines or movies ever? (NOTE: Emphasis on closeted/homosexual stage of model.)

27. Do you ever (have you ever) use(d) classified ads or telephone dating services?

28. Do you avoid certain things/consumer behaviors? Such as?

29. Can you tell me about an experience where you felt bad about being gay? Stigmatized? Oppressed?

30. Can you tell me about an experience where you felt good about being gay? Proud? Elated?

31. Tell me about the gay subculture/community/people in Toronto. What were your first contacts with it?

Appendix 3:
Informant Data

Name	Age	Race/Ethnicity	Occupation	Closeted/ Out
1. A.J.	32	White/Jewish	Unemployed	Somewhat out
2. Alex	45	White/Italian	Interior designer/ decorator	Flamboyantly out
3. Antonio	38	White/Italian	Translator	Quite out; not out to parents
4. Arnold	16	White/Polish	Student	Coming out
5. Ben	53 ·	White	Counselor	Very out
6. Brendan	28	White	Student	Very out
7. Cameron	22	Chinese	Graphic designer	Very out
8. Carl	16	Black	Student	Very out
9. Chretien	28	Native/ Quebecois	Human resources manager	Somewhat out
10. Chuck	50	White	Civil servant	Quite closeted
11. Cody	31	White	Student; substitute teacher	Very out
12. Corey	23	White	Law student	Very out
13. Danny	19	White	Market research supervisor	Very out

Name	Age	Race/Ethnicity	Occupation	Closeted/ Out
14. David	17	White	Student	Quite out
15. Dirk	45	White	Accountant	Very out
16. Don	45	White/Jewish	Real-estate agent	Quite out
17. Eilert	32	Eurasian	Systems designer	Very out
18. François	50	White/French	Dental technician	Quite closeted
19. Gareth	34	White	Social work student	Becoming a "fag"; very out
20. Godfrey	43	White/ New Zealander	Doctor	Quite out
21. Ian	22	White/Russian	Engineering student	Quite closeted
22. Isaac	25	Arab	Law student	Very out
23. Jacob	28	White/Jewish	Lawyer	Very out
24. Jeff	25	White	Warehouse worker	Very out
25. Jim	24	White/Italian	Tour guide	Quite out
26. Johnny	29	Chinese	Magazine publisher	Very out
27. Jordan	26	Eurasian	Systems analyst	Quite out; not out to father
28. Lance	24	Black/Caribbean	Actor/waiter	Very out; not out to parents
29. Lennie	32	White/Jewish	Real-estate manager	Very out
30. Mario	27	White/Italian	Psychology student	Very out

Name	Age	Race/Ethnicity	Occupation	Closeted/ Out
31. Marshall	28	White	Waiter	Somewhat out; not out to family
32. Martin	25	White	Student	Very out
33. Nelson	19	Black/Caribbean	Dance instructor	Somewhat out; not out to parents
34. Nigel	28	White	Unemployed; just graduated teachers college	Very out
35. Pat	23	White	Massage therapist	Somewhat out
36. Paul	37	White/Italian	Economist	Somewhat out
37. Roger	26	White	Graphic designer	Very out
38. Ron	29	White	Waiter	Very out
39. Russ	29	White	Accountant	Very out
40. Sam	16	White	Student	Coming out; not out to parents
41. Simon	25	White	In recovery	Very out
42. Sylvio	44	White/Italian	Hairdresser	Very out
43. Tim	34	White	Teacher	Somewhat closeted
44. Tom	32	White	Actor/ receptionist	Very out

Appendix 4:
Informants and Consumer Ritual Stages

Hiding   François, Tim

Disclosure to Gays   Arnold, Chuck, David, Ian,
Marshall, Pat, Paul, Sam

Disclosure to Heterosexuals   Ben, Brendan, Cody, Danny,
Jordan, Lance, Martin, Roger,
Ron, Simon, Tom

Symbolic Resistance   Cameron, Carl, Corey, Dirk,
Eilert, Gareth, Isaac, Jeff,
Lennie, Mario, Nelson, Nigel

Identity Synthesis   A.J., Alex, Antonio, Chretien,
Don, Godfrey, Jacob, Jim,
Johnny, Russ, Sylvio

Appendix 5:
Informants and Conformity Strategies

The Conformists   Ben, Brendan, Gareth, Ian, Jeff,
                             Martin, Nelson, Sam, Simon

The Anticonformists   Cody, David, Don, François, Jacob,
                             Marshall, Nigel, Paul, Roger, Tim

The "Mixed"   A.J., Alex, Antonio, Cameron, Carl,
                             Chuck, Dirk, Eilert, Godfrey, Isaac,
                             Jim, Jordan, Lance, Mario, Pat, Ron,
                             Russ, Sylvio, Tom

The Independents   Arnold, Chretien, Corey, Danny,
                             Johnny, Lennie

Bibliography

Abrahams, Roger D., and Richard Bauman (1978). "Ranges of Festival Behavior." In *The Reversible World: Symbolic Inversion in Art and Society*, ed. Barbara A. Babcock. Ithaca, NY: Cornell University Press, pp. 193-208.

Abrams, Dominic (1992). "Processes of Social Identification." In *Social Psychology of Identity and the Self-Concept*, ed. Glynis Breakwell. London: Surrey University Press, pp. 57-99.

Aguero, J., L. Bloch, and D. Byrne (1984). "The Relationship Among Sexual Beliefs, Attitudes, Experience, and Homophobia," *Journal of Homosexuality* 3:95-107.

Allen, Chris T. (1982). "Self-Perception Based Strategies for Stimulating Energy Conservation," *Journal of Consumer Research* 8:381-390.

Altman, Dennis (1982). *The Homosexualization of America, the Americanization of Homosexuality.* New York: St. Martin's Press.

Arnould, Eric J., and Linda L. Price (1993). "River Magic: Extraordinary Experience and the Extended Service Encounter," *Journal of Consumer Research* 20 (1):24-45.

Babcock, Barbara A. (1978). "Introduction." In *The Reversible World: Symbolic Inversion in Art and Society*, ed. Barbara A. Babcock. Ithaca, NY: Cornell University Press, pp. 13-36.

Baker, Daniel B., Sean O'Brien Strub, and Bill Henning (1995). *Cracking the Corporate Closet.* New York: Harper Business.

Bakhtin, Mikhail (1984). *Rabelais and His World.* Trans. Helen Iwolsky. Cambridge, MA: MIT Press.

Banaji, Mahzarin R. (1994). "The Self in Social Contexts," *Annual Review of Psychology* 45:297-332.

Bawer, Bruce (1993). *A Place at the Table: The Gay Individual in American Society.* New York: Poseidon Press.

Bearden, William O., and Michael J. Etzel (1982). "Reference Group Influence on Product and Brand Purchase Decisions," *Journal of Consumer Research* (September 1982) 9:183-194.

Bearden, William. O., Richard G. Netemeyer, and Jesse E. Teel (1989). "Measurement of Consumer Susceptibility to Interpersonal Influence," *Journal of Consumer Research* (March 1989) 15:473-481.

Bearden, William O., and Randall L. Rose (1990). "Attention to Social Comparison Information: An Individual Difference Factor Affecting Consumer Conformity," *Journal of Consumer Research* (March 1990) 16:461-471.

Becker, Howard S. (1963). *Outsiders: Studies in the Sociology of Deviance.* New York: Free Press.

————. (Ed.) (1964). *The Outsiders: Perspectives on Deviance.* New York: Free Press.

————. (1967). "Whose Side Are We On?" *Social Problems* (Winter) 14: 239-247.

Belk, Russell W. (1981). "Determinants of Consumption on Cue Utilization in Impression Formation: An Associational Deviation and Experimental Verification." In *Advances in Consumer Research* 8, ed. Kent B. Munroe. Ann Arbor, MI: Association for Consumer Research, pp. 170-175.

————. (1987). "A Child's Christmas in America: Santa Claus as Deity, Consumption as Religion," *Journal of American Culture* (Spring) 10:87-100.

————. (1987). "Material Values in the Comics: A Content Analysis of Comic Books Featuring Themes of Wealth," *Journal of Consumer Research* 14:26-42.

————. (1988). "Possessions and the Extended Self," *Journal of Consumer Research* 15:139-168.

————. (1990). "Hallowe'en: An Evolving American Consumption Ritual." In *Advances in Consumer Research* 17, eds. Richard Pollay, Jerry Gorn, and Marvin Goldberg. Provo, UT: ACR, pp. 506-517.

————. (1992). "Moving Possessions: An Analysis Based on Personal Documents from the 1847-1869 Mormon Migration," *Journal of Consumer Research* 19(3):339-361.

————. (1993). "Materialism and the Making of the Modern American Christmas." In *Unwrapping Christmas*, ed. Daniel Miller. Oxford: Clarendon Press, pp. 75-104.

————. (1994). "Carnival, Control, and Corporate Culture in Contemporary Hallowe'en Celebrations." In *Hallowe'en and other Festivals of Death and Life*, ed. Jack Santino. Knoxville, TN: The University of Tennessee Press, pp.105-132.

Belk, Russell W., Kenneth D. Bahn, and Robert N. Mayer (1982). "Developmental Recognition of Consumption Symbolism," *Journal of Consumer Research* 9:4-17.

Belk, Russell W., and Gregory S. Coon (1993). "Gift Giving as Agapic Love: An Alternative to the Exchange Paradigm Based on Dating Experiences," *Journal of Consumer Research* 20(3):393-417.

Belk, Russell W., and Richard W. Pollay (1985). "Images of Ourselves: The Good Life in Twentieth Century Advertising," *Journal of Consumer Research* 11:887-897.

Belk, Russell, John F. Sherry, Jr., and Melanie Wallendorf (1988). "A Naturalistic Inquiry into Buyer and Seller Behavior at a Swap Meet," *Journal of Consumer Research* (March) 14:449-470.

Belk, Russell, and Melanie Wallendorf (1994). "Of Mice and Men: Gender Identity in Collecting." In *Objects and Collections*, ed. Susan Pearce. London: Routledge, pp. 1-120.

Belk, Russell, Melanie Wallendorf, and John F. Sherry, Jr. (1989). "The Sacred and the Profane in Consumer Behavior: Theodicy on the Odyssey," *Journal of Consumer Research* (June) 16:1-38.

Bell, A.P., and M.S. Weinberg (1978). *Homosexualities: A Study of Diversity Among Men and Women.* New York: Simon and Schuster.

Bell, A.P., M.S. Weinberg, and S.K. Hammersmith (1981). *Sexual Preference: Its Development in Men and Women.* Bloomington, IN: Indiana University Press.

Berlin, Isaiah (1969). "Two Concepts of Liberty." In *Four Essays on Liberty.* New York: Oxford University Press, pp. 118-172.

Bharati, Agehananda (1985). "The Self in Hindu Thought and Action," *Culture and Self: Asian and Western Perspectives,* eds. Anthony J. Marsella, George Devos, and Francis Hsu. New York: Tavistock Publications, pp. 78-101.

Bhat, Subodh (1996). "Some Comments on 'Marketing to the Homosexual (Gay) Market: A Profile and Strategy Implications'." In *Gays, Lesbians, and Consumer Behavior: Theory, Practice, and Research Issues in Marketing,* ed. Daniel L. Wardlow. Binghamton, NY: The Haworth Press, Inc., pp. 213-217.

Blair, M. Elizabeth (1993). "Commercialization of the Rap Music Youth Subculture," *Journal of Popular Culture* 27(3):21-34.

Bleicher, Josef (1980). *Contemporary Hermeneutics.* London: Routledge and Kegan Paul.

Blumer, H. (1969). *Symbolic Interactionism: Perspective and Method.* Englewood Cliffs, New Jersey: Prentice-Hall.

Brake, Michael (1985). *Comparative Youth Culture: The Sociology of Youth Cultures and Youth Subcultures in America, Britain, and Canada.* Boston: Routledge and Kegan Paul.

Braun, Otmar, and Robert A. Wicklund (1989). "Psychological Antecedents of Conspicuous Consumption," *Journal of Economic Psychology* 10:161-167.

Breakwell, Glynis M. (1983). *Threatened Identities.* New York: John Wiley and Sons.

————. (1986). *Coping with Threatened Identities.* New York: Methuen.

Brewer, Marilynn B. (1993). "Social Identity, Distinctiveness, and In-group Homogeneity," *Social Cognition* 11(1):150-164.

Brown, Stanley A., Marvin B. Martenfeld, and Allan Gould (1990). *Creating the Service Culture: Strategies for Canadian Business.* Toronto: Prentice-Hall Canada Inc.

Browning, Frank (1993). *The Culture of Desire: Paradox and Perversity in Gay Lives Today.* New York: Crowne Publishers.

Burrell, Gibson, and Gareth Morgan (1979). *Sociological Paradigms and Organizational Analysis.* Portsmouth, NH: Heinemann Educational Books.

Caplan, Pat (1987). "Introduction." In *The Cultural Construction of Sexuality,* ed. Pat Caplan. New York: Routledge, pp.1-16.

Caplow, Theodore, Howard M. Bahr, Bruce A. Chadwick, Reuben Hill, and Margaret H. Williamson (1982). *Middletown Families: Fifty Years of Change and Continuity.* Minneapolis, MN: University of Minnesota Press.

Carrier, J.M. (1976). "Family Attitudes and Mexican Male Homosexuality," *Urban Life* (October) 50:359-375.

Carrier, James G. (1993). "The Rituals of Christmas Giving." In *Unwrapping Christmas,* ed. Daniel Miller. Oxford: Clarendon Press, pp. 55-73.

————. (1995). *Gifts and Commodities: Exchange and Western Capitalism Since 1700*. New York: Routledge.

Cass, V.C. (1979). "Homosexual Identity Formation: A Theoretical Model," *Journal of Homosexuality* 4(3):143-167.

————. (1984). "Homosexual Identity: A Concept in Need of Definition," *Journal of Homosexuality* 9(2/3):105-126.

Celsi, Richard L., Randall L. Rose, and Thomas W. Leigh. (1993). "An Exploration of High Risk Leisure Consumption Through Skydiving," *Journal of Consumer Research* 20(1):1-23.

Cheal, David (1995). "The Postmodern Origin of Ritual," *Journal for the Theory of Social Behavior* 18(3):269-290.

————. (1988). *The Gift Economy*. London: Routledge.

Childers, Terry L., and Akshay R. Rao (1992). "The Influence of Familial and Peer-based Reference Groups on Consumer Decisions," *Journal of Consumer Research* 19(2):198-212.

Cohen, Albert (1955). *Delinquent Boys: The Culture of the Gang*. New York: Free Press.

Cohen, Anthony (1985). *The Symbolic Construction of Community*. London: Tavistock Publications.

————. (1986). *Symbolising Boundaries: Identity and Diversity in British Cultures*. Manchester: Manchester University Press.

Cooley, C.H. (1902). *Human Nature and the Social Order*. New York: Scribners.

Cooper, Martha (1991). "Ethical Dimensions of Political Advocacy from a Postmodern Perspective." In *Ethical Dimensions of Political Communication*, ed. Robert Denton. New York: Praeger, pp. 262-279.

Corbin, Juliet, and Anselm Strauss (1990). "Grounded Theory Research: Procedures, Canons, and Evaluative Criteria," *Qualitative Sociology* 13(1):3-20.

Corfman, Kim P., and Donald R. Lehmann (1987). "Models of Cooperative Group Decision-Making and Relative Influence: An Experimental Investigation of Family Purchase Decisions," *Journal of Consumer Research* 14:1-13.

Costa, Janeen Arnold (1996). "Foreword." In *Gays, Lesbians, and Consumer Behavior: Theory, Practice, and Research Issues in Marketing*, ed. Daniel L. Wardlow. Binghamton, NY: The Haworth Press, Inc., pp. xix-xxii.

Creswell, John W. (1994). *Research Design: Qualitative and Quantitative Approaches*. London: Sage Publications.

Csikszentmihalyi, Mihaly, and Eugene Rochberg-Halton (1981). *The Meaning of Things: Domestic Symbols and the Self*. Cambridge, MA: Cambridge University Press.

De Cecco, John P. (1982). "Definition and Meaning of Sexual Orientation," *Journal of Homosexuality* 6(4):51-67.

DeLozier, M. Wayne, and Jason Rodrigue (1996). "Marketing to the Homosexual (Gay) Market: A Profile and Strategy Implications." In *Gays, Lesbians, and Consumer Behavior: Theory, Practice, and Research Issues in Marketing*, ed. Daniel L. Wardlow. Binghamton, NY: The Haworth Press, Inc., pp. 203-212.

D'Emilio, John (1983). *Sexual Politics, Sexual Communities: The Making of a Homosexual Minority in the United States 1940-1970.* Chicago, IL: The University of Chicago Press.

D'Emilio, J., and E. Freedman. (1988). *Intimate Matters: A History of Sexuality in America.* New York: Harper and Row.

Dickerson, Mark O., and Thomas Flanagan (1994). *An Introduction to Government and Politics: A Conceptual Approach.* Calgary: Nelson Canada.

Douglas, Mary, and Baron Isherwood (1979). *The World of Goods: Toward an Anthropology of Consumption.* New York: Norton.

Dubay, William H. (1987). *Gay Identity: The Self Under Ban.* London: McFarland and Company.

Eriksen, Thomas H. (1993). *Ethnicity and Nationalism: Anthropological Perspectives.* Boulder, CO: Pluto Press.

Erikson, Erik (1959). *Identity and The Lifecycle.* New York: W.W. Norton and Co.

———. (1968). *Identity: Youth and Crisis.* London: Faber Faber.

———. (1977). *Toys and Reasons: Stages in the Ritualization of Experience.* Toronto: W.W. Norton and Co.

Foucault, Michel (1980). *The History of Sexuality, Part One.* New York: Vintage Books.

Fox, Kathryn Joan (1987). "Real Punks and Pretenders: The Social Organization of a Counterculture," *Journal of Contemporary Ethnography* 16(3):344-370.

Freitas, Anthony, Susan Kaiser, and Tania Hammidi (1996). "Communities, Commodities, Cultural Space and Style." In *Gays, Lesbians, and Consumer Behavior: Theory, Practice, and Research Issues in Marketing,* ed. Daniel L. Wardlow. Binghamton, NY: The Haworth Press, Inc., pp. 83-107.

Frenzen, Jonathan K. and Harry L. Davis (1990). "Purchasing Behavior in Embedded Markets," *Journal of Consumer Research* (June) 17:1-12.

Fugate, Douglas L. (1993). "Evaluating the U.S. Male Homosexual and Lesbian Population as a Viable Target Market Segment," *Journal of Consumer Marketing* 10(4):46-57.

Fuss, Diana (1991). "Inside/Out." In *Inside/Out,* ed. Diana Fuss. New York: Routledge, pp. 1-10.

Gainer, Brenda J. (1992). "The Impact of Between-Buyer Relationships on Consumer Behavior." Unpublished doctoral dissertation, York University, New York, Canada.

Gainer, Brenda J. and Eileen Fischer (in review). "Community and Consumer Behavior." Unpublished manuscript, York University, North York, Canada.

Gecas, Viktor (1982). "The Self-Concept," *Annual Review of Sociology* 8(1):1-33.

Geertz, Clifford (1973). *The Interpretation of Cultures.* New York: Basic Books.

Giddens, Anthony (1991). *Modernity and Self-Identity: Self and Society in the Late Modern Age.* Cambridge, MA: Polity Press.

Glaser, B. and A. Strauss (1967). *The Discovery of Grounded Theory.* Chicago, IL: Aldine.

Globe and Mail, June 27, 1992. "How gay society is blazing a trail for the future," D1-D2.

————. August 15, 1992. "Gay marketing is in the pink," D4.

————. September 2, 1992. "Ontario told to expand gay employee's benefits," A1.

————. September 3, 1992. "The rights of homosexual couples," A14.

————. November 24, 1992. "Courts set seal on gay revolution," A1, A8.

————. October 21, 1993. "Customs' last stand," A32.

————. November 10, 1993. "Year's AIDS death count tops 1000 for first time," A3.

————. August 10, 1995. "The State of Women," A18.

————. October 4, 1995. "The Decency of Davis Elhins," A20.

Gluckman, Max (1954). *Rituals of Rebellion in South-East Africa.* Manchester: Manchester University Press.

————. (1959). *Custom and Conflict in Africa.* Glencoe, IL: Free Press.

Goffman, E. (1951). "Symbols of Class Status," *British Journal of Sociology* (December) 2:294-304.

————. (1959). *The Presentation of Self in Everyday Life.* New York: The Overlook Press.

————. (1961). *Asylums.* Garden City, NY: Doubleday.

————. (1963). *Stigma: Notes on the Management of Spoiled Identity.* Englewood Cliffs, NJ: Prentice-Hall.

————. (1963a). *Behavior in Public Places.* New York: Free Press.

Gollwitzer, Peter M., and Robert A. Wicklund (eds.). (1985). "The Pursuit of Self-defining Goals." In *Action Control: From Cognition to Behavior.* New York: Springer-Verlag.

Goode, Erich (1975). "On Behalf of Labelling Theory," *Social Problems* (June) 22:570-583.

————. (1990). *Deviant Behaviour.* Englewood Cliffs, NJ: Prentice-Hall.

Gough, Jamie (1989). "Theories of Sexual Identity and the Masculinization of the Gay Man." In *Coming on Strong: Gay Politics and Culture*, eds. Simon Shepherd and Mick Wallis. London: Unwin Hyman, pp. 213-236.

Gottdiener, M. (1985). "Hegemony and Mass Culture: A Semiotic Approach," *American Journal of Sociology* 90(5):979-1001.

————. (1995). *Postmodern Semiotics: Material Culture and the Forms of Postmodern Life.* Cambridge, MA: Blackwell.

Gould, Stephen J. (1991). "The Self-Manipulation of My Pervasive, Perceived Vital Energy Through Product Use: An Introspective-Praxis Perspective," *Journal of Consumer Research* (September) 18:194-207.

Granovetter, Mark S. (1985). "Economic Action and Social Structure: The Problem of Embeddedness," *American Journal of Sociology* (May) 78:1360-1380.

Gross, Alan (1978). "The Male Role and Heterosexual Behaviour," *Journal of Social Issues* 34(1):424-431.

Grubb, Edward L., and Harrison L. Grathwhohl (1967). "Consumer Self-Concept, Symbolism, and Market Behaviour: A Theoretical Approach," *Journal of Marketing* 31:22-27.

Hartley, Robert F. (1992). *Marketing Mistakes*. Toronto: John Wiley and Sons.

Hebdige, Dick (1979). *Subculture: The Meaning of Style*. New York: Routledge.

Held, David (1980). *Introduction to Critical Theory*. Berkeley, CA: University of California Press.

Herdt, Gilbert (1992). "'Coming Out' as a Rite of Passage: A Chicago Study." In *Gay Culture in America: Essays from the Field*, ed. Gilbert Herdt. Boston, MA: Beacon Press, pp. 29-67.

Herdt, Gilbert, and Andrew Boxer (1992). "Introduction: Culture, History, and Life Course of Gay Men." In *Gay Culture in America: Essays from the Field*, ed. Gilbert Herdt. Boston, MA: Beacon Press, pp. 1-28.

————. (1993). *Children of Horizons: How Gay and Lesbian Teens Are Leading a New Way Out of the Closet*. Boston, MA: Beacon Press.

Herrell, Richard K. (1992). "The Symbolic Strategies of Chicago's Gay and Lesbian Pride Day Parade." In *Gay Culture in America: Essays from the Field*, ed. Gilbert Herdt. Boston, MA: Beacon Press, pp. 225-252.

Herrmann, Robert O. (1992). "The Tactics of Consumer Resistance: Group Action and Marketplace Exit." In *Advances in Consumer Research*, eds. Leigh McAlister and Michael L. Rothschild. Provo, UT: Association for Consumer Research, pp. 130-134.

Hetrick, William P., and Hector R. Lozada (1994). "Construing the Critical Imagination: Comments and Necessary Diversions," *Journal of Consumer Research* (December) 21:548-558.

Hill, Ronald Paul (1991). "Homeless Women, Special Possessions, and the Meaning of 'Home': An Ethnographic Case Study," *Journal of Consumer Research* (December) 18:298-310.

Hill, Ronald Paul, and Mark Stamey (1990). "The Homeless in America: An Examination of Possessions and Consumption Behaviors," *Journal of Consumer Research* (December) 17:303-321.

Hirschman, Elizabeth C. (1985). "Primitive Aspects of Consumption in Modern American Society," *Journal of Consumer Research* 12:142-154.

————. (1986). "Humanistic Inquiry in Marketing Research: Philosophy, Method, and Criteria," *Journal of Marketing Research* (August) XXIII: 237-249.

————. (1988). "The Ideology of Consumption: A Structural-Syntactical Analysis of 'Dallas' and 'Dynasty'," *Journal of Consumer Research* 15:344-359.

————. (1990). "Secular Immortality and the American Ideology of Affluence," *Journal of Consumer Research* 17:31-42.

————. (1991). "Point of View: Sacred, Secular, and Mediating Consumption Imagery in Television Commercials," *Journal of Advertising Research*: 38-43.

————. (1992). "The Consciousness of Addiction: Toward a General Theory of Compulsive Consumption," *Journal of Consumer Research* (September) 19:155-179.

————. (1993). "Ideology in Consumer Research, 1980 and 1990: A Marxist and Feminist Critique," *Journal of Consumer Research* 19(4):537-555.

Hirschon, Renee (1984). "Introduction: Property, Power and Gender Relations." In *Women and Property—Women as Property*, ed. Renee Hirschon. New York: St. Martin's Press, pp. 173-202.

Holbrook, Morris B., and Elizabeth C. Hirschman (1982). "The Experiential Aspects of Consumer Behavior: Consumer Fantasies, Feelings, and Fun," *Journal of Consumer Research* (September) 9:132-140.

Holman, Rebecca H. (1980). "Clothing as Communication: An Empirical Investigation." In *Advances in Consumer Research* 7, ed. Jerry C. Olson. Ann Arbor MI: Association for Consumer Research, pp. 372-377.

————. (1981). "Product Use as Communication: A Fresh Look at a Venerable Topic." In *Review of Marketing*, eds. Ben M. Enis and Kenneth J. Roering. Chicago IL: American Marketing Association, pp. 106-119.

Horkheimer, Max (1972). *Critical Theory*. New York: Seabury.

Huberman, Michael A., and Matthew B. Miles (1994). "Data Management and Analysis Methods." In *Handbook of Qualitative Research*, eds. Norman K. Denzin and Yvonna S. Lincoln. London: Sage, pp. 428-444.

Jackson, Margaret (1987). "'Facts of Life' or the eroticization of women's oppression? Sexology and the social construction of heterosexuality." In *The Social Construction of Sexuality*, ed. Pat Caplan. New York: Routledge, pp. 121-138.

James, W. (1890). "The Consciousness of Self." In *Principles of Psychology* 1. New York: Holt, Rinehard, and Winston.

Janus, Samuel S. and Cynthia L. Janus (1993). *The Janus Report on Sexual Behaviour*. Toronto: John Wiley and Sons.

Johnson, Frank (1985). "The Western Concept of Self." In *Culture and Self: Asian and Western Perspectives*, eds. Anthony J. Marsella, George Devos, and Francis Hsu. New York: Tavistock Publications, pp. 17-36.

Johnson, William (1971). "The Gay World." In *Social Deviance in Canada*, ed. W. Mann. Toronto: Copp Clark.

Johnson-Brown, Jacqueline, and Peter H. Reingen (1987). "Social Ties and Word-of-Mouth Referral Behaviour," *Journal of Consumer Research* (December 1987) 14:350-362.

Jorgensen, Danny L. (1989). *Participant Observation: A Methodology for Human Studies*. London: Sage Publications.

Kaplan, Howard B. (1986). *Social Psychology of Self-referent Behavior*. New York: Plenum Press.

Katz, Donald R. (1987). *The Big Store: Inside the Crisis and Revolution at Sears*. New York: Viking.

Kinsey, Barry A. (1982). "Killum and Eatum: Identity Consolidation in a Middle-class Poly-Drug Abuse Subculture," *Symbolic Interaction* 5(2):311-324.

Kinsey, A.C., W.B. Pomeroy, and C.E. Martin (1948). *Sexual Behavior in the Human Male*. Philadelphia, PA: W.B. Saunders.

Kinsey, A.C., W.B. Pomeroy, C.E. Martin, and P.H. Gebhard (1953). *Sexual Behavior in the Human Female*. Philadelphia, PA: W.B. Saunders.

Kinsman, Gary (1991). "Homosexuality Historically Reconsidered Challenges Heterosexual Hegemony," *Journal of Historical Sociology* 4(2):91-111.

————. (1992). "Men Loving Men: The Challenge of Gay Liberation." In *Men's Lives*, eds. M. Kimmel and M. Messner. Toronto: Maxwell MacMillan Canada, pp. 91-111.

Kirk, Marshall, and Hunter Madsen (1989). *After the Ball: How America Will Conquer its Fear and Hatred of Gays in the 90s*. New York: Plume.

Klein, Alan M. (1985). "Pumping Iron," *Society* 22(6):68-75.

————. (1986). "Pumping Irony: Crisis and Contradiction in Bodybuilding," *Sociology of Sport Journal* 3(2):112-133.

Kleinberg, S. (1992). "The New Masculinity of Gay Men, and Beyond." In *Men's Lives*, eds. M. Kimmel and M. Messner. Toronto: Maxwell MacMillan Canada, pp. 103-118.

Kugelmass, Jack (1994). Wishes Come True: Designing the Greenwich Village Hallowe'en Parade." In *Hallowe'en and other Festivals of Death and Life*, ed. Jack Santino. Knoxville TN: The University of Tennessee Press.

Kvale, Steinar (1983). "The Qualitative Research Interview: A Phenomological and Hermeneutical Mode of Understanding," *Journal of Phenomenological Psychology* (Fall) 14:171-196.

Larsen, Val, and Newell D. Wright (1993). "A Critique of Critical Theory: Response to Murray and Ozanne's 'The Critical Imagination'." In *Advances in Consumer Research* 20, eds. Leigh McAlister and Michael L. Rothschild. Provo, UT: Association for Consumer Research, pp. 439-443.

Larson, Paul C. (1981). "Sexual Identity and Self-concept," *Journal of Homosexuality* 7(1):15-32.

Lasch, Christopher (1979). *The Culture of Narcissism: American Life in an Age of Diminishing Expectations*. New York: Warner Books.

Lee, Dong Hwan (1990). "Symbolic Interactionism: Some Implications for Consumer Self-concept and Product Symbolism Research." In *Advances in Consumer Research* 17, eds. M. Goldberg, G. Gorn, and R. Pollay. Provo UT: Association for Consumer Research, pp. 386-393.

Lee, John A. (1977). "Going Public: A Study in the Sociology of Homosexual Liberation," *Journal of Homosexuality* 3(4):9-78.

————. (1978). *Getting Sex*. Toronto, Canada: General Publishing.

Lemert, Edwin M. (1951). *Social Pathology*. New York: McGraw-Hill.

————. (1972). *Human Deviance, Social Problems, and Social Control*, Second edition. Englewood Cliffs, NJ: Prentice-Hall.

Leonard, Peter (1984). *Personality and Ideology: Toward a Materialist Understanding of the Individual*. London: MacMillan.

Levy, Sidney J. (1959). "Symbols for Sale," *Harvard Business Review* (July/August) 37:117-124.

Lewis, Robert A. (1978). "Emotional Intimacy Among Men," *Journal of Social Issues* 34(1):108-121.

Lincoln, Yvonna S., and Egon G. Guba (1987). *Naturalistic Inquiry*. Beverly Hills, CA: Sage Publications.

Lukenbill, Grant (1995). *Untold Millions*. New York: Harper Business.

Lurie, Alison (1981). *The Language of Clothes*. London: Heinemann.

Lynch, Frederick R. (1987). "Non-ghetto Gays: A Sociological Study of Suburban Homosexuals," *Journal of Homosexuality* 13(4):13-42.

MacLean's, November 4, 1996. "How Very Different We Are," pp. 36-40.

Marketing, June 10, 1991. "Stirring Up the Marketing Mix," pp. 1, 3.

Marketing News, July 20, 1992. "Quayle's Comments Fuel Boycott Against Three Firms," A1.

Markus, Hazel, and Paula Nurius (1986). "Possible Selves," *American Psychologist* (September):954-969.

————. (1987). "Possible Selves: The Interface between Motivation and the Self-Concept," In *Self and Identity: Psychosocial Perspectives,* eds. K. Yardley and T. Honess. New York: John Wiley and Sons, pp. 157-172.

Marsella, Anthony J., George Devos, and Francis Hsu (1985). *Culture and Self: Asian and Western Perspectives.* New York: Tavistock Publications.

Matza, David (1969). *Becoming Deviant.* Englewood Cliffs, NJ: Prentice-Hall.

McCracken, Grant (1986). "Culture and Consumption: A Theoretical Account of the Structure and Movement of the Cultural Meaning of Consumer Goods," *Journal of Consumer Research* (June) 13:71-84.

————. (1988). *The Long Interview.* Newbury Park: Sage Publications.

————. (1988a). *Culture and Consumption: New Approaches to the Symbolic Character of Consumer Goods and Activities.* Indianapolis, IN: Indiana University Press.

————. (1989). "Who is the Celebrity Endorser? Cultural Foundations of the Endorsement Process," *Journal of Consumer Research* 16:310-321.

Mead, G.H. (1934). *Mind, Self, and Society.* Chicago: University of Chicago Press.

Mehta, Raj and Russell W. Belk (1991). "Artifacts, Identity, and Transition: Favorite Possessions of Indians and Indian Immigrants to the United States," *Journal of Consumer Research* (March) 17:398-411.

Merton, Robert K. (1957). *Social Theory and Social Structure.* New York: Free Press.

Mick, David Glen (1986). "Consumer Research and Semiotics: Exploring the Morphology of Signs, Symbols, and Significance," *Journal of Consumer Research* 13:196-213.

Miles, Matthew B., and A. Michael Huberman (1994). *Qualitative Data Analysis.* Second edition. London: Sage Publications.

Miller, Daniel (1993). "A Theory of Christmas." In *Unwrapping Christmas,* ed. Daniel Miller. Oxford: Clarendon Press, pp. 1-31.

————. (1993a). "Christmas against Materialism in Trinidad." In *Unwrapping Christmas,* ed. Daniel Miller. Oxford: Clarendon Press, pp. 1-31.

Millett, Kate (1969). *Sexual Politics.* Garden City, NY: Doubleday.

Minton, Henry L., and Gary J. McDonald (1984). "Homosexual Identity Formation as a Developmental Process," *Journal of Homosexuality* 4(20):91-103.

Morgan, Gareth (1991). DCAD 7010, a course wherein he taught of the philosophy underlying sociology. Personal communication.

Morin, Stephen F. (1978). "Male Homophobia," *Journal of Social Issues* 34(1): 29-47.

Muchmore, Wes, and William Hanson. (1986). *Coming Along Fine: Today's Gay Man and His World*. Boston, MA: Alyson Publications.

Murray, Jeff B., and Julie L. Ozanne (1991). "The Critical Imagination: Emancipatory Interests in Consumer Research," *Journal of Consumer Research* (September) 18:129-144.

Murray, Jeff B., Julie L. Ozanne, and Jon M. Shapiro (1994). "Translating the Critical Imagination into Action: Unleashing the Crouched Tiger," *Journal of Consumer Research* 21(3):559-565.

Murray, Stephen O. (1992). "Components of Gay Community in San Francisco." In *Gay Culture in America: Essays from the Field*, ed. Gilbert Herdt. Boston, MA: Beacon Press, pp. 107-146.

Myers, James (1992). "Nonmainstream Body Modification: Genital Piercing, Branding, Burning, and Cutting," *Journal of Contemporary Ethnography* (October) 21:267-306.

Myers, Robert J. (1982). *Celebrations: The Complete Book of American Holidays*. Garden City, NY: Doubleday.

Netemeyer, Richard G., William O. Bearden, and Jesse E. Teel (1992). "Consumer Susceptibility to Interpersonal Influence and Attributional Sensitivity," *Psychology and Marketing* 9(5):379-394.

Nungesser, Lon G. (1983). *Homosexual Acts, Actors, and Identities*. New York: Praeger.

O'Guinn, Thomas C., and Russell W. Belk (1989). "Heaven on Earth: Consumption at Heritage Village, USA," *Journal of Consumer Research* (September) 16:227-238.

O'Guinn, Thomas C., and Ronald J. Faber (1989). "Compulsive Buying: A Phenomenological Exploration," *Journal of Consumer Research* (September) 16:147-157.

Paul, William (1982). "Minority Status for Gay People: Majority Reaction and Social Context." In *Homosexuality: Social, Psychological, and Biological Issues*, eds. W. Paul, J.D. Weinrich, J.C. Gonsiorek, and M.E. Hotvedt. Beverly Hills, CA: Sage Publications, pp. 203-228.

Pearce, Susan M. (1995). *On Collecting: An Investigation into Collecting in the European Tradition*. New York: Routledge.

Pearson, Anthony (1987). "The Grateful Dead Phenomenon," *Youth and Society* (June) 18:418-432.

Peñaloza, Lisa (1994). "Atravesando Fronteras/Border Crossings: a Critical Ethnographic Exploration of the Consumer Acculturation of Mexican Immigrants," *Journal of Consumer Research* 21(1):32-54.

————. (1996). "We're Here, We're Queer and We're Going Shopping: A Critical Perspective on the Accommodation of Gays and Lesbians in the U.S. Marketplace." In *Gays, Lesbians, and Consumer Behavior: Theory, Practice, and Research Issues in Marketing*, ed. Daniel L. Wardlow. Binghamton, NY: The Haworth Press, Inc., pp. 9-41.

Peñaloza, Lisa, and Linda L. Price (1992). "Consumer Resistance: A Conceptual Overview." In *Advances in Consumer Research*, eds. Leigh McAlister and Michael L. Rothschild. Provo: UT: Association for Consumer Research, pp. 123-128.

Pfohl, Stephen (1994). *Images of Deviance and Social Control: A Sociological History,* Second edition. New York: McGraw-Hill.

Pfuhl, E. H. (1986). *The Deviance Process*, Second edition. Belmont, CA: Wadsworth Publishing Company.

Phelan, Shane (1989). *Identity Politics: Lesbian Feminism and the Limits of Community.* Philadelphia: Temple University Press.

Plummer, K. (1975). *Sexual Stigma: An Interactionist Account.* London: Routledge and Keagan Paul.

Porter, J.R., and R.E. Washington (1993). "Minority Identity and Self-Esteem," *Annual Review of Sociology* 19:139-161.

Pronger, Brian (1990). *The Arena of Masculinity: Sports, Homosexuality, and the Meaning of Sex.* Toronto: Summerhill Press.

Reingen, Peter H., Brian L. Foster, Jacqueline Johnson-Brown, and Stephen B. Seidman (1984). "Brand Congruence in Interpersonal Relations: A Social Network Analysis," *Journal of Consumer Research* (December) 11:771-783.

Richins, Marsha (1991). "Social Comparison and the Idealized Images in Advertising," *Journal of Consumer Research* 12:71-83.

———. (1994). "Valuing Things: The Public and Private Meanings of Possessions," *Journal of Consumer Research* 21(3):504-521.

———. (1994a)."Special Possessions and the Expressions of Material Values," *Journal of Consumer Research* 21(3):522-534.

Ricoeur, Paul (1976). *Interpretation Theory.* Forth Worth, TX: Texas Christian University Press.

Rook, Dennis W. (1985). "The Ritual Dimension of Consumer Behaviour," *Journal of Consumer Research* 12:251-264.

Rose, Randall L., William O. Bearden, and Jesse E. Teel (1992). "An Attributional Analysis of Resistance to Group Pressure Regarding Illicit Drug and Alcohol Consumption," *Journal of Consumer Research* (June) 19:1-13.

Rosenberg, Morris, and Howard B. Kaplan (eds.). (1982). *Social Psychology of the Self-Concept.* Arlington Heights, IL: Harlan Davidson.

Rubington, Earl (1987). "Theory of Deviant Subcultures." In *Deviance: The Interactionist Perspective*, Fifth edition, eds. Earl Rubington and Martin S. Weinberg, New York: Macmillan Publishing Co., pp. 203-205.

Rubington, Earl, and Martin S. Weinberg (eds.). (1987). *Deviance: The Interactionist Perspective*, Fifth edition New York: Macmillan Publishing Co.

Rudd, Nancy A. (1996). "Appearance and Self-Presentation Research in Gay Consumer Cultures: Issues and Impact." In *Gays, Lesbians, and Consumer Behaviour: Theory, Practice, and Research Issues in Marketing*, ed. Daniel L. Wardlow. Binghamton, NY: The Haworth Press, Inc., pp. 109-134.

Sanders, Clinton R. (1988). "Marks of Mischief: Becoming and Being Tattooed," *Journal of Contemporary Ethnography* 16(4):395-432.

————. (1989). *Customizing the Body: The Art and Culture of Tattooing.* Philadelphia, PA: Temple University Press.

Schmidt, Leigh E. (1991). "The Commercialization of the Calendar: American Holidays and the Culture of Consumption, 1870-1930," *The Journal of American History* (December):887-916.

Schouten, John W. (1990). *Selves in Transition.* Unpublished dissertation, University of Utah.

————. (1991). "Selves in Transition: Symbolic Consumption in Personal Rites of Passage and Identity Reconstruction," *Journal of Consumer Research* (March) 17:412-425.

Schouten, John W., and James H. McAlexander (1993). "Market Impact of a Consumption Subculture: The Harley-Davidson Mystique" In *European Advances in Consumer Behavior,* eds. W. Fred van Raaij and Gary J. Bamossy. Provo, UT: Association for Consumer Research, pp. 389-393.

————. (1995). "Subcultures of Consumption: An Ethnography of the New Bikers," *Journal of Consumer Research* 22 (1):43-61.

Seabrook, Jeremy (1976). *A Lasting Relationship: Homosexuals and Society.* London: Lane Co.

Seidler, Victor J. (1987). "Reason, Desire, and Male Sexuality." In *The Cultural Construction of Sexuality,* ed. Pat Caplan. New York: Routledge, pp. 187-204.

Shallenberger, David (1994). "Professional and Openly Gay: A Narrative Study of the Experience," *Journal of Management Inquiry* 3(2):119-142.

Shilts, Randy (1987). *And the Band Played On.* New York: St. Martin's Press.

Simmons, J.L. (1987). "The Nature of Deviant Subcultures." In *Deviance: The Interactionist Perspective,* Fifth edition. Earl Rubington and Martin S. Weinberg. New York: Macmillan Publishing Co, pp. 18-23.

Sirgy, Joseph M. (1982). "Self-concept in Consumer Behavior: A Critical Review," *Journal of Consumer Research* 9:287-300.

Sirgy, Joseph M, J.S. Johar, and Michael Wood (1986). "Determinants of Product Value Expressiveness: Another Look at Conspicuousness, Differentiation, and Common Usage." In *Developments in Marketing Science* 9, ed. Naresh Malhotra. Atlanta GA: Academy of Marketing Science, pp. 9:35-39.

Smith, M.B. (1975). "Perspectives on Selfhood," *American Psychologist* 33: 1053-1063.

Solomon, Michael R. (1983). "The Role of Products as Social Stimuli: A Symbolic Interactionism Perspective," *Journal of Consumer Research* (December): 319-329.

————. (1988). "Building Up and Breaking Down: The Impact of Cultural Sorting on Symbolic Consumption." In *Research in Consumer Behavior,* eds. J. Sheth and E.C. Hirschman. Greenwich, CT: JAI Press, pp. 325-351.

————. (1994). *Consumer Behavior: Buying, Having, and Being.* Toronto: Allyn and Bacon.

Sontag, Susan (1964). "Notes on Camp." In *Against Interpretation.* New York: Doubleday, pp. 275-292.

Stratton, Jon (1985). "Youth Subcultures and their Cultural Contexts," *Australian and New Zealand Journal of Sociology* 21(2):194-218.

Strauss, Anselm, and Juliet Corbin (1994). "Grounded Theory Methodology." In *Handbook of Qualitative Research,* eds. Norman K. Denzin and Yvonna S. Lincoln. London: Sage Publications, pp. 273-285.

Stryker, Sheldon (1968). "Identity Salience and Role Performance." In *Journal of Marriage and the Family* 30:558-564.

————. (1980). *Symbolic Interactionism: A Social Structural Version.* Menlo Park, CA: Benjamin/Cummings.

————. (1987). "Identity Theory: Developments and Extensions," In *Self and Identity: Psychosocial Perspectives,* eds. Yardley and T. Honess. Toronto: John Wiley and Sons, pp. 89-103.

Tar, Zoltan (1977). *The Frankfurt School.* New York: Wiley and Sons.

Tepper, Kelly (1994). "The Role of Labeling Processes in Elderly Consumers' Responses to Age Segmentation Cues," *Journal of Consumer Research* 20(4):503-519.

Thompson, Craig J., William B. Locander, and Howard R. Pollio (1989). "Putting Consumer Experience Back into Consumer Research: The Philosophy and Method of Existential Phenomenology," *Journal of Consumer Research* (September) 16:133-146.

————. (1990). "The Lived Meaning of Free Choice: An Existential-Phenomenological Description of Everyday Consumer Experiences of Contemporary Married Women," *Journal of Consumer Research* (December) 17:346-361.

Tonnies, Ferdinand (1957). *Community and Society.* New Brunswick, NJ: Transaction Books.

Toronto Star, August 8, 1992. "Metro's 300,000 gays, lesbians struggle for respect," A1.

————. August 9, 1992. "The persecution of the gays," B1, B7.

————. September 2, 1992. "Gay ruling on benefits seen costing 'millions'," A1.

Traub, Stuart H. and Craig B. Little (1994). *Theories of Deviance,* Fourth edition. Itasca, IL: F.E. Peacock Publishers.

Tripp, C.A. (1987). *The Homosexual Matrix.* Scarborough, Ontario: New American Library.

Troiden, Richard R. (1987). "Becoming Homosexual." In *Deviance: The Interactionist Perspective,* Fifth edition, eds. Earl Rubington and Martin S. Weinberg. New York: Macmillan Publishing Co., pp. 296-306.

————. (1989). "The Formation of Homosexual Identities," *Journal of Homosexuality* 5(3):43-73.

————. (1990). "Self, Self-concept, Identity, and Homosexual Identity: Constructs in Need of Definition and Differentiation," *Journal of Homosexuality* 10:97-109.

Turner, Barry A. (1981). "Some Practical Aspects of Qualitative Data Analysis: One Way of Organizing the Cognitive Processes Associated with the Generation of Grounded Theory," *Quality and Quantity* 15:225-247.

Turner, Victor (1969). *The Ritual Process: Structure and Anti-Structure.* Chicago, IL: Aldine.

———. (1982). *From Ritual to Theatre: The Human Seriousness of Play.* New York: PAJ Publications.

van Gennep, Arnold (1960). *The Rites of Passage,* trans. M.B. Vizedom and G.L. Caffee. Chicago, IL: University of Chicago Press.

Visano, Livy A. (1987). *This Idle Trade: The Occupational Patterns of Male Prostitution.* Concord, Ontario: Vitasana Books.

Wallendorf, Melanie, and Eric J. Arnould (1988). "'My Favourite Things': A Cross-Cultural Inquiry into Object Attachment, Possessiveness, and Social Linkage," *Journal of Consumer Research* (March) 14:531-554.

———. (1991). "'We Gather Together': Consumption Rituals of Thanksgiving Day," *Journal of Consumer Research* 18:13-31.

Wallendorf, Melanie, and Russell W. Belk (1989). "Assessing Trustworthiness in Naturalistic Consumer Research." In *Interpretive Consumer Research,* ed. Elizabeth C. Hirschman. Provo, UT: Association for Consumer Research, pp. 69-84.

Wallendorf, Melanie, and Merrie Brucks (1993). "Introspection in Consumer Research: Implementation and Implications," *Journal of Consumer Research* 20(3):339-359.

Ward, James C., and Peter H. Reingen (1990). "Sociocognitive Analysis of Group Decision Making Among Consumers," *Journal of Consumer Research* 17: 245-262.

Wardlow, Daniel L. (1996). "Introduction." In *Gays, Lesbians, and Consumer Behavior: Theory, Practice, and Research Issues in Marketing,* ed. Daniel L. Wardlow. Binghamton, NY: The Haworth Press, Inc., pp. 1-8.

Warren, C.A.B. (1974). *Identity and Community in the Gay World.* New York: John Wiley and Sons.

Weeks, Jeffrey (1985). *Sexuality and its Discontents: Meanings, Myths, and Modern Sexualities.* London: Routledge and Kegan Paul.

———. (1987). "Questions of Identity." In *The Cultural Construction of Sexuality,* ed. Pat Caplan. New York: Routledge, pp. 137-149.

Weinberg, Thomas S. (1986). "Love Relationships and Drinking Among Gay Men," *Journal of Drug Issues* 16(4):637-648.

Whitehead, Ann (1984). "Men and Women, Kinship and Property: Some General Issues." In *Women and Property—Women as Property,* ed. Renee Hirschon. New York: St. Martin's Press, pp. 124-146.

Wicklund, Robert A., and Peter M. Gollwitzer (1982). *Symbolic Self Completion.* London: Lawrence Erlbaum and Associates.

Widdicombe, Sue, and Rob Wooffitt (1990). "'Being' versus 'Doing' Punk: On Achieving Authenticity as a Member," *Journal of Language and Social Psychology* 9(4):257-277.

Willis, Susan (1993). "Hardcore: Subculture American Style," *Critical Enquiry* (Winter) 19:365-383.

Wilson, Elizabeth (1993). "Deviancy, Dress, and Desire." In *Negotiating at the Margins: The Gendered Discourses of Power and Resistance*, ed. Sue Fisher. New Brunswick, NJ: Rutgers, pp. 48-65.

Wolf, Naomi (1990). *The Beauty Myth.* Toronto: Vintage Books.

Wright, Newell D., C.B. Claiborne, and M. J. Sirgy (1992). "The Effects of Product Symbolism on Consumer Self-concept." In *Advances in Consumer Research* 19, eds. John F. Sherry and Brian Sternthal. Ann Arbor, MI: Association for Consumer Research, pp. 311-318.

Index

For Product Safety Concerns and Information please contact our EU
representative GPSR@taylorandfrancis.com Taylor & Francis Verlag GmbH,
Kaufingerstraße 24, 80331 München, Germany

Batch number: 08158221

Printed by Printforce, the Netherlands